D0908120

The
Institutional
Context of
Population
Change

Population and Development

A series edited by Richard A. Easterlin

Previously Published:

Fertility Change in Contemporary Japan
Robert W. Hodge and Naohiro Ogawa

Social Change and the Family in Taiwan
Arland Thornton and Hui-Sheng Lin

Sing Low, Sweet Chariot:
The Mortality Cost of Colonizing Liberia in the Nineteenth Century
Antonio McDaniel

From Parent to Child:
Intrahousehold Allocation and Intergenerational Relations
in the United States
Jere R. Behrman, Robert A. Pollak, and Paul Taubman

Anthropological Demography:
Toward a New Synthesis
Edited by David I. Kertzer and Tom Fricke

FRED C. PAMPEL

The Institutional Context of Population Change

*Patterns of Fertility
and Mortality across
High-Income Nations*

The University of Chicago Press
Chicago and London

Fred C. Pampel is research associate in the Population Program of the Institute of Behavioral Science and Professor of sociology at the University of Colorado at Boulder. He is the author of *Social Change and the Aged* and coauthor of *Old Age Security in Comparative Perspective* and *Age, Class, Politics, and the Welfare State.*

The University of Chicago Press, Chicago 60637
The University of Chicago Press, Ltd., London
© 2001 by The University of Chicago
All rights reserved. Published 2001
Printed in the United States of America

10 09 08 07 06 05 04 03 02 01   1 2 3 4 5

ISBN: 0-226-64525-8 (cloth)

Library of Congress Cataloging-in-Publication Data

Pampel, Fred C.
    The institutional context of population change : patterns of
fertility and mortality across high-income nations / Fred C. Pampel.
        p. cm. — (Population and development)
    Includes bibliographical references and index.
    ISBN 0-226-64525-8 (alk. paper)
    1. Population Policy—Cross-cultural studies.   2. Fertility,
Human—Cross-cultural studies.   3. Economic development—
Cross-cultural studies.   I. Title.   II. Population and development
    (Chicago, Ill.)

    HB883.5 .P35 2001
    304.6′09172′2—dc21
                                                            2001023054

Contents

Tables and Figures   vii

Preface   xi

PART I. THE INSTITUTIONAL CONTEXT OF POPULATION CHANGE

1   The Demographic Consequences of Changing Cohort Size and Female Work   3

2   Sociopolitical Sources of Demographic Divergence   27

PART II. FERTILITY

3   Contextual Variation in the Determinants of Fertility   55

4   Relative Cohort Size and the Total Fertility Rate   77

5   Female Labor Force Participation and the Total Fertility Rate   96

PART III. MORTALITY

6   Cohort Size and Suicide and Homicide Mortality   121

7   Age-Specific Suicide Rates   140

8   Age-Specific Homicide Rates   160

PART IV. SEX DIFFERENCES IN MORTALITY

9   Sex Differences in Suicide and Homicide Mortality   185

10   Sex Differences in Suicide Rates   205

11   Sex Differences in Homicide Rates   223

Conclusion   243

Appendix A: Statistical Models and Estimation I   249

Appendix B: Statistical Models and Estimation II   253

Notes   257

References   273

Index   293

Tables and Figures

Tables

Table 1. Nation Scores for Collectivism and Women-Friendly
Institutions Scales   45

Table 2. Mean Total Fertility Rates and Related Characteristics by
Nation and Time Period   78

Table 3. Unstandardized Coefficients for Regression of the Total
Fertility Rate on Relative Cohort Size—Additive Models   83

Table 4. Unstandardized Coefficients for Regression of the Total
Fertility Rate on Relative Cohort Size—Nation-Specific Effects   84

Table 5. Unstandardized Coefficients for Regression of the Total
Fertility Rate on Relative Cohort Size—Time-Specific Effects   86

Table 6. Unstandardized Coefficients for Regression of the Total
Fertility Rate on Relative Cohort Size—Interaction Models   87

Table 7. Effects of Relative Cohort Size on Fertility by Time and
Collectivism   89

Table 8. Unstandardized Coefficients for Regression of the Total
Fertility Rate on Cohort Size and Other Variables—Additive
and Interaction Models   91

Table 9. Effects of Relative Cohort Size on Fertility by Collectivism
and Female Labor Force Participation   92

Table 10. Mean Female Labor Force Participation Rates by Nation
and Time Period   98

Table 11. Unstandardized Coefficients for Regression of the Total
Fertility Rate on the Female Labor Force Participation Rate—
Additive Models   102

Table 12. Unstandardized Coefficients for Regression of the Total
Fertility Rate on the Female Labor Force Participation Rate—
Nation-Specific Effects   103

Table 13. Unstandardized Coefficients for Regression of the Total

Fertility Rate on the Female Labor Force Participation Rate—
Time-Specific Effects   105
Table 14. Unstandardized Coefficients for Regression of the Total
Fertility Rate on the Female Labor Force Participation Rate—
Collectivism and Time Interaction Models   108
Table 15. Effects of Female Labor Force Participation on Fertility
by Time and Collectivism   109
Table 16. Unstandardized Coefficients for Regression of the Total
Fertility Rate on the Female Labor Force Participation Rate—
Gender and Time Interaction Models   112
Table 17. Effects of Female Labor Force Participation on Fertility
by Time and Gender Equality   113
Table 18. Mean Male and Female Suicide Rates and Age Group
Sizes by Nation, Time Period, and Age Group   145
Table 19. Correlation Coefficients of Suicide Rates and Cohort
Size by Age and Sex   147
Table 20. Unstandardized Coefficients for Regression of Age-
Specific Suicide Rates on Cohort Size—Age Interaction Models   150
Table 21. Unstandardized Coefficients for Regression of Age-
Specific Male Suicide Rates on Cohort Size—Age, Nation, and
Time Interaction Models   154
Table 22. Unstandardized Coefficients and t-Ratios for Regression
of Age-Specific Suicide Rates on Cohort Size and Other
Variables—Age Interaction Models   156
Table 23. Mean Male and Female Homicide Rates and Age Group
Sizes by Nation, Time Period, and Age Group   163
Table 24. Correlation Coefficients of Homicide Rates and Cohort
Size by Age and Sex   167
Table 25. Unstandardized Coefficients for Regression of Age-
Specific Homicide Rates on Cohort Size—Age Interaction
Models   170
Table 26. Age-Specific Effects on Homicide Rates of Population
Percentage   172
Table 27. Age-Specific Effects on Homicide Rates of Relative
Cohort Size   172
Table 28. Unstandardized Coefficients for Regression of Age-
Specific Homicide Rates on Cohort Size—Sex, Age, Nation,
and Time Interaction Models   173
Table 29. Unstandardized Coefficients and t-Ratios for Regression

of Age-Specific Homicide Rates on Cohort Size and Other
Variables—Age Interaction Models 176
Table 30. Regression Coefficients and *t*-Ratios for Regression of
Age-Specific Homicide Rates on Cohort Size and National
Context Measures—Nation Interaction Models 178
Table 31. Unstandardized Coefficients and *t*-Ratios for Regression
of Combined Age-Specific Homicide and Suicide Rates on
Cohort Size and Other Variables—Age Interaction Models 180
Table 32. Mean Relative Suicide Rates by Nation and Time Period 208
Table 33. Mean Relative Suicide Rates by Age and Time Period 210
Table 34. Unstandardized Coefficients and *t*-Ratios for Regression
of Measures of Relative Suicide Rates on Female Work and
Family Variables—Additive Models 213
Table 35. Unstandardized Coefficients and *t*-Ratios for Regression
of Measures of Relative Suicide Rates on Time, Collectivism,
and Gender Scale—Nation Interaction Models 215
Table 36. Unstandardized Coefficients for Regression of the
Logged Suicide Ratio on Time and Female Labor Force
Participation Polynomials—Nation-Specific Models 217
Table 37. Mean Relative Homicide Rates by Nation and Time
Period 225
Table 38. Mean Relative Homicide Rates by Age and Time Period 229
Table 39. Mean Female Homicide Rates and Logged Rates by Age
and Time Period 232
Table 40. Unstandardized Coefficients and *t*-Ratios for Regression
of Measures of Relative and Absolute Female Homicide Rates on
Female Work and Family Variables—Additive Models 234
Table 41. Unstandardized Coefficients and *t*-Ratios for Regression
of Measures of Relative and Absolute Female Homicide Rates on
Time, Collectivism, and Gender Scale—Nation Interaction
Models 235
Table 42. Unstandardized Coefficients for Regression of Measures
of Relative and Absolute Female Homicide Rates on Time
Polynomials—Nation-Specific Models 237

Figures

Figure 1. Fertility and Cohort Size Trends, United States 80
Figure 2. Fertility and Cohort Size Trends, Sweden 81

Figure 3. Fertility and Cohort Size Trends, 18-Nation Means   82
Figure 4. Fertility and Female Work Trends, 18-Nation Means   99
Figure 5. Fertility and Female Work Trends, United States   100
Figure 6. Fertility and Female Work Trends, Sweden   100
Figure 7. Fertility and Female Work Trends, Italy   101
Figure 8. Female Labor Force Participation and Fertility, by
    Collectivism   110
Figure 9. Female Labor Force Participation and Fertility, by
    Gender Equality   114
Figure 10. Male Suicide Rate Trends, 18-Nation Means   144
Figure 11. Female Suicide Rate Trends, 18-Nation Means   145
Figure 12. Male Homicide Rate Trends, 18-Nation Means   164
Figure 13. Female Homicide Rate Trends, 18-Nation Means   165
Figure 14. Male/Female Suicide Ratio Trends, 18-Nation Means   211
Figure 15. Male/Female Suicide Ratio Trends by Collectivism   216
Figure 16. Relative Homicide Trends, 18-Nation Means   227
Figure 17. Homicide Rate Trends, 18-Nation Means   231

Preface

Despite having similar industrial economies that scholars once thought would produce convergence in economic, demographic, and political institutions, high-income democracies show persistent diversity. While they all have mature and stable democratic systems, for instance, they differ in their welfare state policies and institutions of public social protection. While they have all passed through the demographic transition, they differ in the size of cohorts and age groups in their populations and the patterns of fertility and mortality. And while they have all experienced changes in the status and roles of women, they differ in the size of the female labor force and their programs to support working mothers. In recent years, comparative political, sociological, and demographic studies have done much to describe and explain enduring differences among high-income democractic nations in the areas of politics, population, and gender inequality.

Consistent with this attention to cross-national diversity, this book explores how sociopolitical institutional features of high-income nations shape the influence of two population characteristics—cohort size and female labor force participation—on the demographic outcomes of fertility and mortality. I thus combine, in this study, politics and demography, topics all too rarely made the subject of a single study. Despite a division of labor in research, the two topics (and their special perspectives on social life) can inform each other. One can best understand the demographic consequences of changes in cohort size and female work (or any variety of other changes) by recognizing the importance of national sociopolitical context. Conversely, one can best understand the importance of national differences in sociopolitical environments by recognizing the special problems presented by varied patterns of demographic change within nations.

Although politics and demography intersect in many areas, my study of the consequences of institutional context and changes in cohort size and female work concentrates on three types of demographic outcomes: fertility levels; mortality from suicide and homicide (or "suicide mortality" and "homicide mortality," for short); and sex differences in suicide and homicide mortality. Despite the use of the summary term "mortality" in the title, the book focuses on two causes of death of special importance. Compared to mortality from all causes, suicide and homicide mortality respond more immediately to social relationships in society, relate more closely to social problems of youth and violence, and better reflect the importance of institutional context. Although other mortality outcomes may also deserve study because they relate to both politics and demography, these two offer sufficient diversity and complexity for a single study. In combination with the study of family decisions concerning childbearing, the study of social and personal conflict in the form of lethal violence and of sex differences in victimization by lethal violence covers a wide range of behaviors.

In fact, a large research study like this one may work best when it investigates a single sociological or demographic outcome and devotes each chapter to a particular set of influences. That is, a common dependent variable lends unity to the effort. The task I have taken on, however, is different in that a set of common determinants contributes to a variety of outcomes. Cohort size, female work, and sociopolitical institutional contexts of high-income nations combine to influence a variety of separate but related outcomes. Levels of fertility, patterns of suicide and homicide mortality, and sex differences in suicide and homicide mortality—although distinct phenomena that are rarely the subject of a single study—turn out to respond similarly to the combined influences of social, political, and demographic determinants. In other words, it is the common determinants of diverse outcomes—rather than a single outcome—that give unity to this book.

Although the book covers topics of interest to readers from a wide variety of backgrounds, the statistical models in some chapters become technical and can make for difficult reading. Chapters 1–3, 6, and 9 present the theoretical arguments and methodological approach in a way understandable to most readers, and the conclusion summarizes the results of the book in nontechnical language. In contrast, the empirical chapters 4, 5, 7, 8, 10, and 11 include much statistical detail in order to explain the results fully, defend the models, and justify the conclusions. The detail provides sufficient information to understand and evaluate the choices made in testing the theoretical arguments but is balanced by nonstatistical summaries of the findings in the introduction and conclusion of each empirical chapter.

Since some of the material in this book appeared in earlier journal articles, I owe the editors and reviewers for those journals thanks for their efforts. Although I have since extensively revised the journal articles and updated the data and analyses for this book, parts of the chapters that follow appeared earlier in "Relative Cohort Size and Fertility: The Socio-Political Context of the Easterlin Effect," *American Sociological Review* 58 (1993): 496–514; with Rosemary Gartner, "Age Structure, Socio-Political Institutions, and Homicide," *European Sociological Review* 11 (1995): 243–60; "Cohort Size and Age-Specific Suicide Rates: A Contingent Relationship," *Demography* 33 (1996): 341–56; and "National Context, Social Change, and Sex Differences in Suicide Rates," *American Sociological Review* 63 (1998): 744–58. For more recent help, I thank Richard Easterlin, editor of this series on population studies for the University of Chicago Press, and anonymous reviewers of the manuscript. Finally, I thank the Institute for Behavioral Science at the University of Colorado for general support, and the National Institute on Aging (07683), the National Institute for Child Health and Development (28985), and the National Science Foundation (SBR-9729922) for external grant support.

PART I

The Institutional Context of Population Change

CHAPTER 1

The Demographic Consequences of Changing Cohort Size and Female Work

Patterns of Demographic Change

Fertility and Mortality. Despite having passed through a demographic transition to low fertility and mortality rates, the high-income nations of Western Europe, North America, Oceania, and Japan have nonetheless experienced notable and often puzzling demographic changes in recent decades. Fertility rates have shown substantial fluctuation: after a period of low birth rates during the economic Depression of the 1930s, an unexpectedly sharp rise in fertility occurred in the 1950s, followed by an equally unexpected and sudden drop in fertility in the mid-1960s, and then a leveling off of the decline and a small increase in fertility during the 1980s and 1990s. The United States, Canada, Australia, and New Zealand exhibited the greatest post–World War II fluctuations in fertility (Lesthaeghe 1983), while less striking patterns emerged in European nations (Chesnais 1992; Guibert-Lantoine and Monnier 1997).

In addition to the level of fertility, the age pattern of childbearing also changed. The shift from the high fertility of the 1950s to the low fertility of later decades resulted, in large part, from women in high-income nations delaying first births to older ages. Accordingly, fertility rates have fallen more among women ages 15–24 than among women 25–34. Here again, however, differences exist across nations (Morgan 1996). The United States, for example, has relatively high birth rates among teenagers compared to European nations. At the other extreme, Irish women have a particularly high proportion of births at the oldest ages. Even holding fertility levels constant, the age pattern of births represents a dimension of demographic behavior that varies across time and nations.

Trends in mortality rates have not fluctuated like fertility but, averaged across all causes, show steady declines. During the 40 years from 1950 to 1990, life expectancy at birth rose from 68 to 75 in the United States, from 72 to 77 in Sweden, and from 63 to 79 in Japan. Despite some noted exceptions—such as the prevalence of heart disease deaths among middle-aged males in the 1960s or rising deaths from violence and AIDS among young males since the late 1980s—continued decline in mortality characterizes the high-income nations in the last half of the twentieth century. Perhaps equally notable, the decline in mortality for women—at least until recently—substantially exceeded that for men, thus generating a sex differential in mortality that has received much popular and scholarly attention.

In contrast to the overall downward movement in mortality rates, trends in certain kinds of mortality reveal larger fluctuations over time and greater variation across nations. Deaths from such external causes as suicide and homicide, in particular, relate more closely to problems of daily living than to the steady improvements in medical care. Deaths from violence respond directly and immediately to economic conditions, social integration, alcohol and drug use, group conflict, inequality, and availability of weapons. Given varied trends in these social conditions in modern societies, suicide and homicide can change in unexpected and nonlinear ways. Further, the social nature of violent deaths means that they vary widely across nations with diverse cultures and patterns of social behavior. Homicide in the United States and suicide in Sweden, for example, reach much higher levels than in most other nations.

Deaths from violence also vary by age. Suicide and homicide kill persons at all ages but represent leading causes of death for persons under age 45 and contribute more than most other causes to premature loss of life (Rockett 1998). Deaths from homicide are highest among young people, while deaths from suicide are highest among older persons. Still, deaths from both have risen among youth in the United States, even creating a sense of crisis about the conditions of younger generations. Although less severe in European nations, problems of lethal violence also occur outside the United States. Again, variation in age patterns exists both over time and across nations for these causes of death.

Along with variation by age, lethal violence varies by sex. By a large margin, males at all ages die from suicide and homicide more often than do females. The sizes of sex differences in these types of mortality no doubt vary across nations and change over time, but sex differences have not been investigated to the same extent as the level of violent mortality. Likely, sex differentials remain smaller in nations with overall low levels of violent mortality and have increased over time as the sex differential for all causes has increased. Thus, sex differentials in violent deaths may represent another important dimension of demographic change in high-income nations.

Age Structure and Its Demographic Consequences. Changes in fertility and, to a lesser degree, changes in mortality contribute to another component of demographic variation among the high-income nations: uneven age structures and contrasting cohort sizes (Lutz 1991). The general decline in fertility over the past century and the specific decline in mortality among the elderly in recent decades have contributed to a long-term trend of population aging (Kannisto 1994). Within that long-term trend, however, low birth rates during the Great Depression followed by baby booms and then baby busts have produced bottom-heavy age structures in the 1950s, large youth populations in the 1960s and 1970s, and increasingly middle-age structures in the 1980s and 1990s and, in the next century, will produce huge elderly populations.

Along with the general trend in age structure, variation also exists across the high-income nations. Those nations experiencing the largest fluctuations in fertility, with the largest baby booms and subsequent baby busts, also exhibited more widely varying cohort sizes in the decades that followed. Because of their high fertility peaks in the late 1950s and early 1960s, for example, the former English colonies, particularly the United States, experienced uneven age structures and contrasting cohort sizes more so than most European nations did.

Changes in the age distribution of populations can in turn influence the demographic behavior and social well-being of cohorts. Although such influences remain the subject of much debate (which this book aims to address), they suggest—in even a qualified form—some interesting sources of social and demographic change in modern societies. First, changes in the relative size of age groups and cohorts affect levels of fertility and mortality. Although accumulated fertility and mortality rates in the long run shape the age structure, the relative sizes of cohorts reflected in the age structure can have more immediate impacts on fertility and mortality rates. According to Easterlin (1987a), cohort size affects the supply of workers, opportunities for promotion, wage levels, and relative economic well-being of individuals and families. Relative economic well-being in turn influences the propensity toward marriage, divorce, and fertility. It also affects certain kinds of mortality, such as suicide and homicide, that involve violence, social pathology, and immediate personal problems. The different experiences across cohorts of different sizes may help define identities, cultural values, and social behaviors of generations—including values and behaviors related to family goals and personal health—and contribute to concerns about generation-based social inequality.

Second, changes in the relative size of age groups and cohorts may affect sex differences in mortality. Although important for all members of a cohort, size may have greater, more immediate influences on males than on females. Again based on Easterlin's (1987a) arguments, to the extent that roles for men more strongly relate to occupational success than do roles for women, men may more strongly feel the impact, for better or worse, of cohort-driven changes in opportunities for promotion, wage levels, and relative economic well-being of individuals and families. That claim does not deny the importance of work and financial success for women and the importance of family life and child rearing for men, nor does it minimize the obvious changes that have taken place toward greater gender equality in social life. It does, however, recognize that men and women have not yet reached full equality and likely respond differently to demographic changes. In regard to mortality, then, this reasoning suggests that cohort size may increase suicide and homicide, but may do so more for men than for women.

Female Employment and Its Demographic Consequences. Other changes besides those involving age and cohort structure contribute to variation across nations and over time in fertility and mortality outcomes. Of most importance is the expansion of the female labor force. Like cohort size, trends and patterns of female work both respond to and cause changes in fertility and mortality. The long-term downward trend in fertility freed women from family duties that had prevented participation in the paid labor force (Oppenheimer 1982) and, ultimately, contributed to the emergence of the women's movement and made work acceptable for married mothers (Mason 1997). Lengthened life expectancy, by extending the years of potential work after the growth of children, similarly contributed to the reentrance of women into the labor force during middle age (Davis and van den Oever 1982).

In turn, however, female employment and independence can have more immediate influences on fertility and mortality. Again, these influences remain subject to debate but raise important issues that need study. One such issue is that increased desires of and opportunities for women to work outside the family may have contributed to declining fertility. According to economic arguments, women lose more in potential wages from having children when they have better work and career opportunities and, according to sociological arguments, gain less in terms of personal and social satisfaction from children in societies that value autonomy, careerism, and materialism. In the short run, having children limits work opportunities, but in the longer run women's commitment to work and desire for economic independence appear to limit fertility.

Another issue needing study is that changes in women's work may affect sex differences in mortality—although the direction of change is less clear. On one side, some argue that equalizing gender and work roles equalizes conditions that cause mortality and reduces the sex differential in mortality in general and violent mortality in particular. On the other side, some argue that equalizing gender and work roles gives women the status advantages that men have traditionally enjoyed and, therefore, further expands the female mortality advantage. Either way, social changes in the gender composition of the labor force can alter the relative mortality rates of men and women.

To summarize, changes and national differences in fertility and in mortality from violence, along with sex differences in mortality from violence in modern societies, raise important and sometimes puzzling questions. Of particular interest to many scholars, these changes and national differences may relate to age structure, cohort size, female work, and gender equality. In fact, issues concerning these relationships have, in high-income nations, come to replace issues of population growth as dominant population concerns among policy makers. Although crucial for the experiences of Third World countries, population size seems less important for nations with relatively low rates of population growth and current fertility below replacement rates. Instead, much popular attention these days focuses on the baby-boom and baby-bust generations, on the relative size and well-being of child and elderly populations, and on youth violence—all issues relating to generational and cohort inequality. Similar popular attention focuses on promoting gender equality, the consequences of female labor force participation for family formation, the availability and quality of day care for children with working parents, and the harm or benefit to women's health, well-being, and mortality from new social roles.

As already noted, however, claims about cohort size and recent changes in fertility, mortality, and sex differences in mortality have produced more controversy than acceptance. The links between cohort size and demographic outcomes, although an accepted part of the field, prove quite complex. Indeed, scholars offer divergent views of the consequences of changes in cohort size for demographic behavior. The links between female work and fertility or mortality prove similarly complex and also involve theoretical and empirical controversy. The next sections review these controversies in more detail, first considering the consequences of cohort size for fertility and mortality and then considering the consequences of female work for fertility and the sex differential in mortality. The concluding sections of the chapter then suggest ways to make sense of divergent theoretical views and empirical results and provide a general hypothesis to guide the analysis in the chapters to come.

Debate over the Consequences of Cohort Change

On one side, Easterlin (1973, 1976, 1978, 1987a, 1987b) presents and most strongly defends the claim that large cohort size lowers fertility and raises mortality. He argues that, because of competition over increasingly scarce resources, members of large cohorts experience shortages of teachers and schools when young, labor market competition and unemployment in early adulthood, low pay and few promotions during adulthood, and tight public retirement benefits in old age. The deprivation felt by members of large cohorts results in late marriage, low fertility, high divorce, and high levels of suicide and homicide. Just the opposite occurs for smaller cohorts, whose members enjoy greater economic success, more stable and satisfying family lives, and lower rates of suicide and homicide.[1]

On the other side, Preston (1984) cites improvements in the status of a growing elderly population relative to a declining child population to make the more general point that large cohorts benefit from their ability to influence public policy and garner consumer resources. Because large cohorts represent potentially large voting blocs and purchasing segments, their political and economic concerns become societal concerns. Moreover, when smaller cohorts follow larger ones, the larger cohorts continue to dominate the economy and fill most of the jobs. All this may contribute to the well-being of an increasingly large older generation and the large baby-boom generation relative to the younger baby-bust generation.

To complicate the debate further, many researchers discount altogether the influence of cohort size. For example, researchers find inconsistent and weak relationships of cohort size with fertility, earnings, unemployment, and labor force participation in European countries (Bloom, Freeman, and Korenman 1987; Wright 1989). Similarly, studies in the past decade find that the expected benefits of small cohort size among young people have yet to emerge (Olsen 1994). More generally, cohort effects have little influence relative to age and period effects on fertility (Bhrolcháin 1992). As a result, a number of scholars suggest that cohort size contributes little to recent social and demographic trends. Instead, much attention has focused on the impact of changes in female work and wages (Butz and Ward 1979; Robinson 1997; Schultz 1981) and in individualist and secular values (Lesthaeghe 1995; Lesthaeghe and Surkyn 1988; Westoff 1991) that affect members of cohorts of all sizes.

In addition, debate over the importance of cohort size for fertility and mortality relates to the mortality differential between men and women. Easterlin (1987a) argues that, given the gender inequality that continues to characterize social life, cohort size has greater effects on male than on female mortality. For large cohorts, suicide and homicide mortality will increase more quickly for men than for women, thereby widening gender differences in mortality. Small cohorts, in contrast, will enjoy similarly low mortality rates for both men and women. The competing arguments about cohort size, however, might posit the opposite. For instance, as large cohorts come to gain the benefits of social well-being and public support, men may gain relative to women in their rates of mortality, causing the gender gap to decline. Small cohorts may show the largest gender difference in mortality rates. Or, if cohort size has little effect on male mortality, it likely will have little effect on female mortality and no effect on the sex differential in mortality. The negative evidence for the influence of cohort size may apply to sex differences in mortality and negate claims about the special harm of large cohort size for men relative to women.

Overall, theory and research on the impact of cohort size on fertility and mortality exhibit wide divergence. Not only do scholars typically disagree over the importance of cohort size, but they disagree as well on the direction of the impact. Some claim that large cohort size lowers fertility and raises mortality, while others claim that large cohort size brings economic benefits. The theoretical disagreement likewise spills over into empirical studies. Much evidence shows negative effects of cohort size, other evidence shows positive effects, and still other evidence shows no effects at all (Pampel and Peters 1995).

Debate over the Consequences of Female Work

Arguments at one end of the spectrum emphasize the negative influences for family formation and female mortality of the entrance of women into the labor force. In regard to fertility, the arguments stress that the movement toward gender equality in work roles creates more transitory family bonds, below-replacement fertility, and problems of child care. As family, community, and religious support for childbearing declines, shifts toward personal fulfillment and female careerism make family and children less important and more costly in terms of lost work opportunities and wages. These changes can drive fertility down to levels that eventually produce a negative rate of natural population increase. In regard to mortality, the arguments claim that movement toward gender equality in work roles exposes women to greater risks of death. In the past, women's less intense involvement outside the family protected them from certain causes of death most common among men. Social changes that integrate women into the world of work, politics, and social life end that protection and promote convergence over time in male and female death rates.

Arguments at the other end of the spectrum emphasize the positive influence of female labor force participation on family formation and female mortality. Because traditional marriage and family roles benefit men more than they do women, changes in those roles harm men more than women. In regard to fertility, better and more egalitarian marriages, improved public institutions for child care, and public policies in support of the family may increase fertility among working women. In other words, it is the absence of substantial advances in equality for women, rather than the limited improvements that have taken place, that limits family formation and fertility in modern society (Goldsheider and Waite 1991). In regard to mortality, the unequal benefits of marriage to men and women and the limited roles reserved for women have in the past harmed women's health and well-being and restrained any potential female advantage in mortality. Social changes toward gender equality in work roles thus lead to further divergence in men's and women's life expectancy.

The general debate about the consequences of gender equality for mortality also applies to those violence-based causes that prove important at the younger ages in high-income nations. For suicide, convergence arguments suggest that, with increased labor force involvement, women will come to lose the integrative ties to the family that have protected them from self-harm. As their integrative ties to groups come to resemble those of men, their suicide rates will also approach the levels found among men. For homicide, the arguments submit that traditional family arrangements have socialized women to avoid risk, thereby reducing the likelihood of their participation in social conflict. Removing women from this constraining but protective patriarchal family environment increases their potential to become involved in conflict and their participation in or vulnerability to crime. Further, to the extent that homicide stems from threat and competition, women's improved position outside the family may threaten traditional status hierarchies, challenge male dominance over resources, and cause an increase in the killing of women.

For each of these types of mortality, the competing arguments predict divergence between men and women. For suicide, if traditional marriage and family roles do more to integrate men than women and if men gain more protection from family life than women do, gender equality will increase male suicide rates more than female rates. In contrast to men, women develop multiple sources of integration outside the family so that they suffer less than men from family change and in fact may benefit directly from expanding roles. For homicide, traditional gender inequality makes women vulnerable to violence by partners: lacking power within the traditional male-dominated relationship, women have few options for avoiding intimate violence. Reducing gender stratification, giving women more power, resources, and control within family relationships, and providing sources of work, income, and protection outside the traditional family should reduce the vulnerability of women to homicides and reduce their victimization levels relative to men.

Existing studies of fertility and mortality have not provided clear support for either set of arguments. Research on fertility generally demonstrates a negative relationship between female work and fertility, but in recent years some intriguing exceptions to the relationship have emerged. Fertility in Sweden, for instance, where women make up a large share of the labor force, increased in the 1990s, while fertility in Italy, where female labor force participation remains less common relative to Sweden and other nations, has reached levels that are among the lowest in the world. Theories and research need to incorporate such anomalies into their understanding of the relationship between female work and fertility. Research on gender differences in mortality provides even more ambiguity and inconsistency. While some studies find positive effects of female labor force participation on suicide and homicide, others find negative effects and still others find no effect.

Overall, theory and research on the influence of female work on fertility and mortality, like research on the influence of cohort size, exhibit wide divergence. Scholars often disagree over the direction of the impact, and empirical studies thus far have not settled the disagreements. Some claim that female labor force participation lowers both fertility and the female mortality advantage, while others suggest the opposite. Perhaps the theoretical controversy and inconsistent results indicate the need to move beyond comparisons of competing and exclusive alternative theories.

Convergence and Divergence among the High-Income Nations

One limitation of existing theory and research on—and a source of the debates over—the consequences of cohort size and gender equality relates to the lack of attention to the institutional contexts in which the demographic changes take place. In studying the sources and consequences of population changes in high-income nations, demographers often assume that the changes have proceeded similarly across this group of economically similar nations. They assume that the nations of Western Europe, Japan, the United States, Canada, Australia, and New Zealand—having all reached high levels of economic development and passed through the demographic transition to low birth and death rates—have also become demographically homogeneous. The homogenizing forces of capitalist economies and individualist or secular cultural values minimize the importance of national idiosyncrasies and make generalizations across high-income nations meaningful. Differences may exist but can be understood best as peculiar to individual nations—worth noting but not appropriate for meaningful generalization.

Some describe these nations as experiencing a second demographic transition to below-replacement fertility, the postponement of mortality until old age, and an unprecedentedly large aged population (Cliquet 1991; Lesthaeghe 1995; van de Kaa 1987, 1988). The transition stems from a cultural shift to individuation and secularization that makes children a means to parental self-fulfillment rather than a community obligation. In addition, rising wages for women workers and normative environments supportive of working women raise the cost of childbearing and maternal child care in all modern societies. Similarly, the development and diffusion of medical technology and the understanding and promotion of the importance of healthy lifestyles reduce differences in premature mortality across the high-income nations. As a consequence of converging trends, high-income nations have similar levels of fertility and mortality.

Like arguments about the second demographic transition, population projections sometimes assume that nations are moving toward a common fertility rate, life expectancy, and percentage of the population age 65 and over (Demeny 1997; Valkonen 1991). Similarly, the 1998 revised projections from the United Nations (1999) allow for differences across the high-income nations in the total fertility rate and life expectancy but nonetheless assume decreasing national differences in the next century. The range of values predicted for fertility and mortality decline from 1994 to 2045 as nations move toward a projected average fertility rate of 1.77 and a projected average life expectancy of 82.3. These projections minimize enduring demographic variation across the high-income nations in the potential for a substantial rise in future fertility, the ability to continue to extend life expectancy, and the relative rates of mortality for men and women.

With respect to cohort change and female work, the assumption of homogeneity leads to a search for relationships and consequences that are the same across all contexts. Demographic change is assumed to have similar meaning and more or less automatic consequences across diverse nations and time periods. Scholars differ on just what direction and form these consequences take, but they still aim for establishing lawlike relationships that generalize across contexts and give little attention to variation from the average.

In contrast, literatures outside of demography have done much in recent years to both identify and explain heterogeneity among the high-income nations. These nations exhibit distinct and enduring cultural values, political ideologies, and government policies. For example, Esping-Andersen (1990, 1999) and Castles (1993) distinguish regimes or families of nations that vary in geographic, linguistic, cultural, and historical attributes, the organization of classes and the relative power of workers, and the structure of public policies. These attributes in turn affect the partisan composition of government (Esping-Andersen 1985, 1990; Stephens 1979), family change (Castles and Flood 1993; Clark 1992; Gauthier 1996a, 1996b; Therborn 1993), and equality across classes and genders (Castles and Mitchell 1993; Korpi and Palme 1998; Lewis 1993; Norris 1987; Sainsbury 1994; Schmidt 1993).

Of special importance, scholars distinguish sociopolitical contexts across nations and over time in terms of the institutional environments for social protection. Institutions can protect citizens to varying degrees from dependence for their economic well-being on market forces and on other family members. First, institutions can insulate citizens in general, and wage workers and the disadvantaged in particular, from market forces. These institutions, which promote class equality, collective solidarity, and universal public benefits that aid persons at all income levels, strengthen the welfare state relative to the market in economic support of the population. They emerge most strongly in combination with powerful working-class organizations, popular social democratic or leftist parties, and procedures for cooperative decision making. All nations have to some degree expanded public benefits for social protection from the 1950s to at least the 1980s, but the Nordic nations have done more than the central European and English-speaking nations to develop broad-based public institutions of social protection. As a result of these institutional differences, the meaning of quite similar income levels differs across nations and time periods and can affect the demographic consequences for citizens of similar social and economic changes.

Second, institutions can also insulate citizens in general, and women and mothers in particular, from dependence on other family members and encourage individual autonomy (Mósesdóttir 1995; O'Connor 1993). These institutions moderate the conflict between work and family by providing support for working women. They emphasize gender equality, involvement of a strong welfare state in the lives of women, and universal public benefits that aid homemakers as well as workers. According to Norris (1987), non-Catholic nations with strong unions and leftist parties do the most to advance female independence with their public policies. Attending more to qualitative differences in policies, Lewis (1992, 1993, 1997) distinguishes among nations such as the United Kingdom, whose institutions are characterized by reliance on a traditional male-breadwinner model, nations such as France, whose institutions modify the traditional male-breadwinner model, and nations such as Sweden, whose institutions promote a dual-breadwinner model. Others have similarly evaluated nations according to how well their policies reduce female dependence on traditional family sources of income support (Gauthier 1996b; Gornick and Jacobs 1998; Lewis 1993; Sainsbury 1996; Siaroff 1994; Singh 1998).

The relationship between class-based and gender-based institutions remains unclear. On the one hand, feminist scholars claim that institutional sources of gender equality differ from sources of class equality (Chamberlayne 1993; Orloff 1993; Williams 1995). They identify nations such as the Netherlands, which do much to equalize class differences but little to equalize gender differences (Sainsbury 1996), and nations such as the United States, which do as much for gender equality as class equality (Gelb 1989). On the other hand, many nations have policies that favor both disadvantaged classes and women (Esping-Andersen 1999). The Nordic nations in particular remain the most equalizing on dimensions of both class and gender, and their institutions for class and gender protection have expanded over time. Whether class-based and gender-based institutions correspond closely remains an empirical question, but the potentially separate dimensions further highlight variation in sociopolitical contexts. Along with institutional differences across nations in the treatment of classes, institutional differences in the treatment of women identify crucial sources of contextual divergence.

If divergence characterizes nations in the sociopolitical realm, it may characterize the demographic realm as well—the existence of distinct families of nations may imply the existence of distinct families of demographic regimes. Institutional heterogeneity certainly raises the question about whether it can be assumed that demographic convergence results from common economic and productive pressures. It also raises issues of whether a single pattern of demographic change can describe all nations going through the second demographic transition and suggests that sociopolitical context may crucially shape each of the components of demographic change. As nation-specific institutional factors affected the timing of mortality and fertility transitions in the distant past (Gillis, Tilly, and Levine 1992; Lesthaeghe 1983; Watkins 1991), they may have done the same in more recent decades. In Lesthaeghe's (1992) words, "Conceptual models of demographic choices cannot be restricted to the individual level and household decisions, but need to take [into account] the institutional agencies . . . shaped by political and religious interests and ideologies" (39).

In summary, demographic studies of cohort size, female work, fertility, and mortality, although addressing crucially important issues, tend to minimize the differences across high-income nations in processes and structures and to assume demographic homogeneity or convergence. Even those studies that describe and explain national demographic peculiarities often do so in isolation from other single-nation studies and without attempts to fit the national characteristics into a larger scheme. Yet, as the high-income nations vary meaningfully and systematically in their social, political, and economic institutions, they may also show demographic variation that corresponds closely to sociopolitical institutional variation.

Divergence in the Consequences of Cohort Change

Attending to the institutional sources of divergence in demographic outcomes has implications for the study of the impact of cohort change. Rather than assuming cohort size has the same influence in all nations and time periods, one could begin with the possibility that it has different meanings and consequences in different contexts. Taking the influence of cohort size as itself varying across contexts relates demographic processes to national and temporal differences in the institutional environments of the high-income nations. It also helps explain the source of debates over the importance and direction of the effects of cohort size on diverse demographic outcomes and the failure of research to produce a consensus. The competing arguments and results may in fact relate to the divergent sociopolitical contexts across the nations and years in which researchers have studied the impact of cohort change.

In essence, the thesis of this book concerning cohort size, sociopolitical context, and demographic outcomes can be stated as follows: *the influence of cohort change on demographic outcomes varies across institutional environments for social protection.* Institutional environments differ most clearly across nations and time periods but may also differ across age groups that depend to varying degrees on market sources of income. Each component of the institutional environment shapes or specifies the relationship between cohort change and fertility, certain types of mortality, and sex differences in these types of mortality.

To illustrate in broad terms what later chapters consider in more detail, arguments for the importance of institutional context in shaping the influence of cohort size take the following form. As large cohort size becomes harmful to economic well-being in relation to success in private labor markets, institutions that reduce the dependence of citizens on market work may also reduce the impact of large cohort size on demographic behavior. Universal programs of public social protection would mitigate the influences of cohort size, while the less interventionist policies of other nations would exacerbate them. Thus, the larger the role that welfare-state support plays relative to the market, the less the harm of belonging to a large age group or cohort will be. Conversely, the larger the role of earnings and the market, the greater the disadvantage of belonging to a large cohort.

Consider the implications of this argument for variation in the meaning and importance of cohort size for fertility and mortality rates across nations, time periods, and ages. Across nations, public policies and cultural values create diverse institutions of social protection in Scandinavia, central Europe, and North America. Both Easterlin (1987a) and Preston (1989) limit their arguments to the United States, a nation with relatively weak institutions of social protection. However, critics point to the lack of evidence for the importance of cohort size in either direction in European nations. Based on a contextual argument, both the positive and negative effects of cohort size will emerge less strongly in European nations because of their stronger welfare-state institutions, and more strongly in nations like the United States with weaker welfare-state institutions.

Across time periods, changes in the strength of institutions of social protection during the expansion of the welfare state over the post–World War II period should reduce the importance of cohort size. Much of Easterlin's evidence in support of the importance of cohort size comes from fertility trends during the 1950s–1970s. The weaker evidence for later periods may result from the concurrent growth of public programs that cushion the harm of a poor job market. Similarly, the increase over time in gender equality within nations may modify the potential for cohort size to influence fertility and mortality. Women's increasing commitment to work rather than family may moderate the harm for family income of large cohort size and low relative income of males.

Across ages, varying sources of income mean that arguments about cohort size should fit some groups better than others. Easterlin applies his arguments about the harmful effect of cohort size most strongly to young persons entering the labor market and adults depending on private market income for their economic well-being. Both groups occupy their lives with efforts to complete school, attain occupational success, and build a family. Preston applies his arguments about the benefits of large cohort size to children and the elderly, who have weak attachments to the labor force, depend more on government income transfers, and (at least for the elderly) involve themselves with public policy and politics. Age groups dependent on market income suffer economic harm and social costs from large size, while age groups more dependent on transfers recoup benefits from large size.

Consider, too, how these same arguments for the importance of institutional context also apply to sex differences in mortality. Since the harm of large cohort size on economic well-being comes in relation to success in private labor markets, men and women respond differently to cohort change. Nations, time periods, and being of an age that reduces one's dependence on market work may also reduce the impact of large cohort size on differences in male and female demographic behavior. Universal programs of public social protection would mitigate the special influence of cohort size on men, while the less interventionist policies of other nations would exacerbate them. Thus, the larger the role of the welfare state relative to the market, the weaker the differences in how cohort size affects the suicide and homicide rates of men and women and the smaller the sex differential in suicide and homicide mortality. The larger the role of earnings and the market, the greater the disadvantage of belonging to a large cohort for men relative to women and the larger the sex differential. The same argument would imply that sex differences in the effect of cohort size on suicide and homicide mortality will decline over time with expansion of the welfare state and improvement in gender inequality and will appear more strongly for age groups that are more dependent on the market than age groups that are more dependent on transfers.

In summary, the differences across high-income nations and over time in the strength of institutions of social protection and in the relative roles of the welfare state and market—and the differences across ages in the dependence on those institutions and the state—shape the kinds of influences that cohort size may have on demographic outcomes. This claim implies that cohort changes and sociopolitical context have a combined, interactive, or contingent influence rather than a separate, additive, or invariant influence. I later define more precisely the dimensions of sociopolitical context in terms of collectivism and individualism and the temporal dimensions of context in terms of welfare-state expansion. At this stage, however, the argument that the consequences of changing cohort sizes for several demographic and social outcomes depend on the varied sociopolitical institutions across nations, time periods, and ages provides a general perspective to make sense of complex demographic processes.

This preliminary statement of the context-specific influence of population change thus brings together the several arguments presented in this chapter. Despite the importance attributed to cohort size by many theories, the empirical literature has found only mixed support, in large part because both theorists and researchers expect the processes to work identically across all high-income nations and all time periods. However, since institutions of social protection differ across nations, time, and ages, demographic processes may vary as well. The sources of institutional divergence help explain demographic divergence in the effects of cohort change on fertility, mortality, and sex differences in mortality.

Divergence in the Consequences of Female Work

The same logic applied to cohort change implies divergence in the consequences of female work for fertility and mortality. If female work has different, rather than identical, meanings and consequences in different contexts, its influence can be treated as a variable (Mason 1997). Such an approach would help make sense of anomalous findings in the importance and direction of the effects of changing female labor force participation on diverse demographic outcomes. Inconsistent empirical results may again relate to the divergent sociopolitical contexts across the nations and time periods in which researchers have studied the impact of gender equality. To restate the basic thesis of this book in a slightly revised version, *the influence of female work on demographic outcomes varies across institutional environments for social protection.* Institutional environments that differ across nations, time periods, and ages shape or specify the relationships between female work and fertility, certain types of mortality, and sex differences in these types of mortality.

For fertility, the argument claims in general terms that the institutional environment may affect the degree of role incompatibility and conflict between work and family duties of women, which in turn shapes the relationship between female labor force participation and fertility. Fertility should rise or at least remain stable in response to women's changing work roles where and when institutions moderate the work-parenting conflict but should decline where and when institutions do little to deal with this conflict. Institutions that favor flexible job schedules, part-time work, paid parental leave, and access to child care outside the family should, for example, reduce the harm for fertility of women's work (Bernhardt 1993).

Applied to changes over time, the argument predicts that female labor force participation initially reduces fertility but later comes to have no effect on or increases fertility. The initial entrance of large numbers of women of childbearing age into the labor force initially conflicts with traditional family responsibilities but later generates institutional changes that accommodate work to family care needs. Initially, changes that move women out of traditional family roles make childbearing more expensive and difficult. Female work will have, according to this supposition, the strongest negative effect from the 1950s to the 1970s when pioneering changes in women's roles conflicted most with traditional ways of raising children. During the 1980s and 1990s, however, as institutions and policies became more favorable to combining roles of work and family, female work comes to have a different effect on fertility. With reduced inequality, women's new roles make for less conflict as institutions adapt to pressures for change and become more supportive of fertility.

Applied to differences across nations, the argument predicts that adjustments in institutional supports for working women, and the declining harm of female work for fertility, will occur more quickly in some nations than in others. Female work may have curvilinear effects on fertility, but the initial negative effects will reverse quickly with egalitarian policies. As nations with strong institutions of social protection do the most to moderate the risks of income loss for workers, they may do the most to ease the conflict between the dual roles of women. Indeed, the Nordic nations offer not only generous benefits for retirement, unemployment, and sickness but also paid maternity leave, opportunities for part-time work, and access to high-quality day care to working mothers. Institutions for both class protection or gender equality, then, may weaken the harm of rising female work on fertility and produce a quicker shift from negative to zero or positive effects.

For mortality, the contextual argument specifies similar patterns of change in the relative rates of suicide and homicide of women. Since new roles initially disrupt traditional values and create normative uncertainty, entering the labor force in an institutional environment generally unsupportive of women's independence creates problems for women. Hence, initial movement toward equality may raise female suicide and homicide mortality rates. However, institutions of social protection eventually adapt to pressures for change, new norms gain wide acceptance, and women benefit more completely from their new opportunities. As the environment becomes more supportive of women's independence, continued movement toward increased work and higher female status brings mortality benefits to women. Thus, institutional adjustment posits a process of adaptation that produces patterns of convergence, then divergence, in suicide and homicide mortality rates of women relative to men.

The argument likewise suggests differences across nations in the effect of female work on gender differences in mortality. Those nations with the strongest institutions of social protection will show a quicker adjustment of relative violent mortality rates of women to social change. All nations will experience the curvilinear effect of female work and status on relative mortality, but the initial decline will be smaller in some nations than in others. The Nordic nations do the most to support women and will likely experience smaller effects of female work and smaller convergence in relative mortality rates. Other nations likely will show slower adjustment in the effects of female work.

To recap, the differences in institutional support for women across time periods and high-income nations shape the kind of influence that female labor force participation has on demographic outcomes. Like the argument about cohort size, this argument implies that female work and sociopolitical context have combined, interactive, or contingent influences rather than separate, additive, or invariant influences on fertility and mortality. The next chapter does more to define the dimensions of sociopolitical context relevant to female work and demographic outcomes. For now, the argument takes into consideration that since sociopolitical institutions of social protection relevant to gender equality differ crucially across nations and over time, demographic processes relating female work, fertility, and mortality may vary as well and may help explain empirical divergence in the effects of female work.

The claim for context-specific influences of female work also helps explain some unexpected or ambiguous findings in the literature on fertility and mortality. Despite the often-demonstrated negative relationship between female work and fertility, some studies unexpectedly find a positive relationship at the macrolevel. Similarly, researchers have found both negative and positive relationships between female work and sex differences in mortality. Rather than expecting the same relationship across all high-income nations and time periods, institutional adjustment predicts variation in the direction of the relationships across contexts.

Politics and Demography

These arguments that institutional contexts shape the nature and even the direction of the influences of cohort size and female work on fertility and mortality link sociopolitical context and demographic relationships in a special way. Rather than claiming that context directly influences fertility and mortality, the arguments claim that context affects the relationships between cohort size or female work and fertility or mortality. By specifying interactive or contingent relationships rather than additive or invariant relationships, I aim to do more than add one more variable to a list of determinants. I address, instead, the differences across institutional contexts in the processes determining fertility and mortality. The theoretical arguments and hypotheses thus specify interactive effects rather than additive effects.

Public policies may sometimes directly influence fertility and mortality, but the evidence does not demonstrate consistent direct effects and suggests another approach. Egalitarian institutions of social protection in Sweden, for example, seem to have lowered fertility during the early post–World War II decades but to have raised fertility in more recent decades; and less egalitarian institutions in Italy kept fertility high until recent years but then contributed to lower fertility. To make sense of contradictory direct effects, it is necessary to consider more complex arguments. I suggest that institutions of social protection affect how fertility and mortality respond to changes in cohort size and female work. Conversely, changes in cohort size and female work can facilitate the importance of sociopolitical context for fertility and mortality. The emphasis on interactive or contingent rather than additive or invariant relationships will remain central throughout this study.

Although applied specifically to relationships involving fertility and mortality, these theoretical arguments may provide a more general framework to understand how demographic and political forces work together. On the one hand, demographic arguments tend to assume that changes in the characteristics of a population produce automatic effects on the outcomes of demographic behavior.[2] Further, they assume contextual invariance: relationships operate in much the same way across a variety of nations and periods. Indeed, comparisons across space and time assume that population characteristics have similar meanings and reflect similar social needs. This sort of determinism aims for developing lawlike relationships but gives little attention to variation from the average.

On the other hand, political explanations tend to emphasize the importance of national differences more than invariance of processes (Steinmo, Thelan, and Longstreth 1992). Political perspectives often reject structural determinism in favor of a view of political contingency and contextual variability (Ragin 1987). The complexities of the political environments—the varied mix of interest groups, parties, ideologies, and policy-making institutions across nations—make broad generalizations difficult. Understanding the constellation of these forces often requires detailed national case studies (e.g., O'Connor, Orloff, and Shaver 1999).

Given their different assumptions of invariance and particularity, demographic and political perspectives have led many to view them as mutually exclusive. Yet efforts to combine the advantages of both strategies, even if they fail wholly to maintain the strengths of each, may help make sense of competing theories and inconsistent evidence (Kertzer 1997; Pollack and Watkins 1993). An integrative approach can begin with the abstract relationships among variables favored by the demographic approach but can then, in order to incorporate some of the insights of the case-based political approach, consider how the contexts of nations and time periods affect those relationships. This interactive or contextual approach negates any hope for a simple direct conclusion in the form of a single proposition. Something more than the statement "the greater X, the greater Y" is needed to make sense of varied empirical results. Instead, the relationships between variables vary systematically with contextual characteristics. While complicating the theoretical and empirical tasks facing scholars, the contingent approach helps move distinct and sometimes competing perspectives toward integration and a more complete understanding of the phenomena under study. At the same time, it attempts to make sense out of cross-national and temporal patterns rather than merely to describe a set of unique country or time-specific processes.

Tilly (1995) argues for these sorts of contingent explanations: "The construction of invariant models of revolution—which remains a major activity among American sociologists—is a waste of time. . . . The same conclusions hold for a wide range of social phenomena, including most or all large-scale political processes" (1605). Claiming that few political processes conform to invariant models, he advocates attempting to understand variations in sequences of causal processes across macrolevel phenomena rather than searching for similarities. Some demographers make the same point. Lee and Casterline (1996) and Morgan (1996), for example, criticize linear and additive models of fertility that generalize across diverse contexts. They favor nonadditive models that reflect radical discontinuities, floors, ceilings, and feedback effects in the determinants of fertility.

Overview

The importance of the institutional or political context in shaping the relationship between demographic causes and outcomes has obvious implications for the study of national patterns of fertility and mortality. It not only requires comparison of the varied levels of demographic and social variables but also requires comparison of how relationships vary across nations and time. However, limits exist in making such comparisons. For several reasons, the contextual approach, at least in regard to the issues concerning cohort size and female work, applies best to the advanced industrial or capitalist democracies. First, these nations have reached the levels of industrial development and high income needed for the development of the welfare state and for the emergence of large differences in public policy. Second, these nations have passed through the first demographic transition, experiencing population change as a result of low fertility and low mortality—precisely the demographic conditions presumed to exist by the theories discussed in the previous sections. Although substantial variation in demographic conditions remains among the sample countries, they still differ from developing countries, where high fertility and mortality dominate. Third, the high-income nations have enjoyed political democracy at least since shortly after World War II. Sociopolitical institutions and their consequences for class and gender equality vary most in nations that allow groups to organize and mobilize politically.

Limiting the study to nations with a population of at least 1 million leaves 18 nations that meet the above conditions. This includes the 13

Western European nations of the United Kingdom, Ireland, the Nether-lands, Belgium, France, German Federal Republic (later Germany), Swit-zerland, Austria, Italy, Denmark, Norway, Sweden, and Finland. It also includes Canada, the United States, Australia, New Zealand, and Japan but excludes Eastern European nations or newly democratic nations (Spain, Portugal, and Greece) that do not meet conditions of political de-mocracy during most of the postwar period.

Although only one of 18 nations in the sample, the United States gets special attention by virtue of its extreme position along many social, polit-ical, and demographic dimensions. Showing wide swings in cycles of fer-tility and cohort size, special political, cultural, and institutional traits, and extremely high levels of homicide mortality, the United States stands out from other high-income nations. Yet understanding demographic change in the United States can best come from comparisons with other high-income nations and from models that generalize beyond the experiences of a single nation.

For this set of high-income democracies, the chapters to follow examine several demographic-related outcomes: fertility, suicide and homicide mor-tality, and sex differences in suicide and homicide mortality. If the socio-political institutional contexts similarly shape the determinants of all these outcomes, it will demonstrate robustness of the results and the generality of the theory. Despite the use of the summary term "mortality" in the book title, suicide and homicide mortality deserve special attention for several reasons. One reason is that, in examining age differences in mor-tality and giving special attention to youth, cohort size, and female work, the theory and analyses need to highlight mortality that varies across the life course. Among the high-income and low-mortality nations, age pat-terns in lethal violence may vary more than age patterns in mortality from all causes. While the age trajectory of mortality from all causes is heavily weighted by deaths from degenerative diseases closely related to physio-logical and developmental changes during old age, the age trajectories of mortality from suicide and homicide relate less directly to biological resis-tance (Horiuchi and Wilmoth 1998). Instead, they relate more immedi-ately to social conditions involving group integration and interpersonal conflict and, therefore, may vary widely with temporal and national differ-ences in social conflict.

Another reason to focus on suicide and homicide mortality is that, whereas deaths from degenerative diseases at the older ages result primarily from the long-term accumulation of the effects of certain behaviors, suicide and homicide respond more immediately to social circumstances and do not require decade-long lags to observe the consequences of social behavior. The daily problems of living and personal distress, risky behaviors and lifestyles, and the degree of social integration and support will have immediate effects that can be observed in suicide and homicide rates but in few other forms of mortality. Without data over a much longer time span, the study of cancer, heart disease, and all causes of mortality combined do not prove as suitable.

Finally, as argued by Durkheim ([1897] 1966), suicide rates (and perhaps homicide rates as well) relate to fertility rates. Although I focus on the consequences of relative cohort size and female labor force participation for fertility and mortality rather than on the consequences of social integration and regulation, the links between fertility, suicide, and homicide offer some justification for their common study. Moreover, the study of all three topics contributes to generality in the conclusions: the demographic outcomes differ enough that applying the contingent or contextual argument to them should provide a stringent test of the theory behind them. Further, if the integrative arguments apply not only to multiple dependent variables but also to different independent variables, their validity will be strengthened.

With this framework in mind, the next chapter examines the demographic and political backgrounds of the high-income nations during the post–World War II period. It highlights, through discussion of previous research, both the convergence and divergence in national demographic trends. It also includes a general description of social and political differences across the high-income nations. Although all high-income nations are democracies with mature welfare states, they differ in the strength of their institutions for social protection from dependence on the market or family support and in their universalist or solidaristic public policies in support of workers and women. Finally, it constructs measures of these institutional differences across nations for use in subsequent chapters.

The second section of the book considers the contingent determinants of fertility. Chapter 3 presents the theoretical arguments about cohort size, female work, fertility, and institutional context in more detail. Chapter 4 examines cohort size and the total fertility rate, and chapter 5 examines female labor force participation and the total fertility rate.

The third section of the book considers the determinants of suicide and homicide mortality. Chapter 6 applies the general theoretical arguments about sociopolitical context and cohort size to these types of mortality.

Chapter 7 examines the determinants of age-specific suicide rates for males and females, and chapter 8 does the same for age-specific homicide mortality rates.

The fourth section of the book considers sex differences in suicide and homicide mortality. Chapter 9 presents the theoretical arguments, and chapters 10 and 11 analyze the contingent effects of female employment.

CHAPTER 2

Sociopolitical Sources of Demographic Divergence

The thesis of this study—that the influence of cohort size and female work on demographic outcomes varies across nations and time periods with different institutional environments—implies the existence of both sociopolitical and demographic variation across the otherwise relatively homogenous high-income nations.[1] This chapter considers the evidence of this variation. In my review here of several research literatures, I find that, despite pressures toward convergence, high-income nations exhibit substantial diversity in national institutions and offer many exceptions to general demographic patterns. This divergence deserves attention along with efforts to generalize about the consequences of economic and demographic modernization to all nations.

Toward that end, I describe, in the first section, national differences in institutional strategies of political decision making and public policies that may affect the influence of cohort size on fertility and mortality. In the next section, I examine national differences in institutional strategies of promoting gender equality through public policy that may affect the influence of female work on fertility and mortality. Having identified the sociopolitical sources of divergence, I then describe differences across nations in fertility and mortality. The existence of national divergence in fertility and mortality may at least potentially correspond to divergence in institutions of social protection and gender equality. Finally, I construct scales that measure national differences in institutions of social protection and gender equality and that may shape the influence of cohort size and female work on divergence in fertility and mortality.

Divergence in National Institutions of Social Protection

Arguments for convergence in welfare-state institutions stem from theories of industrialism popular several decades ago. According to the theories, common imperatives of industrial technologies—including the need for social protection of skilled workers subject to employment dislocations, of groups poorly prepared for industrial work, and of older persons facing mandatory retirement or health problems—generate similar social, political, and economic institutions to deal with problems of the labor force (Inkeles 1981; Kerr et al. 1964). Common pressures reduce the importance of traditional cultural differences across nations, and produce quite similar institutions of social protection. Although some nations began public programs by providing universal flat-rate benefit payments, and others began by providing unequal benefits based on wage contributions, the two systems tend to become more alike as the former adds special benefits for high-wage workers and the latter adds minimum benefits for the poor. Similarly, primarily public-pension systems tend to add private pension options, and primarily private-pension systems add government guarantees and supervision. The convergence argument recognizes differences across nations in the generosity of welfare benefits but views them primarily as the result of variation in the size of the aged population and other groups in need (Wilensky 1976).

The past several decades of research, however, have rejected such claims. Comparisons of the levels of public spending for social protection programs of retirement, unemployment, health, and family expenses reveal differences across nations that have remained steady or have increased in recent years. Indeed, nations have responded to recent fiscal problems in contrasting ways, with some trying (with varied success) to cut benefits, and others trying (again, with varied success) to increase taxes to maintain the benefit levels (Castles and Pierson 1996).

More important, nations differ qualitatively as well as quantitatively in their institutions of social protection. Esping-Andersen (1990, 1999) argues that, based on underlying social philosophies, nations vary in the extent to which policies provide universal protection to persons from contingencies of old age, sickness, and unemployment (see also Korpi 1989; Palme 1990; Wennemo 1992). For example, in contrast to nations with contribution-based insurance benefits or means-tested benefits, nations with universal coverage guarantee protection without regard to prior market participation. Regardless of common economic pressures, then, nations maintain different types of welfare-state institutions because they have incommensurate underlying philosophies of social protection. Rather than converging toward a single model, nations have followed multiple paths to reach capitalist social and economic goals (Korpi and Palme 1998).

Several kinds of institutional differences among the high-income nations may contribute to the lack of convergence in welfare states. Institutions refer here to stable structures and roles linking the exercise of political power and authority to the distribution of goods and services. They include both procedures for decision making and the policy outcomes for social protection that come from the decision making. For example, nations with institutions that promote collective solidarity in decision making, encompassing group interests, and social and economic equality across classes do most to protect citizens from dependence on the market and contribute most to economic well-being with public social provision. In contrast, nations with institutions that promote direct political competition, diverse and numerous group interests, and social and economic individualism do less to protect citizens from dependence on the market and provide less in the way of public social provision. These institutional differences are numerous and complex, but scholars have highlighted several more specific dimensions of comparison.

First, the historical presence of corporatist organization of classes in some nations helps make class associations the primary sources of group identification and mobilization. Schmitter (1979) defines democratic corporatism as a system in which interest groups are organized into centralized and monopolistic, class-based peak associations that participate in state policy formation and implementation (see Williamson [1989] for a review of competing definitions). Corporatist bargaining arrangements require the existence of a unified, centrally organized labor movement that can use its power to force capitalist compromise. This arrangement, which contrasts with the existence of numerous, fragmented, nonhierarchal, and specialized interest groups in noncorporatist nations, promotes cooperation within and compromise across classes. Cooperative decision making in turn promotes universal and egalitarian programs for social protection.

Second, nations differ in the constitutionally mandated procedures for democratic rule. At one extreme, majoritarian democracies govern with one-party rule, fusion of the cabinet and legislature, and plurality election systems. At the other extreme, consensus democracy involves partisan parties acting in concert to reconcile conflicting interests (Lijphart and Crepaz 1991). Consensus democracies have institutional structures that promote collaboration and cooperation rather than majoritarian decision making. When dispersed and shared in a variety of ways, political power encourages coalition formation rather than direct electoral competition as a means to solve conflicts. It tends to result in public programs favoring collective rather than particular group interests and universal rather than market-based benefits.

Third, nations differ in the electoral success of social democratic, social-ist, or labor parties relative to liberal, conservative, or Christian democratic parties (Western 1991). As illustrated by the contrasting characteristics of social welfare states in Scandinavian and English-speaking nations, pow-erful leftist parties promote strongly egalitarian, generous, and universal social policies. Their policies aim to reduce the dependence of workers on the market and to moderate class differences in economic well-being.

Fourth, Esping-Andersen's (1990, 1999) three welfare-state regimes are based on differing institutions of social protection. Social democratic na-tions treat universal welfare programs as a means to promote solidarity and equality across classes; conservative nations provide benefits in order to maintain existing status differentials between occupational and industrial social groups; and liberal nations reinforce the free market by providing benefits on the basis of wage contributions or means tests. These welfare-state philosophies and the resulting policy types promote (or discourage) collective solidarity and egalitarianism in social protection.[2]

Fifth, Schmitter (1981) emphasizes national differences in the degree to which citizens initiate efforts to influence public choices through violent or illegal ways. He argues that "governability" stems from the consolida-tion of interests into groups that can resolve political conflicts peacefully through collective compromise. As such, governability reflects both nor-mative commitments and structural institutions to avoid political vio-lence. Like the other components, governability incorporates diverse soci-etal groups into collective decision making and produces egalitarian and universal public programs.

Together, these institutional characteristics define diverse sociopolitical contexts. At one extreme, nations with collectivist sociopolitical and eco-nomic institutions stress social solidarity and universalism in social protec-tion. Collectivist institutions typified in the Nordic nations of Sweden, Norway, Denmark, and Finland promote class equality, universal coverage for welfare-state programs, and independence from market forces. At the other extreme, nations with individualist institutions emphasize individual property rights more than equality, work-based and means-tested eligi-bility more than universal qualifications for welfare-state programs, and dependence on market forces more than politically based social protec-tion. Individualist institutions emerge most strongly in English-speaking nations. In between these two extremes fall the central European nations such as Germany, France, and Italy. These nations rely on a strong state relative to the market as in collectivist Nordic nations but are less committed to equality than to maintaining traditional hierarchal social organization as in the individualist English-speaking nations.

I use the terms "collectivism" and "individualism" to refer to the extremes of this dimension. Collectivism does not, in this context, refer to state ownership and control of the means of production but to variation among capitalist democracies in strategies of social protection. It highlights the distinction among capitalist democracies between institutions that promote communal bonds in political life and institutions that promote market competition.[3] Although this discussion compares ideal types at the extremes of the dimension, nations in fact represent points somewhere between the extremes and differ in quantity as well as quality. The dimension thus highlights sources of institutional divergence across the high-income nations and, later in the chapter, will provide the basis for a comparative measure of sociopolitical context.

The collectivist-individualist dimension of social protection likely relates to divergence in the influence of relative cohort size on fertility and mortality. It may shape the vulnerability of cohorts to fluctuations in size, the supply of workers, and opportunities for employment, promotion, and high wages. As presented in the last chapter, the argument suggests that collectivist nations moderate the negative effect of large cohort size on fertility and the positive effect of large cohort size on mortality. Since the consequences of cohort size stem from its influence on market opportunities, collectivist institutions that reduce dependence on the market should also reduce the importance of relative cohort size for demographic outcomes.

Divergence in National Institutions Supporting Gender Equality

Women in high-income, low-fertility nations have moved toward greater equality with men over the past several decades. After a period of quiescence during the 1950s, feminism reemerged forcefully during the 1960s and has continued since then to promote female independence and economic advancement. Less clear has been the contribution of the state to these changes. Initial feminist theory debated claims that the state either reproduced and reinforced women's dependence or empowered women by acting in their interests (Misra and Akins 1998), but such theory too often generalized across all nations in making these claims. More recently, scholars have rejected claims of homogeneity in the treatment of women across nations and devoted attention to national differences in how state policies advantage or disadvantage women (Mósesdóttir 1995; Sainsbury 1996).

As some nations have done more than others to equalize class differences, they may have also done more to transform gender relations, respond to pressures for gender equality, and ameliorate gender inequalities in work and income. Such differences produce variation in the relative power of men and women and shape the context in which decisions to have children are made and in which sex differences in mortality occur. The key to variation in institutions of social protection is the extent to which policies insulate citizens from dependence either on work or on other family members (Lewis 1993). Institutions that insulate women from involuntary dependence on the family complement those that insulate men and women from involuntary dependence on the labor market.

Consider two general strategies to reduce involuntary female dependence—a liberal feminist strategy and a state feminist strategy—and their effectiveness in reaching this goal. A liberal feminist strategy focuses on ensuring individual rights to equal opportunity and nondiscrimination primarily in the public spheres of school, work, and politics. The state should regulate competition for valued economic and social goods by guaranteeing that laws, employers, and administrators treat gender neutrally. Laws should eliminate exclusionary rules based on size, strength, or fetal protection, mandate antidiscrimination programs to give women access to jobs from which they traditionally have been excluded, and require equal pay for equal work. The focus on individual rights and the neutral treatment of gender ignores reproductive differences, leaving problems of family and home for women to solve individually. It also tends to leave intact the values that dominate the workplace and to require women to adapt to the status quo.

In contrast, a state feminist strategy focuses on efforts to socialize child care and housework in ways that make work and family less incompatible. Less neutral in orientation than the liberal strategy, the statist strategy recognizes and attempts to compensate for reproductive differences between men and women (Heitlinger 1993; Hernes 1987). In aiming more for equality of result than equality of opportunity, the state not only should eliminate direct discrimination against individuals but should also minimize indirect discrimination against women as a group. To do so, the state intervenes in the domestic sphere as well as in the public sphere (Hewlett 1986). Laws give preferential treatment to women to redress past inequalities, counter male domination in positions of power, and integrate work and family responsibilities. Paid pregnancy and maternity leave, child-care services, flexible work hours, and special social security and tax laws help reconcile women's domestic responsibilities with desires for employment (Kamerman and Kahn 1991). The strategy expands state power and may latently legitimize other forms of discrimination by recognizing the special needs of women. Yet it does so with the goal of equalizing the ability of women to compete with men in the labor market.

These two approaches to gender equality correspond to larger philosophies of state action to redress class inequality. Despite disputes within and across nations over the efficacy of each strategy, one strategy tends to dominate in particular nations and to emerge in response to existing institutions. The liberal strategy has emerged most strongly in individualist nations such as the United States, where the women's movement maintains autonomy from traditional parties and class-based interest groups. These nations tend to have decentralized political opportunity structures in which numerous and specialized interest groups compete for resources. As a result, women's movements avoid close collaboration and can press their demands for equal opportunity across party boundaries (Gelb 1989). Independence from traditional male power structures in parties and unions may give women's movements greater ability to influence policy but can sometimes result in disenfranchisement.

The reformist strategy of state feminism tends to emerge in collectivist, egalitarian, and interventionist nations (Karvonen and Selle 1995) that maintain institutions for cooperative decision making and universal policies (Matland 1995). Alliances of women with workers, the poor, and other disadvantaged groups make sense in nations substantially committed to collective efforts to reduce inequality. As they transformed the relationship between state and market, social democracy and worker movements may help transform the relationships among state, market, and family (Lewis 1992; Orloff 1993).

Although some dispute exists (Gelb 1989), cross-national comparisons suggest that state feminism common in the collectivist nations does the most to create conditions for gender equality. Norris (1987) finds smaller pay differentials, less occupational segregation, more liberal reproductive rights, better public child care, and more egalitarian attitudes in nations with strong leftist parties than in nations with strong rightist parties. She suggests that working within organized socialism offers an effective route to the economic and social goals of the women's movement. Case studies of the Nordic nations, particularly Sweden, also identify the progress made by the state in reducing female dependence. By encouraging paid work for women and addressing family obstacles to paid work, social democratic

governments have substantially improved women's social and economic independence (Chamberlayne 1993; Kolberg 1991; Lewis 1993). Also, entitlements in these nations, based on citizenship rather than on status as
wives or mothers, do much to neutralize women's dependence on work or
partners for income support (O'Connor 1993; Sainsbury 1996). Complete equality between men and women does not exist in Sweden or the
other Nordic nations—occupational segregation remains high (Charles
1992; Hoem 1995), part-time rather than full-time work predominates
(Rosenfeld and Birkelund 1995), and the burden of caring for others persists for women (Borschost 1994)—but movement toward gender equality
has proceeded farther than in other nations.

In classifying the European nations according to how well their policies promote female autonomy, Singh (1998) makes much the same point
about the progressivism of collectivist nations (also see Gauthier [1996b]
for a similar classification). Reviewing policies in the areas of social protection, legal rights, tax incentives, sexual discrimination, maternity benefits,
child care, divorce, reproductive rights, and legislative representation, she
identifies four groups of European nations. First, advanced nations—best
exemplified by Sweden but also including Norway, Denmark, and Finland—do the most to promote gender autonomy. Second, potentially progressive nations, including Belgium, France, and Italy, offer family-friendly
policies that often have traditional, profamily motivations but help women
realize goals of work and family. Third, conservative nations, which include Austria, Germany, the Netherlands, and the United Kingdom, remain committed to the traditional gender-based division of family labor
and to a limited role of the state in addressing women's problems. Fourth,
Ireland and Switzerland represent nations that exhibit hostility to gender
change.

In updating his 1990 work, Esping-Andersen (1999) extends his concept of the decommodification of labor to address national differences in
women's family roles. As the state can contribute to decommodification of
labor by protecting workers from the loss of wage employment, the state
can contribute to defamilialization—the unburdening of household duties
and the diminishing of individual dependence on kin for social and economic welfare. State policies contribute to defamilialization by providing
opportunities for women to enter the labor force and support an independent household.

Although classifications of nations such as these roughly correspond
to the collectivist-individualist distinction based on redistribution across
classes, differences exist. Sainsbury (1996) notes that the Netherlands, con-

sidered a social democratic or collectivist nation in class-based schemes, consistently disadvantages women compared to Sweden. O'Connor, Orloff, and Shaver (1999) also claim that the United Kingdom differs substantially from other liberal nations, such as the United States, by making its benefits widely available to women. Finally, conservative nations that fall in the middle of the collectivism dimension may do less to protect women and more to maintain traditional family roles than liberal nations at the individualist extreme of the collectivism dimension. These inconsistencies imply the need to identify separate gender- and class-based institutions of social protection.

Esping-Andersen (1999) also highlights differences as well as similarities between his concepts of decommodification and defamilialization. Scandinavian nations in particular use social policy to ease both the risk of loss of market work and the dependence of women without market work on family support. The liberal nations—the United Kingdom, Ireland, Australia, New Zealand, Canada, and the United States—offer, in contrast, little in the way of public support for wage or home workers, but the low cost of hired child care and the reliance on private social protection increase the likelihood that mothers will work. The conservative nations of central and southern Europe do the most to maintain the traditional family and have low rates of female labor force participation. They, more than the liberal nations, may differ most from social democratic nations.

Whatever the relationship between collectivism and gender equality, the attention to national differences in institutions for gender-based social protection again demonstrates cross-national divergence. Further, differences in institutional strategies may relate to national differences in how fertility, suicide, and homicide rates respond to the modernizing influences of women's work and family change. Collectivism, or state feminism, and individualism, or liberal feminism, may specify the impact of changes in women's work and family roles on these demographic outcomes. If, however, feminist critics of the class-based collectivism scheme are correct, a different pattern of nation-specific effects on fertility and mortality may emerge: the adjustment process may occur less quickly in conservative nations than in liberal nations. In other words, institutions that reduce class inequality will have less relevance to defining the context of social protection for women, and alternate measures of institutional context will do better than measures of collectivism in specifying the influence of female work on fertility and mortality. Context remains important, but empirical investigation is needed to define the contextual characteristics relevant to gender inequality.

Fertility

Having demonstrated national variation in institutions and policies promoting class and gender equality, I can proceed to a similar task for demographic outcomes. Differences across nations exist in fertility and lethal violence in the forms of suicide and homicide. Further, these demographic differences may relate to sources of divergence in class and gender institutions. Later chapters develop the link between political context and demographic outcomes in more detail, but the overview of demographic variation in this section on fertility and the next section on mortality can offer some insights into the link.

Arguments for convergence in fertility levels stem from claims that high income generates desires for individual autonomy from traditional family, community, and religious authority (Cliquet 1991; Lesthaeghe 1995; van de Kaa 1987, 1988). As cultures shift to individual and nonreligious values and as women become more attached to the labor force, the demand for children and the level of fertility fall. In relation to convergence, these forces exerting downward pressure on fertility in the high-income nations seem to cross national boundaries. Because of increased international communication across nations through movies, media, technology, and trade, the economic structures, cultural values, and contraceptive technologies responsible for low fertility diffuse quickly across high-income nations. Efforts toward European economic and political unification in the past decade may accelerate such diffusion. As a result, historically large national differences in fertility converge.

When fertility falls to below replacement levels, less room exists for it to fall much further. Although tolerant of fertility modestly below the replacement level, policy makers and citizens seem more troubled by total fertility rates that fall closer to 1 than 2 and threaten to produce negative rates of natural increase in the immediate future. These contrasting pressures—a floor below which societies and their members seem not to want to fall and desires for individual freedom and female equality—produce similar fertility levels in high-income nations that fluctuate slightly below replacement (Keyfitz 1991). They limit the potential for national differences in the levels and age patterns of fertility. In part as a result of these pressures, the total fertility rate has, since the mid-1960s, declined synchronically in nearly all high-income nations to levels varying from 1.3 to slightly over 2 (Chesnais 1992). According to this view, although the nations show some differences, no clear pattern of variation has emerged in the past decade: random fluctuation in the range of below replacement-level fertility seems to characterize the high-income nations.

A review of the evidence, however, suggests some important deviations from the expected convergence, with the trends in total fertility rates showing at least some variation among the relatively homogeneous set of high-income nations (Coleman 1996; Klinger 1991). For example, fertility rates in the more traditional and largely Catholic nation of Italy have recently fallen to near the world's lowest levels, contrasting with resurgent fertility levels in Sweden and Norway (Chesnais 1992; Pinelli 1995). Perhaps in part the result of high teenage birth rates, the United States has relatively high fertility rates, while other nations such as Germany have relatively low rates.

If these differences reflect more than national idiosyncrasies, they would prove consistent with longer-term demographic processes. Viewed over the past 150 years, convergence may reflect only a short-term and temporary synchronicity during the late 1960s and early 1970s. For example, Watkins (1991) demonstrates that from 1860 to 1960, variation in fertility declined within nations but increased across nations. She argues that community networks became increasingly bounded by national identities and account for national divergence in the timing of fertility declines in the first demographic transition. Such arguments also are consistent with the findings of the importance of culture-specific diffusion for the decline of European fertility identified by the Princeton project (Coale and Watkins 1986). Low mortality and high income may be prerequisites for a transition to low fertility, but they still leave much opportunity for nation-specific diversity (Chesnais 1992; Lesthaeghe 1995). More recently, transnational economic competition and the emergence of the European community actually highlight the salience of national identity rather than eliminating it in favor of some sort of postnational identity (Deflem and Pampel 1996). Despite globalization, "the peoples of different societies are characterized by enduring differences in basic attitudes, values, and skills: in other words, they have different cultures" (Inglehart 1990, 3).

These sources of divergence in fertility levels and patterns may relate to the two components of institutions for collective protection discussed in the previous sections. One component involving collective, solidaristic, and egalitarian institutions for social protection may affect the social context of family decision making by encouraging bonds across as well as within generations. Since raising the next generation contributes to the reproduction of the population and labor force and in the long run provides workers to support future retirees, it may be viewed as a collective responsibility. Those without children should contribute to the expensive tasks of those who do have children since all citizens will benefit from the entrance of new generations into adulthood. Nations with collectivist institutions thus do more to distribute the costs of child rearing across generations with their social programs (Pampel and Adams 1992). Nations that treat family support as a private matter, in contrast, do little to reduce the costs of childbearing.

Institutions for social protection in general and family support in particular do not, however, appear to raise fertility levels greatly. Cross-national studies that measure family benefits in some detail find a significant but quite small positive effect on fertility (Blanchet and Ekert-Jaffé 1994; Cliquet 1991; Gauthier and Hatzius 1997; Höhn 1991). Studies of individual nations sometimes reveal more evidence of the ability of public programs to affect fertility (Hoem 1990, 1993; Whittington, Alm, and Peters 1990) but only within a small range. Another type of effect may instead contribute to national diversity. Rather than directly raising or lowering fertility, collectivist family support may make fertility levels less susceptible to fluctuations in economic circumstances across cohorts. The ability to support children partially with public income sources makes dependence on private income sources less crucial and low income less harmful to childbearing. If fertility levels in collectivist nations relate less closely to changes in cohort size, unemployment, and income than in individualist nations, institutions for social protection contribute to demographic diversity.

The second component involving gender-based institutions for social protection also differs across countries in ways that may affect fertility. The recent rise of fertility in egalitarian Sweden and the decline in Italy, where the state has done little to support combined work and child-rearing roles for women, appear consistent with this thesis (Chesnais 1996; Day 1995). Also, despite high national income, German-speaking nations show considerably lower rates of female labor force participation and higher levels of gender inequality than Scandinavian or English-speaking nations (Schmidt 1993). In part because of limited policy efforts to combine work and family, Germany has low rates of both fertility and female labor force participation (Hantrais 1994). Finally, a detailed comparison of fertility in the Netherlands and France demonstrates that lower institutional support for women in the Netherlands led to an earlier and larger drop in fertility during the 1960s (Nimwegen, Chesnais, and Dykstra 1993).

Similar national differences may contribute to varied age patterns of fertility. Economic opportunities in general, and for young women in particular, likely have some influence on the propensity to have children at young ages. By improving educational and job opportunities for young women, institutions can encourage them to postpone births. Through their effects on teen fertility, then, economic and labor market conditions can contribute to national differences in overall fertility. Accordingly, rates of teenage conception and birth appear much higher in the United States than in more egalitarian European nations (Jones et al. 1985, 1989).

In terms of changes over time, gender-based institutions may have another effect on fertility. As institutional supports for women improve over time, the fertility-inhibiting effects of women's work should decline over time. Quicker adjustment would occur in nations with women-friendly institutions of social protection, and the negative effects of women's work would reverse sooner. Slower adjustment would occur in nations that treat women's problems of combining work and family roles as a private matter.

In summary, both types of institutions contribute to diversity in fertility determinants and outcomes across nations. Collectivist institutions might moderate the negative effect of limited job opportunities, low wages and salaries, and high risks of unemployment that relate to large cohort size on fertility. Women-friendly institutions might also limit the negative effect on fertility of female labor force participation.

Mortality

As demonstrated for fertility, the national patterns of mortality in general and suicide and homicide in particular show divergence despite predictions to the contrary. Predictions of convergence follow from arguments specifying the compression of mortality into the oldest ages as life expectancy continues to rise. Fries (1980, 1989) claims that as life expectancy approaches its projected maximum of 85, variability around that limit declines, and the age curve of survivorship increasingly comes to resemble a rectangle. The ceiling limits the potential for national differences in mortality and for variation across nations in age patterns of mortality. With the quick diffusion of modern medical technology in recent decades, the decline in deaths from infectious diseases, and improved medical care, sanitation, and nutrition, the cause-specific patterns of mortality should become more alike and produce similar age patterns of mortality.

Studies of age-specific changes in mortality, however, fail to support predictions of compression. Life expectancy has increased steadily without as yet reaching an apparent limit (Manton, Stallard, and Tolley 1991), rates of decline in mortality are higher at older ages than at younger ages (Himes, Preston, and Condran 1994), and variability in rates around the mean age of death seems to have increased rather than declined (Rothenberg, Lentzer, and Parker 1991).

At the national level, studies also fail to support predictions of convergence. National rates of decline in mortality relate only weakly to previous levels, and the coefficient of variation across nations increases (Kannisto 1994; Kannisto et al. 1994). In addition, cross-national differences remain in the size and rate of change in the sex differential in mortality (Nathanson 1995), the age pattern of mortality (Himes, Preston, and Condran 1994), and the survival rates after age 80 (Manton and Vaupel 1995). Enduring national differences in mortality levels and patterns may result in part from varied distributions by cause of death: Brouard (1990) identifies clusters of high-income nations that have diverse cause-based mortality profiles as a result of health-related cultural and behavioral differences.

The lack of convergence in the levels of mortality results in part from the increasing importance of behavioral rather than medical sources of longevity (Rogers and Hackenberg 1987). Even if medical technologies diffuse quickly across nations, behavioral differences disappear less quickly. Educational, occupational, and income status differentials in mortality appear to have persisted or even widened rather than disappeared, perhaps because of enduring status differentials in smoking, diet, alcohol consumption, and risk taking (Christenson and Johnson 1995; Feldman et al. 1989; House, Kessler, and Herzog 1990; Mare 1990; Pappas et al. 1993; Preston and Taubman 1993; Rogers 1995). Although stronger in the United States, status differentials in mortality exist in European nations as well (Fox 1989; Kunst and Mackenbach 1994; Lopez, Caselli, and Valkonen 1995).

Even more so than for mortality from all causes, these differences across nations in social conditions and behavioral norms exert a crucial influence on suicide and homicide mortality. As national diversity in social and political conditions endures, so will diversity in these types of mortality. Indeed, the diffusion across nations of advanced medical techniques for treatment of infectious and degenerative diseases may make lethal violence an increasingly large component of all mortality. As medical care becomes similar, nations come to vary most in socially determined types of mortality such as suicide and homicide. At the younger ages in particular, where deaths from infectious or chronic diseases rarely occur and where deaths from suicide and homicide have increased in many nations over the past decade, lethal violence has become a major source of national diversity. The importance of behavioral sources of national mortality differences helps justify further the focus on suicide and homicide. Although arguments about the social determinants of mortality apply to lifestyle-related causes of death such as heart disease and lung cancer, suicide and homicide mortality rates are particularly well-suited for comparative study and may most strongly demonstrate differences across nations.

As with fertility, the sources of divergence in suicide and homicide mortality may relate to institutions for social protection. For one thing, collectivist, solidaristic, and egalitarian motivations in public policy should reduce status and income differentials and thereby affect homicide. Universal programs for social protection in collectivist nations—including unemployment, social assistance, family allowances, retirement, medical care, public employment, and public infrastructure—may help moderate income inequality, economic stress, and lack of opportunities that contribute to crime in general and homicide in particular. Lowering class differences in homicide by bringing the number of lower-status victims closer to the smaller number of high-status victims should lower homicide overall. With regard to suicide, the differing degrees of solidarity, egalitarianism, and identification with larger collective interests across nations may affect the nature of social integration and the determinants of suicide. Arguments about economic equality and suicide have received less attention than those for economic equality and homicide but nonetheless underscore the potential for collectivism to reduce class differences in suicide and produce diversity across nations in suicide rates.

Collectivist institutions not only reduce the disparities in suicide and homicide mortality across class and status groups but can also reduce age differences. Suicide and homicide mortality vary by age, with homicide victimization concentrated at the younger ages and suicide at the older ages. Yet, as exhibited by public support for children and the elderly, age patterns of stratification differ significantly across nations and may relate to age differences in victimization by lethal violence (Pampel 1994; Preston 1984). In nations that attempt to equalize social conditions across ages, patterns of suicide and homicide mortality may reveal relatively few age differences. In contrast, in nations with greater inequality across the life course, homicide rates may reach relatively high levels among the young and suicide rates may reach relatively high levels among the old.

A second possible connection is that, if national institutions of collectivism and individualism produce varied rates of suicide and homicide, they may also produce varied rates of suicide and homicide for women relative to men. Perhaps even more likely, women-friendly institutions may affect sex differences in suicide and homicide rates. To the extent that institutions reduce the conflict between work and family roles, they can reduce the difficulties that contribute to women's suicide. Similarly, by protecting women from vulnerability to violence of male partners, collectivist and women-friendly institutions may reduce homicide deaths of women relative to men. Sex differences thus define another dimension of divergence in mortality across high-income nations that may relate to contextual national differences.

More specifically, the structures of national institutions may relate to a pattern of social change in which women's relative mortality increases initially but later declines. The less support a nation's institutions provide for women's new roles, the longer and more difficult the adjustment of relative violence-based mortality rates to social change. Quicker adjustment (i.e., less negative impact of changes in work and family roles of women) will likely occur among nations with collectivist or women-friendly institutions of social protection.

In short, suicide and homicide mortality patterns may relate in theoretically meaningful ways to institutional divergence. National characteristics involving class equality, universalistic welfare states, and collectivism facilitate egalitarianism and solidarity across classes, ages, genders, and other dimensions of social structure. As social conditions across social groups become more similar, they become less powerful determinants of suicide and homicide mortality.

Measuring National Differences in Institutions of Social Protection

Given meaningful and measurable differences in the sociopolitical institutional environments of high-income nations described earlier in the chapter, scholars have developed numerous measures of various aspects of institutional context and used them in a variety of studies. Indeed, without such measures, the analysis of contextual determinants of demographic outcomes makes little sense. Corresponding to the review of institutional divergence, the review of measures in this section and the next describes, in specific terms, the differences across nations that will be examined in the analyses to follow.

Since certain types of institutional characteristics tend to emerge together, these measures relate closely to one another. Focusing on measures of institutions for collective social protection, this section identifies several national characteristics commonly employed in the literature on comparative politics, demonstrates similarities in the measures of these characteristics, constructs a scale based on the measures, and describes national variation in the scale. The chapters that follow can then connect the institutional collectivism scale to the relationships between cohort size, female work, and demographic outcomes.

In contrast to data updated yearly by statistical gathering agencies, institutional characteristics do not lend themselves to simple reporting and presentation. Instead, measures must come from judgments of experts culled from the relevant literature rather than from standardized sources. To simplify the task, most of the institutional variables, if not completely constant over the full time span, nonetheless change slowly because they reflect enduring national structures. The component variables and the resulting scale therefore vary across but not within countries. In choosing institutional characteristics to study, one could develop a list that well exceeds the number of the high-income nations available for study. Therefore, I limit myself to a set of five measures related most directly to the concept of collective social protection.

1. Corporatism. Corporatist arrangements for bargaining among centralized classes reflect class solidarity and class compromise conducive to collectivism. The measure is based on an index constructed from five expert-based scales (Pampel, Williamson, and Stryker 1990). It has a correlation of .983 with another corporatism scale constructed by Lijphart and Crepaz (1991) from 12 expert ratings.

2. Consensus Government. This measure sums the five related components identified by Lijphart (1984) into a single scale. The measure assigns a high score on consensus democracy to nations with coalition cabinets, balanced legislative-executive relations, proportional representation, multidimensional issue salience, and a large number of parties. In contrast, nations with majoritarian systems, typified by executive dominance, two parties, plurality or majority electoral systems, and divisions based on socioeconomic cleavages, receive low scores. A consensus government creates structural conditions conducive to cooperation between classes and parties.

3. Years Leftist Rule. This measure cumulates years of leftist rule since 1949. If demographic change has little to do with yearly changes in government or periodic elections, it may respond indirectly to support for collective social protection and interventionist policies common among nations with powerful leftist parties.

4. Universalism. Esping-Andersen's (1990) index for each nation circa 1980 includes the replacement rate of benefits, the extent of qualifying conditions for receipt of those benefits, minimum benefit levels, the percentage of contributions paid by individuals, and coverage of programs for pensions, sickness, and unemployment. A high score reflects universality of benefits and market independence, and a low score reflects restrictions on benefits and market dependence.

5. Governability. Schmitter (1981) rank orders nations during the 1960s according to the number of collective protests (i.e., riots, antigovernment demonstrations and political strikes, armed attacks in the form of attempted or actual assassinations and deaths from intergroup conflict, and strike volume in terms of worker days lost). A high score indicates low political conflict and high governability.

In previous studies, I have used these items to construct a collectivism scale. When included in a principle components factor analysis, the items produce only one significant factor, and each loads strongly on this factor. The loadings are as follows: corporatism, 0.950; universalist benefits, 0.912; governability, 0.847; leftist rule, 0.794; and consensus democracy 0.642. The high factor loadings result in high reliability (Cronbach's alpha equals 0.887). A scale computed from the factor loadings has a mean of 0 and a standard deviation of 1. Table 1 lists the values and rankings of the collectivism scale for the 18 high-income nations. The Scandinavian nations score highest, and the English-speaking nations score lowest. Among the other nations, the Netherlands, Austria, Switzerland, and Finland score relatively high, while France, Italy, and Ireland score relatively low. These rankings reflect a well-known emphasis on egalitarianism in the Scandinavian nations, perhaps stemming back to the legacy of an independent agriculture (Stephens 1979). The other end of the continuum reflects an antistatist tradition in English-speaking nations, with an emphasis on voluntary associations, church life, and intermediating interest groups (Fukuyama 1995). The middle-level nations rely on a strong state, as in the Scandinavian nations, but are less committed to equality than to maintenance of traditional hierarchal social organization. The terms "collectivism" or "individualism" may not convey fully all the relevant differences between nations implied by the measure but nonetheless provide a useful short-hand terminology.

Despite use of different names and attempts to capture different concepts, each of the items used in the scale reflects underlying commonality.

Table 1. Nation Scores for Collectivism and Women-Friendly Institutions Scales

Nation	Collectivism		Women-Friendly Institutions		Rank Difference
	Value	Rank	Value	Rank	
Australia	−1.00	16	−.91	16	0
Austria	.83	5	.81	4	1
Belgium	.23	7	.83	3	4
Canada	−1.23	17	−.68	13	4
Denmark	1.17	3	.69	6	−3
Finland	.53	7	.69	5	2
France	−.84	15	1.29	1	14
Germany	.06	9	.20	7	2
Ireland	−.55	11	−.52	12	−1
Italy	−.65	12	−.06	9	3
Japan	−.32	10	−1.22	18	−8
Netherlands	1.02	4	−.20	10	−6
New Zealand	−.83	14	−.91	17	−3
Norway	1.68	1	.39	7	−6
Sweden	1.51	2	1.15	2	0
Switzerland	.71	6	−.85	15	−9
United Kingdom	−.76	13	−.50	11	2
United States	−1.62	18	−.78	14	4

Whether comparing nations with encompassing or fragmented groups, corporatism or pluralism, cooperation and consensus or conflict and civil disorder, the items tap social and institutional differences in the nature of collectivist or individualist group relations in the political and social realm. Many other similar measures could be constructed, and this measure does not attempt to capture all relevant dimensions of political and social differences across nations. It does, however, reflect one important dimension that has been the subject of much theorizing and measurement. Accordingly, the validity of the scale and its similarity to other measures show in a close relationship ($r = .802$) to a related measure of left corporatism of Hicks and Swank (1992).

A potential source of error comes from the assumed stability of the index and its component items. Although they do not have time series to prove the assumption, comparative scholars (e.g., Esping-Andersen 1990; Hicks and Swank 1992; Lijphart 1984) note that postwar structures for corporatist bargaining, constitutional mandates for consensual government, and universalist strategies of public income redistribution have changed only rarely during the postwar period. These structures may change more dramatically, however, with European integration (Streek and Schmitter 1991). More generally, the assumed stability of these cultural and institutional forces could be relaxed if better measures were available over time. The lack of comparable data, however, requires the approximately correct assumption of stability. To the extent that national experiences violate the assumption that the cultural and institutional environment changes when the collectivism measure does not, the results will bias downward the effect of the scale on demographic outcomes.

To supplement the stable measure, it is possible to use time varying measures of social protection. Spending measures, although generally seen as less adequate in their ability to capture the redistributive aspects of welfare-state programs, nonetheless change over time. Social security spending as a percentage of gross domestic product and total government nonmilitary spending as a percentage of gross national product help define differences across time and nations in public support for social protection.

Despite the absence of change in the measure, collectivism represents a set of powerful, enduring, and broad-based national traits that influence numerous social, political, and economic outcomes. The measure proves reliable, as shown by consistency in scores across multiple measures devised independently by several scholars. The measure proves valid in that, according to numerous studies, the components of the scale (and therefore, by implication, the scale itself) relate closely to a variety of economic and political outcomes. In concrete terms, the measure taps well-known and often-demonstrated differences between Scandinavian nations and other European nations and between European nations and the former English-speaking colonies. The link between collectivism and fertility or mortality may not appear immediately obvious, but this says little about the reliability or validity of the measure. Rather, it emphasizes the benefits from specifying the theoretical mechanisms linking the concepts and from developing a good measure to test for these mechanisms.

Since collectivism obviously represents only one dimension across which national institutions differ, one could also develop institutional or contextual measures precisely tailored to explain a particular demographic outcome. Toward the goal of generality and robustness, however, I take a different strategy. Specific measures would hide the general importance of the broadly defined sociopolitical environment. An advantage of collectivism is that it may affect diverse social and demographic outcomes to which it has no immediate connection. If broad institutional forces shape the processes determining policy outcomes and demographic behaviors, then a similarly broad measure can best represent these arguments and highlight the nonobvious consequences of institutions.

Measuring National Differences in Institutional Supports for Women

To complement the collectivism measure of institutional forces promoting equality across classes, a measure of national differences in institutions promoting gender equality is needed. To some extent, the measure of collectivism may also reflect national differences in state and liberal feminist strategies of promoting gender equality. According to the criticisms made by feminists of class-based measures of policy regimes (Lewis 1993; Orloff 1993; Sainsbury 1996), however, a direct measure of institutional support for women would do better than the collectivism measure. Orloff (1993) specifies in detail a framework for comparing nations in their treatment of gender relations in state social provisions, but no one has yet constructed the data needed to operationalize the concepts. Several other measures of women-friendly policies have been constructed but often use existing data in an ad hoc fashion, lack checks for validity and reliability, and do not include all high-income nations. Some simple efforts at index construction can improve on these measures and usefully complement the collectivism measure in the analyses to come.

Again, note that a scale of institutional support for women faces the same limits as the collectivism scale: it must rely to some extent on expert judgments of national policies and must assume stability over time in national rankings. With these qualifications, I focus on measures of five dimensions of public policy relevant to gender equality. The higher the score of nations on each of these dimensions, the greater the financial support women receive for their special reproductive roles, the lower the dependence of women on a male breadwinner, and the greater the ability of women to combine work and family roles. The dimensions do not measure female equality directly—a more difficult task suited for a separate study—but do measure how government policies and laws make work and mothering more compatible.

1. Child and Family Support. Bradshaw (1994) measures cash benefits for families and children, housing benefits, the value of public preschool education, and the value of health care costs for a two-parent family as

a percentage of gross income net of taxes and social security contributions. Gauthier (1996b) presents two related measures: (1) cash benefits for families as a percentage of average wages in manufacturing and (2) supplementary income, including tax relief as well as cash benefits, available to a two-child family compared to a single worker (again as a percentage of average male wages in manufacturing). Siaroff (1994) ranks nations using a five-point scale on the generosity of family policy spending. An additive scale of child and family support created from these four measures has an alpha reliability coefficient of 0.928.

2. Maternity Leave. Siaroff (1994) ranks nations using a five-point scale on the generosity of public or publicly mandated maternity leave, with high scores indicating the most generous maternity leave policies and low scores indicating the least generous. Gauthier (1996b, 172–77) measures maternity leave benefits for women as a function of two components: the duration in weeks of maternity leave and the percentage of regular earnings available to those on maternity leave. Multiplying the two components measures the number of weeks for which women on leave receive full compensation. An additive scale of maternity leave using the two measures has an alpha reliability coefficient of 0.820.

3. Preschool Access. Siaroff (1994) ranks nations using a five-point scale on child-care availability. Gauthier (1996b, 181) measures the percentage of preschool age children in full- or part-time care, including subsidized family home care and preprimary schools. An additive scale created from these two measures has an alpha reliability coefficient of 0.950.

4. Legal Equality. Charles (1992) constructs an index "based on a principal components analysis, single-factor solution of three variables: (1) a dummy variable coded 1 if abortion is legally available to women on request; (2) a dummy variable coded 1 if marital rape is defined as a crime; and (3) a dummy variable coded 1 if women are guaranteed at least 12 weeks paid pregnancy leave from their job" (491–92). The third component overlaps with the maternity leave measure, but the first two components emphasize additional aspects of legal equality.

5. Employment Support. Gornick, Meyers, and Ross (1998) create an index that includes components of family support, maternity leave, preschool access, and legal equality contained in the previous four scales. Specifically, the index sums eight policies relevant to support of mothers with children under the age of 3, such as the coverage, length, and generosity of parental leave, the existence of tax relief for working mothers, and the access to publicly subsidized child care. They also create a corresponding

index of support for mothers with children ages 3–5. I average the two to obtain a single measure.

All of these scales and their component items correlate closely with one another. The average interitem correlation among the 10 items (four family support items, two maternity leave items, two preschool access items, the Charles index, and the Gornick et al. index) equals .601. If all 10 items are combined into a single scale, the alpha measure of reliability equals 0.938. Further, a principal components factor analysis demonstrates that all items load strongly on a single factor. Because these items relate closely to one another and appear to reflect similar rankings of the 18 nations, a combined index offers a useful summary measure of gender equality that I use in the analyses of fertility to follow.[4]

Table 1 lists the values on this combined index of women-friendly institutional support. Given a correlation of .543 between the scale and collectivism, many nations—such as Australia, Austria, Finland, Germany, Ireland, Sweden, and the United Kingdom—rank similarly on both scales. However, Switzerland, Japan, the Netherlands, and Norway score more highly on collectivism than on the gender-based scale, while France, Belgium, Canada, and the United States rank higher on the gender-based scale than on collectivism.

The United States has the lowest collectivism score in the sample. Whatever the historical causes, the liberalism, individualism, and market orientation in America differentiates it from other nations, especially European nations. However, the United States appears less extreme in its score on women-friendly institutions. Still low relative to Scandinavia, it scores higher than Switzerland, Japan, New Zealand, and Australia.

Like collectivism, the women-friendly institutions scale assumes that differences across nations persist during the post–World War II period. Obvious movement has occurred toward state support of women in all nations, just as obvious movement has occurred toward a more interventionist welfare state during the same period. The stable cross-nation measures do not deny that change but assume that the relative rankings of nations have changed little. As it does now, Sweden no doubt better supported women with its policies than Germany or the United States did in the 1950s (Gauthier 1996b). Other measures used in the analyses to come, particularly female labor force participation, reflect changes over time as well as differences across nations in women's roles, but the stable, cross-national measure of women-friendly institutions represents another important dimension that deserves study. Rather than a substitute measure of female work, national differences in women-friendly institutions may shape the effect of changes in female labor force participation on fertility and mortality.

Like the measure of collectivism, the measure of women-friendly institutions is both reliable and valid. The similarity of scores across measures constructed independently by scholars and focused on different components of public policies to promote gender equality, as shown by the factor analysis and high alpha coefficient, demonstrate the reliability of the scale. The use of the separate components to predict, for example, the ability of women with young children to continue working (Gornick, Meyers, and Ross 1998), equality in occupations of men and women (Charles 1992), and fertility rates (Gauthier and Hatzius 1997) demonstrate the validity of the scale. The measure does not capture all aspects of gender equality but identifies policy differences that make for quite varied work and family experiences of women across nations. Of course, the validity will ultimately show in the ability of the measure to shape the determinants of demographic outcomes in the statistical analyses.

The scale must exclude one component of change in the institutional context of women's work: the support for part-time work. Much of the increase in female labor force participation of mothers in European nations comes from jobs with limited, often flexible hours. With data for nine nations in the 1980s, Rosenfeld and Birkelund (1995, 116) find that the percentage of women with part-time jobs correlates .569 with guaranteed paid maternity leave and .707 with family transfers per child. If measures of part-time work were available for all nations, it would most certainly represent another component of women-friendly institutions. The overlap of part-time work and the scale will, however, prove relevant in understanding how the nature of female labor force participation—including part-time participation—changes in the presence of women-friendly institutions.

Conclusion

The material in this chapter identifies important differences that remain among the high-income democracies in political structures, ruling ideologies, strategies of state action, the organization of economic interests, and policies supportive of women. One dimension of these national differences relates to collectivist versus individualist institutions for social protection, and another relates to state versus liberal approaches to institutional support for women. Although less obvious than political differences, demographic differences in fertility and mortality also persist across the high-income nations. Despite experiencing declining fertility and mortality rates, these nations exhibit exceptions to the general patterns, exceptions that may relate to differences in types of institutions for social protection and gender equality. A review of studies of fertility, suicide, and homicide suggests potential relationships between political and demographic divergence. Although existing evidence remains sketchy, it suggests the need to investigate further how the determinants of fertility and mortality vary across sociopolitical contexts.

In this chapter, I take a first step toward this goal by constructing measures of national differences in institutions for collective social protection and national differences in institutional support for women. The collectivism measure summarizes expert classifications of the potential for government policies to insulate workers from dependence for income on the private market. In contrast to the class focus of the collectivism measure, the measure of women-friendly institutions relates to gender relations. It summarizes expert classifications of the support of government policies for working women and their potential to insulate women from dependence on male family members for income. The two measures relate closely to one another but differ in their rankings of several nations. Debates over the importance of class-based and gender-based institutions to the status and well-being of women warrant the use of both measures in the analyses to come.

Given the demonstrated differences across nations in collectivist and women-friendly institutions, fertility, and certain types of mortality and the evidence of the ability to reliably and validly measure these differences, the chapters to follow can take the next logical steps in the theoretical arguments. They can present in more detail how the institutional context of nations (and of time periods as well) can facilitate or inhibit the determinants of fertility and mortality outcomes. Specifically, the chapters in the next section consider how cohort size and female work have varied effects on fertility across collectivist and individualist nations, women-friendly and unfriendly nations, and early and late time periods. The same logic applies in later chapters that consider how the same determinants have different effects on suicide and homicide and on sex differences in suicide and homicide mortality.

PART II

Fertility

CHAPTER 3

Contextual Variation in the Determinants of Fertility

This chapter further develops the theoretical arguments specifying divergence in the effects of cohort change and female work on fertility rates. Viewed as a facilitating or inhibiting influence, the sociopolitical context may alter the cohort size–fertility relationship and the female work–fertility relationship. Collectivist and women-friendly institutions, as defined and measured in the previous chapter, serve as the primary contextual characteristics that shape the processes determining fertility rates. Although not direct and obvious, the influence of these institutions, in combination with demographic and economic conditions, may generate national differences in demographic outcomes. The first section concentrates on the contingent influence of relative cohort size, and the second section concentrates on the contingent influence of female work.

The Easterlin Effect and Fertility

The impetus for the study of cohort size and fertility comes from the work of Richard Easterlin. To review Easterlin's arguments, couples make decisions about childbearing on the basis of their income potential relative to their expected standard of living. Income potential depends on current income and perceived future earning power, which in turn depend on competition for jobs, opportunities for promotion, and the tightness of the labor market. The expected standard of living comes from childhood economic socialization — the standard of living experienced in childhood and adolescence produces aspirations that individuals and couples can compare to their income potential in young adulthood. The higher the income potential relative to the expected standard of living, the higher the fertility.

To link these arguments to age structure, Easterlin posits that cohort size represents the key determinant of both income potential and expected standard of living. Income potential depends on the size of cohorts entering the labor force, while the expected standard of living depends on the size of cohorts of the previous generation. Large cohorts face a crowded labor market—more workers, stronger competition for jobs, fewer opportunities for promotion, and lower real wages.[1] The size of current cohorts relative to the size of previous cohorts indicates a generation's income potential relative to the income of the parental generation or the expected standard of living. Thus, the size of the cohort entering the labor market relative to the size of previous cohorts yields a rough measure of relative economic status. A large youth cohort relative to the parental cohort results in relatively low income and low fertility. A small youth cohort relative to the parental cohort results in relatively high income and fertility.

The influence of cohort size on fertility can emerge through multiple mechanisms. It may influence the decision making of married couples to postpone or not postpone childbearing and may also affect fertility through decisions to marry and divorce. Members of large cohorts facing poor economic prospects may avoid marriage or, once married, divorce under the strain of economic problems. Despite the rise of extramarital fertility in recent decades, the lack of a stable marriage reduces fertility, so that cohort size has influences involving both the entrance into (or exit from) marriage and fertility decisions within marriage.

Note that Easterlin's theory emphasizes processual rather than compositional arguments. The percentage of the female population at childbearing ages will affect the total number of births or, as in the crude birth rate, the total number of births divided by the total population. However, measures such as the total fertility rate or age-specific fertility rates eliminate the compositional influence of the age distribution of the female population on fertility. According to Easterlin, cohort size has effects controlling for compositional changes in the age structure. By affecting the process of fertility determination, cohort size influences the total fertility rate and age-specific fertility rates.

Easterlin's arguments present an original and appealing perspective that differs from (and in some ways combines) both economic and sociological viewpoints. Although it treats economic status and relative income as central to fertility, Easterlin's argument rejects some assumptions of neoclassical economic models of fertility. Assuming that preferences for children remain constant, neoclassical economic models explain changes in fertility rates as a function of income and prices. According to Becker (1991), the decision to have children requires that the utility parents receive from them exceeds the expenses and lost income needed to raise them. Of special relevance in high-income nations is the fact that increasing female wages have lowered fertility rates by raising the opportunity costs or lost income of having children (Butz and Ward 1979; Robinson 1997).

Easterlin, in contrast, assumes that preferences for children change with material aspirations. Shifting preferences result from childhood economic experiences and, in combination with income and prices, greatly influence fertility decisions. From this perspective, female labor force participation rises and fertility falls because of a gap between material aspirations and economic opportunities brought on by changes in cohort size. Rather than treating fertility as a consequence of rising female labor force participation and female wages, Easterlin views female labor force participation, female wages, and fertility as determined by relative cohort size.

Although deviating from neoclassical economic models, Easterlin's reasoning also contrasts with sociological theories. Sociologists have identified changes in values in high income, postmaterialist, or postdemographic transition societies that involve a shift from an emphasis on community and family norms to an emphasis on personal goals. Values of personal fulfillment increase women's desires for work and independence, make singlehood and marital dissolution more acceptable, and make childbearing more of an individual decision independent of community and family pressures. Although desires for children remain, fertility in these societies declines and more often occurs at older ages.

Easterlin recognizes these same trends but attributes them less to permanent changes in values in high-income nations than to the consequences of reversible cohort-based shifts in preferences. The trends in values, work, and family formation result from the sense of relative deprivation experienced by the large baby boom cohorts that reached adulthood from the 1960s to the 1980s. As smaller, baby-bust cohorts reach adulthood, profamily, profertility values will reemerge. Easterlin thus views changes as cyclical rather than secular.

Empirical Evidence. Decades of research have not produced consistent support for the Easterlin effect. Despite many negative findings (e.g., Elder 1981; MacDonald and Rindfuss 1978; Thornton 1978), Macunovich's (1998) review of micro studies finds that 15 of 22 confirm Easterlin's hypothesis. Further, the negative studies of relative cohort size face two problems: many fail to measure economic status and control accurately for other relevant variables, and variation across individuals within cohorts reflects Easterlin's concepts less well than do aggregate differences between cohorts. If an environment of optimism or pessimism shapes the perceptions of all cohort members, even couples with high subjective relative income may hesitate to have children when they see the financial struggles of other members of a large cohort. A process of social contagion may occur in which cohort size changes the environment in which couples evaluate their own relative status (Easterlin 1987a). The contextual argument thus explains the weak cross-sectional microlevel effects within cohorts and can account for similar swings in fertility that researchers have found across diverse socioeconomic groups (Rindfuss and Sweet 1977; Smith 1981; Sweet and Rindfuss 1983).

At the macrolevel, studies generally find supportive results, at least until recently. In the first 3 decades after World War II in the United States, shifts in relative cohort size corresponded closely to shifts in fertility (Ahlburg 1983, 1986; Easterlin and Condran 1976; O'Connell 1978). Relatively small cohorts born during the Depression years, and entering the tight labor market of the 1950s, had high fertility compared to the larger cohorts that entered the labor market during the more depressed economy of the 1970s and the early 1980s. Overall, Macunovich (1998) notes that, similar to the microlevel studies, 15 of 22 macrolevel studies using North American data corroborate the Easterlin hypothesis.

Given the correspondence between period measures of fertility rates and cohort size during this time period, it appears that relative cohort size involves more than the residual influence of cohort net of age and period—it contributes to and overlaps with period effects on fertility. Again reflecting Easterlin's (1987a) social contagion argument, periods with large cohorts of childbearing age have low fertility rates, and periods with small cohorts have high fertility rates. By contributing to period norms, cohort size has influences that involve more than the residual remaining once removing age and period influences and can be studied using time-series data.

More recently, however, the period correspondence between relative cohort size and fertility has ended. Early on, Easterlin bravely and provocatively predicted increases in fertility during the 1980s and 1990s. Based on the measure of relative cohort size, he could project that relative economic status would rise as the baby-bust cohorts reached childbearing ages. Despite their small size relative to the baby-boom generation, however, baby-bust cohorts have experienced only a small elevation in fertility. Perhaps fertility may yet rise further after a lag in the impact of relative cohort size. Yet figures for the United States in the late 1990s indicate a slight drop rather than a rise in the total fertility rate.

Comparative macrolevel studies reveal other exceptions to the Easterlin hypothesis. In general, studies of fertility in European countries do not replicate the findings for the United States. Ermisch (1979, 1980) finds little evidence of a relationship between relative cohort size and fertility in Great Britain and Germany; Ahlburg (1987) finds little evidence in Australia and Britain; and Beer (1991) finds an effect of relative cohort size in the Netherlands that is small compared to the long-term downward trend in fertility. Chesnais (1983) demonstrates graphically that changes in relative cohort size in European countries are generally small and not closely associated with fertility. Finally, Wright (1989) provides a more systematic empirical test of the relationship using models of Granger causality. Since the expected effect of relative cohort size emerged in only about five of the 20 European countries he studied, Wright concludes that future studies need to pay little attention to relative cohort size.[2]

Contextual Influences. Perhaps the inconsistent support for the predictions of the Easterlin effect results from contextual influences. If national social and institutional conditions shape the strength of the relationship between cohort size and fertility, it could explain the different experiences of European nations and the United States. The effects of cohort size on fertility may not occur as directly as naive demographic or economic determinism would suggest but may be mediated by national processes that most studies ignore or assume constant. Similar reasoning applies to changes over time in the relationship between relative cohort size and fertility: the failure of fertility to rise in the 1990s with declining relative cohort size may have resulted from changes in sex roles that transformed the context of decision making about children (Easterlin 1987a).

If this contextual perspective makes sense, models of fertility can take the variation across countries in the Easterlin effect as something to explain. Rather than rejecting the theory on the basis of varied empirical results, a more useful approach might aim to identify the national and temporal conditions that promote or inhibit the expected relationship. As Easterlin (1987a) suggests: "The effect of generation size most likely will take different forms in different environments because of national differences in labor markets and other institutions. . . . [In western Europe] one would not expect a mere replication of the American experiences" (161).

This reasoning identifies the need for a systematic comparative study of the conditions that promote or inhibit the Easterlin effect rather than a blanket rejection or acceptance of the theory.[3]

Following the general theoretical arguments presented in the first two chapters of this book, I present two general hypotheses about variation in the Easterlin effect. First, in regard to contextual differences across nations, societal institutions promoting collective responsibility for living standards and solidaristic policies of social protection may cushion the harmful impact of large cohort size on economic well-being. By attenuating the link between market performance and economic success, institutions in some nations limit the consequences of cohort size, while institutions in other nations exacerbate them. Second, in regard to contextual differences across time, trends toward female independence and gender equality may moderate the harm of large cohort size because women's rising income compensates for low income of male workers. Thus, differences in social and political environments both across nations and over time can mitigate the sensitivity of economic opportunities and fertility rates to changes in cohort size.

Collectivism. To make these hypotheses more specific, consider how institutional differences across nations relate to the dimension of collectivism. In general, government stabilization of the demand for labor in nearly all high-income nations proves crucial for the emergence of the effect of relative cohort size. Easterlin (1987a, 32–35) notes that governments must moderate wide swings in the demand for labor, which may overwhelm the impact of the supply of workers entering the labor force, in order for relative cohort size to affect wages, promotions, and ultimately relative income. At the extreme, however, a strong national commitment to full employment in collectivist nations may minimize the importance of cohort oversupply. Relative cohort size influences fertility only when it translates into poor opportunities for employment, wages, and promotion. If government policies keep unemployment at a minimum and guarantee jobs for those who desire them, they will mitigate the harmful effects of large cohort size. Full employment policies may similarly increase workers' beliefs that fluctuations in the number of entrants into the labor force will not threaten their future income. Initially, then, the stabilization of demand enables the effects of cohort size to emerge, but above a threshold, full employment policies may moderate the effects of cohort size.

Collectivist and individualist nations also differ in the protection they provide for citizens unable to work. Beyond attempts to maintain full employment, governments in collectivist nations aim to reduce the financial consequences of unemployment or job loss from sickness, family duties, or disability. Quantitatively, they provide more generous social benefits or social welfare spending (in relation to the standard of living or gross domestic product [GDP]) for this purpose. Subsidies for housing, energy, and other living expenses may further soften the financial harm of a poor job market. Qualitatively, collectivist nations provide universal entitlements to benefits. Their programs decommodify labor by separating their citizens' economic well-being from the sale of labor in the market. Benefits provided as a social right in collectivist nations afford more protection than benefits earned from wage contributions to a social insurance fund in individualist nations. Because of their generous benefits and universal entitlements, which insulate workers from the financial risks of membership in large cohorts, collectivist welfare states modify calculations of relative economic status and their effects on fertility.

The institutional context shapes the effect of relative cohort size in another less materialistic way: in collectivist nations committed to social protection, citizens may develop a sense of public trust that lessens concern with current economic circumstances. Compared to couples in more market-oriented, individualistic nations, couples in collectivist nations may pay less attention to relative economic status when making childbearing decisions. Ideological differences in decision-making contexts would thus produce different responses to similar economic conditions, and similar swings in cohort size and relative economic status would emerge as less important for fertility in some nations than in others. This line of reasoning takes into consideration the moral and political contexts of economic decision making beyond relative economic status alone (Lesthaeghe and Surkyn 1988; van de Kaa 1987).[4]

Gender Equality. Consider next how changes in institutions within nations might also affect the relative cohort size–fertility relationship. Oppenheimer (1976), noting that Easterlin's theory minimizes the impact of wives' changing economic roles, states, "As long as wives' labor force participation was very limited, fertility would be more likely to vary markedly in response to the mechanisms posited by Easterlin" (43). According to Oppenheimer, the entry of women into the labor force compensates for the low income of males in large cohorts. This raises relative incomes and aspirations in large cohorts and reduces the relative incomes of the smaller cohorts that follow. In this way, changing gender roles and sexual equality tend, over time, to reduce generational differences in economic status and to attenuate the importance of relative cohort size in recent years compared to earlier decades.

In response to Oppenheimer's arguments, Easterlin (1987a) distinguishes between ex ante relative income due to cohort size and ex post relative income, which incorporates the response to low ex ante relative income through increased labor force participation of wives. He suggests that changes in sex roles and ex post relative income dampen, but do not eliminate, the effect of relative cohort size on fertility. As a result, the effect of relative cohort size on the total fertility rate in the 1990s may not emerge as large as originally thought but should still push it above the replacement rate.

In summary, the consequences of relative cohort size on fertility may vary across nations and over time. They should appear weaker in nations with collectivist, solidaristic, and universal policies that promote full employment or protect workers from loss of earning power than in nations with individualistic, market-oriented, and contribution-based policies. They should also prove weaker in more recent periods characterized by relatively high gender equality, female independence, and women's labor force participation than in earlier decades dominated by more traditional roles.

These arguments specify interactive or contingent influences—rather than additive or invariant influences—of national context and relative cohort size on fertility. Sociopolitical context involves national and period differences that may also have additive effects on fertility, just as relative cohort size does. Collectivist institutions may, on average, reduce fertility through their association with income security and progressive values (van de Kaa 1987). Nevertheless, models should not consider the impact of institutions for social protection as independent from other forces that shape childbearing decisions: just as collectivism moderates the influences of cohort size on individual decisions, relative cohort size moderates the influence of collectivism. If the arguments hold, one can interpret the influence of the variables in combination rather than individually and additively.

This approach differs from the tendency to reject cohort size arguments completely. Too often the current disenchantment with cohort size eliminates concern altogether with men's deteriorating economic status (Oppenheimer 1994, 294) and ignores important, albeit not dominant or exclusive, influences on fertility. By rejecting this tendency, the theoretical arguments in this chapter aim to present a more nuanced, qualified approach. They identify social conditions that facilitate or inhibit cohort size influences rather than dismiss such influences altogether.

Female Work and Fertility

Several theoretical arguments explain the negative relationship between female work in the paid labor force and fertility. Some arguments do not specify a causal relationship but treat both female work and fertility as the common consequence of other changes. Easterlin, for example, argues that large relative cohort size and low relative income increase both the propensity of wives to work and desires for a small family. In addition, economic theories of household production view both female work and fertility as responding to changes in female wages relative to male wages. Sociological theories are more likely to treat increased female work and fertility as resulting from changes in attitudes and values. In other ways, however, female work may directly affect fertility: the sheer time demands of work and parenting may prevent working women from having additional children. Whether specifying common causes or direct effects, theories predict a strong negative relationship between female work and fertility.

Having already considered Easterlin's arguments in some detail, I review in this section other economic and sociological theoretical arguments and the predictions they make about the relationship between female labor force participation and fertility. Then, following the logic presented in the previous section concerning the relationship between relative cohort size and fertility, I review discrepancies in the empirical literature on the fertility consequences of female work and suggest the importance of institutional context in shaping those diverse consequences.

Theoretical Arguments. Economic theories of household production claim that changes in female labor force participation and fertility respond to rising female wages and the opportunity costs of lost work (Becker 1991; Robinson 1997). Assuming women who have children must at least temporarily leave the labor force, lose wages, and delay their career progress, higher wages and greater financial opportunities for women make full-time child rearing increasingly expensive. Empirically, then, female wages relative to male wages predict hours worked, female labor participation rates, and fertility during the post–World War II period in high-income nations (Butz and Ward 1979; Ermisch 1979, 1980). Women's wages and work opportunities have risen with the expansion of service-based industries that traditionally have employed women and the contraction of manufacturing and agricultural industries that traditionally have employed men. The resulting higher price of not entering or leaving the labor force to have children explains the decline of fertility since the 1960s and the stable, low levels of fertility in more recent years.

Economic theories also posit a competing determinant of fertility, one based on the ability of couples to afford the high costs of raising children. All else equal, higher income allows men to realize their desires for children. This relationship fits the economic claim that, with higher income, households can purchase more durable goods; although parents consider issues of child quality as well as quantity, and children are not completely analogous to consumer products, the ability of couples to afford children remains crucial. If higher women's wages reduce fertility through the price effect of lost income, higher men's wages increase fertility through an income effect. In recent decades, the price effect has dominated the income effect as female wages have risen faster than have male wages (Macunovich 1996). Still, with controls for female work, rising income should increase and high unemployment should lower fertility. Conversely, controls for rising income and fluctuations in unemployment should strengthen the negative relationship between female work and fertility.

One component of the income effect relates to pronatalist public policies. Public benefits for families with children should reduce the costs of children or raise the income of couples with children (Gauthier and Hatzius 1997; Walker 1995). Some policies provide cash benefits in the form of family allowances for parents with children and increase the benefits substantially for large families, while other policies provide tax deductions for children (Whittington, Alm, and Peters 1990). Paid maternity leave and generous housing, food, and energy subsidies—more general forms of social protection without explicit pronatalist or profamily motivations—can also reduce the costs of children and raise the income of parents. Not only should these policies increase fertility according to economic arguments but, when held constant, they should enhance the negative relationship between female work and fertility.

Sociological explanations posit a strong relationship between rising labor force participation among women of childbearing ages and fertility but attribute the relationship more to changing values and attitudes than to higher wages (Rindfuss, Brewster, and Kavee 1996). Although wages have increased for women, value changes would have led to higher labor force participation and lower fertility even had wages remained unchanged. The spread of values of individual autonomy, self-fulfillment, and postmaterialism have translated into desires for female emancipation (Lesthaeghe 1995). Concern with self-realization in work and in the quality of personal relationships has reduced the centrality of children in the lives of individuals and couples.

Lesthaeghe (1995) discusses three additional specific value changes that contribute to changing patterns of work and fertility in high-income nations. The first of these is that the emphasis on individual autonomy leads to an emphasis on the quality of the dyadic relationship. Since quality involves relationship equality, the personal fulfillment of wives—often in work rather than in family duties—becomes as important as the personal fulfillment of husbands. The changes increase married women's work and reduce their childbearing. A second value change involves rising nonconformity and anti-authoritarianism, which contribute to the rejection of traditional "bourgeois" marriage, female homemakers, and the two-child norm. As conformity to externally defined duties of the extended family, community, or church declines, female work and childlessness increase. Third, postmaterialism strengthens market orientations, careerism, and consumerism of couples. Gender egalitarianism makes the values increasingly as common among women as men, raises the importance of work and earnings, and reduces the importance of children to self-fulfillment.

As a result of value changes, women's desires for independence and their ability to realize those desires through work and earnings become stronger, and beliefs about traditional models of child rearing, where the father works and the mother stays home with the children, become more negative (Beets, Liefbroer, and Gierveld 1997). Besides lowering fertility, value changes have other consequences. They lead to a revolutionary change in the willingness of mothers with young children to work (Rindfuss, Brewster, and Kavee 1996) and to the growth of the feminist movement. Both of these changes in turn further reinforce female independence, the desirability of women's self-realization through careers, and the acceptability of childlessness, as well as work for mothers with young children (Chafetz 1995).[5] The end result is to encourage reproductive freedom and women's autonomy rather than high birth rates.

Given shifts in tastes and preferences, the psychic costs of leaving the labor force to bear and raise children augment the financial costs emphasized by economists. Attitudinal and ideational factors broaden and complement rather than contradict the economic factors of income aspirations, work opportunities, and earnings (Lesthaeghe 1995; Pollack and Watkins 1993). Both arguments recognize the contradiction between work and raising children in modern society. "The energy and commitment required by the family are seen as significantly reducing women's career opportunities, given that traditional definitions of women's obligations to husbands and children persist" (Chafetz 1995, 69).

Neither rising female wages nor changing attitudes have eliminated altogether the preferences for children. Economists recognize the utility children bring to parents (Ermisch 1996), and sociologists recognize the importance of children as a social resource that increases social bonds and integration (Schoen et al. 1997). Changes in female wages and attitudes will not drive fertility to zero. They do, however, affect a variety of behaviors that reinforce one another. They increase women's independence and labor force participation, which contribute to solo living, cohabitation, late marriage, divorce, and delayed or reduced fertility. The changes in family formation in turn contribute further to women's independence and labor force participation. The interconnections among these changes help explain the negative relationship between female work and fertility.

Empirical Evidence. Dozens of micro- and macrolevel studies demonstrate a negative relationship between female labor force participation and fertility. Debate exists over the causal order, with current thinking emphasizing the short-term effect of fertility on work and the longer-term effect of desires for work on fertility. Without disputing these general conclusions, however, the empirical evidence does identify some exceptions to the negative relationship between work and fertility. A brief review of these exceptions can help identify sources of diversity in the relationship and the importance of the contextual environment to decisions about work and children.

Rindfuss and Brewster (1996) find a positive cross-sectional correlation ($r = .628$) between female labor force participation rates and total fertility rates for high-income nations in 1988. The positive correlation reflects the recent upturn in fertility in nations such as Sweden, which has high female labor force participation rates, and declining fertility in nations such as Italy, which has lower female labor force participation rates (Pinnelli 1995). In the past, modernization and rising female status in northern Europe resulted in lower fertility than in the more traditional southern Europe nations (Chesnais 1996). More recently, the pattern has reversed; in fact, some regions of Italy have a total fertility rate of only 0.8 (Golini 1998). Rindfuss and Brewster do not conclude from the correlation that participation itself raises fertility but suggest that the context or meaning of participation likely differs across nations.

Blossfeld (1995) and contributors to a comparative study of nine nations find that women's independence, as reflected in high levels of education, generally does not reduce the propensity to marry and have children. A longer time enrolled in school delays marriage and childbirth but does not make women less interested in marriage and childbearing, as economic arguments imply (see also Oppenheimer, Kalmijn, and Lim 1997). In addition, the comparative study by Blossfeld and colleagues demonstrates disparate effects of education across countries with different values and policies. Education inhibits marriage and childbearing in Italy, France, and the Netherlands but has positive or no effects in Sweden, the United States, and West Germany. Women's independence may suppress marriage and family formation in traditional societies but not elsewhere.[6]

Macunovich (1995, 1996) finds that the effect of female wages changes over time—it shifts from negative to positive as relative cohort income increases. In their classic article, Butz and Ward (1979) demonstrate that female wages relative to male wages account for the rise and decline of fertility in the United States. However, fertility has remained stable or increased in recent years in the United States and Sweden despite continued improvements in female wages (Lee and Casterline 1996)—only in a few nations, such as Italy, has the fertility trend continued downward as predicted by the economic hypothesis. Macunovich argues, instead, that in recent years female wages have come to have a positive income effect rather than a negative price effect on fertility. The meaning and influence of female wages thus vary over time, and the shifting direction of influence explains the stability of recent fertility rates in the face of continuing growth of female wages and work.

Gauthier and Hatzius (1997) find national differences in the effects of family and maternity benefits on fertility. Averaged across 22 nations for the years from 1970 to 1990, their results demonstrate a modest influence: benefits 25% higher than average raise fertility by only .07 children per woman. Other studies find similarly sized effects (Blanchet and Ekert-Jaffé 1994; Ekert 1986; Gauthier 1996a; Hantrais 1994, 1997). However, Gauthier and Hatzius discover stronger effects of family benefits on fertility in Scandinavian nations. After exhibiting one of Europe's lowest fertility rates during the twentieth century, Sweden's total fertility rate moved above the replacement rate and above rates in most other European nations in direct response to legislation in the 1980s that extended parental leave benefits to couples who had a second child within 2 years (Hoem 1993). In contrast, pronatalist policies have had little effect on fertility in Japan despite a sense of crisis over the falling birth rate and an aging population. Boling (1998) attributes the ineffectiveness to other policies that favor wives who stay at home. Thus, family benefits alone will not reverse the downward movement in desired family size but can boost fertility in conjunction with larger efforts (such as in Sweden) to promote women's attachment to the labor force with minimal cost to childbearing and child rearing (Ermisch 1996).

Tsuya and Mason (1995) find that changes in postmaterialist values do not, as predicted by sociological theories, contribute to low fertility in Japan (see also Retherford, Ogawa, and Sakamoto 1996). Rather, traditional family living arrangements and the subordination of the wife in marriage make educated women reluctant to enter into marriage and have children. In Japan, marriage and parenthood conflict with work opportunities because the gendered division of labor in the family has not changed. Tsuya and Mason claim that modern values and economic opportunities alone do not lower fertility but that the downward trend in birth rates comes from the conflict between economic opportunities and traditional conjugal relations.

Contextual Influences. The evidence of diverse and sometimes unexpected consequences of female work, income, and independence for fertility may relate to national differences and temporal changes in the institutional contexts of fertility decisions. The contexts may affect the degree of role incompatibility and conflict between work and family duties for women, which in turn shapes the relationship between various components of female status and fertility.

Rindfuss and Brewster (1996) nicely summarize this argument: "Our thesis is that variation in the degree of role incompatibility experienced by working mothers may be one key to understanding variation in fertility levels across developed countries. . . . Underlying this hypothesis is the assumption that the degree of role incompatibility mediates the relationship between labor force participation and fertility. Fertility should rise in response to easing of the work-parenting conflict, and the constraining influence of female work on fertility should decline. Diversity in role conflict should further explain diversity in fertility levels despite similarly rising female participation rates" (262). Pinelli (1995) makes much the same point: "The factor that seems most important for levels of fertility is the extent to which institutional conditions make it possible for women to reconcile productive and reproductive roles" (84). Female work and fertility rates emerge higher where institutional conditions make work and fertility compatible.

McDonald (1997) states this argument in terms of the incoherence between gender equity in institutions of education and market employment that emphasize individual achievement and in institutions involving public services, government transfers, and the family that treat individuals as group members. Where equity emerges in the former, but not in the latter, it places downward pressure on fertility: desires of men and women for individual achievement in education and the market conflict with the lack of support for equity in public services, government services, and family roles. In contrast, when both institutions adopt models of gender equity (or, as in the past, when both institutions adopt models based on the dominance of a male breadwinner), the coherence across institutions moderates the conflict between desires for individual opportunities and child-rearing duties and reduces the downward pressure on fertility.

Consider several institutional differences across nations and time periods that may ease or aggravate the problems working mothers face (Hantrais 1997; Lewis 1992; Rindfuss and Brewster 1996). First, flexible job schedules and the ability to work at home make it easier to combine work and child-rearing duties. While some nations now allow workers to switch from full time to part time, others lack flexible work schedules and maintain school hours unfavorable to full-time employment (Huinink and Mayer 1995). Contrast, for example, the 55% and 47% of women workers with part-time jobs in Norway and in Sweden, respectively, with the 33% in Canada and the 18% in the United States (Rosenfeld and Birkelund 1995).

Second, paid parental leave policies and flexible career timetables make it possible for women to sequence years devoted to work and family effectively. Sweden has offered paid parental leave for 12 weeks to either parent and an extension of the leave if a second child is born soon after. The United States allows private employees to take a leave for maternity but without pay or public benefits.

Third, access to affordable, high-quality child care makes it possible for mothers to reenter the labor force with confidence that their children will not suffer. Government support of preschool and after-school programs can increase the affordability and quality of child care. Sweden again does more than most nations to subsidize child care and has a higher proportion of young children in child care than other nations (Pinelli 1995). Cash benefits alone may not increase fertility because women work for reasons other than money, but child-care programs that help women combine career and family roles regardless of their motives for working may effectively foster childbearing (Esping-Andersen 1996). As an alternative to public services, market mechanisms can sometimes make it easier to combine work and family roles in liberal nations like the United States with a large supply of low wage workers that parents can afford to hire for child care (Esping-Andersen 1999). Yet these opportunities exist primarily for high-income couples in liberal nations, rather than for couples throughout the status hierarchy, and therefore do less to moderate the fertility consequences of female work than the public services in the Nordic nations.

These arguments about female work and fertility make much the same point as the previous section on relative cohort size and fertility. They suggest that institutions promoting collective responsibility for social protection and supporting women's involvement outside the family cushion the harmful impact of female work on fertility. Both types of institutions may do more than protect workers from loss of income; they may also protect women from loss of income and work due to childbearing. By mitigating the contradiction between female work and home duties, such institutions limit the negative effect of female labor force participation on fertility.

In addition, the recent growth, over time, in policies, institutions, and values in support of working women may further moderate the harm of female labor force participation for fertility. Hoem (1993) argues, "It may be part of this picture that women limited their childbearing during the late 1960s and early 1970s when they felt like pioneers moving into the labor market and reorganizing their home lives, while current cohorts feel less constrained, now that their rights have been firmly established and greatly strengthened" (25). Another mechanism may contribute to the decline over time in the effects of married women's work on fertility. Women who chose to work initially may be less family-oriented and fertility-prone than those who join the labor force later. The growth over time of institutions for the support of working women will contribute to the later entrance of more family-oriented and fertility-prone women and to the weaker influences of work on fertility.

Several predictions about female labor force participation as a determinant of fertility follow. Over time, female labor force participation should come to have less of an inhibiting effect, perhaps even a positive effect, on fertility as institutions change to become more women-friendly. This implies a convex or U-shaped curvilinear relationship. Role incompatibility and conflict emerged with economic growth and labor force changes during the post–World War II period and initially resulted in lower fertility. However, given social concerns with low fertility rates and the problems faced by working mothers, institutions change over time to better accommodate women's dual roles of work and family. Eventually, a rise in women's status makes for less conflict between the roles of parent and worker, and women's work comes to have a zero or even positive relationship rather than a negative relationship with fertility (Chesnais 1996).

Across nations, the speed of adjustment in institutions and changes in the effect of female work on fertility may vary. Since nations with collectivist or women-friendly institutions do more than other nations to ease the conflict between the dual roles of women, they should experience a quicker reversal of the negative effect of female work. Note again the interactive or contingent nature of the predictions. Collectivist and women-friendly institutions may directly affect fertility during the post–World War II period. More likely, however, they may ease the conflict between women's work and family duties and, therefore, weaken the negative effects of female work.

Data and Measures

To review, the theoretical arguments specify four general hypotheses that apply to patterns of fertility: (1) The negative effect of relative cohort size will emerge less strongly in collectivist nations than in other nations. (2) The negative effect of relative cohort size will decline over time. (3) The negative effect of female labor force participation will decline over time and reverse. (4) The reversal of the negative effect of female labor force participation will occur more quickly in collectivist and women-friendly nations than in other nations.

These arguments must be studied across varied national and temporal contexts. Only with such variation can models fully examine how relationships diverge across contexts. Although studies of individuals can do more to understand the sources of family decisions, they lack the variation in the institutional environments across nations and time that is needed to test the hypotheses presented in this chapter. For example, individual-level data for several nations allow comparisons of the timing of specific family events (Blossfeld 1995) but lack information on how long-term trends modify the forces determining these events. In some ways, then, comparative aggregate data over several decades can best examine the influence of the institutional context of work on the determinants of fertility.

The tests of the hypotheses use aggregate data on 18 high-income nations for the years 1951–94 and macrolevel measures of the determinants of fertility. These data offer substantial variation in fertility, its macrolevel determinants, and the institutional context of fertility determination. With 18 nations and 44 years, the potential sample size comprises 792 cases that represent hundreds of millions of people over several decades of change. Along with the substantial variation it provides, the sample has enough cases for multivariate analysis and allows measurement of variables crucial to testing the theories. Although different from individual-level surveys of fertility history, the aggregate data have many strengths and are well suited to the issues raised by the theoretical arguments.

The main dependent variable needed to study the macrolevel determinants of fertility, the total fertility rate, comes from Teitelbaum and Winter (1985), with updating from the United Nations' (1996 and various years) *Demographic Yearbook* and Guibert-Lantoine and Monnier (1997). The total fertility rate, in contrast to the crude birth rate, controls for the number of women at the prime childbearing ages and isolates the effects of the relative income component of cohort size from the counteracting demographic effects of the number of potential parents. A measure of completed cohort fertility would also avoid the problems of the crude birth rate but would not reflect differences in the timing of births due to yearly changes in economic and social circumstances.

One primary independent variable, relative cohort size, replicates Easterlin (1987a, 18–19) by taking the ratio of the number of persons ages 15–29 to the number of persons ages 30–64 (also gathered from the *Demographic Yearbook*). The numerator represents the size of childbearing cohorts during peak fertility years, and the denominator represents the size of parental generations 15–35 years older than the childbearing generation. A high ratio reflects a large childbearing cohort relative to the parental cohort, implies low income for the young cohort relative to income of older generations, and should reduce fertility. A low ratio reflects a small childbearing cohort, high relative income, and high fertility. Further, the measure distinguishes between younger and older segments of the working age population and, thereby, reflects the age-based contrast in economic circumstances brought about by differences in labor supply. In support of the validity of the measure, Easterlin (1987a, 18), demonstrates that it corresponds almost exactly to fertility rates during the years 1950–80.

Other studies have used the measure with similar results but with slightly different age groups (Chesnais 1983; Wright 1989). Some studies use the ratio for males only, but male measures may mask the importance of females for job competition and cohort size. Examining the interaction between relative cohort size and female labor force participation rates makes more sense if the measure of relative cohort size includes both sexes.

The other primary determinant, the female labor force participation rate, equals the number of employed and unemployed women as a percentage of the total female population. Consistent figures exist back to 1960 (Organization for Economic Cooperation and Development [OECD] 1996 and various years), but less complete data for 1950–59 require some estimation.[7] Lacking data on age-specific participation rates and the work circumstances of women of childbearing age, the analysis must treat the total participation rate as only a rough indicator of women's overall involvement in the labor force.[8]

Several additional problems with the measure of female labor force participation may further limit its additive and interactive effects on fertility. For one, the lack of participation rates by marital and family status limits the ability of the measure to capture changes in the dependence of women on the earning power of partners. For another, the rates do not measure the occupational status or earnings of working women. Perhaps more important, the figures do not reflect national differences in the prevalence of part-time work. Much of the increase in female labor force participation in many nations has come from part-time work (Hakim 1997). Some claim that part-time work contributes to the marginalization of women rather than to their equality with men, but Blossfield and Hakim (1997) argue instead that part-time jobs in many nations are high quality, contribute to women's independence, and are highly valued by the women who take them. Rosenfeld and Birkelund (1995) further demonstrate that part-time work emerges most commonly in the otherwise egalitarian Scandinavian nations with powerful labor unions and a strong state sector. Given the advantages of part-time work, the measure of female labor force participation appropriately includes workers of all types.

Comparative data on part-time work is not routinely gathered in international compendiums of labor force statistics (through much effort, Rosenfeld and Birkelund [1995] obtain data on only nine nations for 1 year with the use of separate microlevel labor force surveys). However, as demonstrated in chapter 2, the measure of women-friendly institutions overlaps with the prevalence of part-time work. Measuring labor force participation for part-time and full-time workers but allowing the effects of female labor force participation to vary with the measure of women-friendly institutions will indirectly reflect the growing importance of part-time work in the female participation rate and contribute to the possible changes in the effect of female participation on fertility. The influence of female labor force participation on fertility would no doubt emerge more strongly with precise internationally comparable data on the family, occupational, and part-time status of working women. Despite these limitations, the variation in female labor force participation rates in the sample appears sufficient to expect effects to emerge.

Other measures of possible determinants of fertility come from standard sources. Social security spending measures the generosity of benefits for social protection. It takes spending for programs such as pensions, medical care, sickness, disability, unemployment, and family allowances as a percentage of GDP. Data come from the International Labour Office ([ILO] 1992 and various years). Although not directed to young couples, most of these programs nonetheless reflect a country's broad commitment to social protection. An alternate measure, total government nonmilitary spending as a percentage of GDP, correlates highly with social security spending ($r = .901$). Figures on family allowance spending, more directly relevant to fertility, exist only since 1959 (International Labour Office 1992 and various years). However, because family allowance spending targets parents with young children, its effect may differ from the effect of general social security spending.

The more general economic variables include the unemployment rate and national product per capita. The unemployment rate averaged across all ages and workers captures the impact of exogenous economic cycles as well as the ability of national labor market policies to maintain full employment. Comparable unemployment data for persons of all ages, but not for age-specific rates, exist for the years from 1959 to 1994 (Organization for Economic Cooperation and Development 1996 and various years).

The national product measure equals real GDP per capita in international dollars based on purchasing price parities. The measure allows for more meaningful comparisons across nations and years than provided by measures that rely on reported exchange rates and price deflators. Summers and Heston (1991) present details on construction of the measure, and the data are available up to 1992 from the Penn World Table (Center for International Comparisons 1998). To estimate figures for 1993 and 1994, I use a simple standardization technique: the percentage increases in real GDP per capita in U.S. dollars (using exchange rates and price deflators) from 1992 to 1993 and from 1993 to 1994 are used to project forward the purchasing parity figures for 1993 and 1994, respectively.

To measure stable contextual differences across nations, I focus on the measures of collectivist and women-friendly institutions defined in chapter 2. Recall that these measures do not vary over time like the other measures but vary only across the 18 nations.

Statistical Methods

The next two chapters analyze the data and measures for both nations and years. Rather than analyzing separate models of fertility for each nation or for each time period, I use another approach that pools the two sources of data. Analyzing combined nations and years incorporates both cross-sectional variation across nations and time-series variation within nations. It also increases the potential sample size dramatically; with 44 years and 18 nations, the pooled analyses include 792 cases. By maximizing the variation and degrees of freedom in the multivariate analyses, the pooled data efficiently summarize relationships across a diverse sample of cases.

Pooling data creates the risk of an overly simplified analysis that ignores diversity across nations and time periods by highlighting relationships for the typical or most influential cases. Yet with appropriate care to model specification and robustness, the pooled approach offers much flexibility. It allows the analyst to concentrate primarily on time-series models, primarily on cross-sectional models, or on both combined. It can attend to unusual as well as typical cases and to variations from the average as well as to average relationships. Indeed, the models must incorporate this flexibility because the theory specifies processes determining fertility that vary across nations and time; a crude pooled analysis cannot test such hypotheses.

The analyses begin with simple, general models but then, by relaxing the assumption of identical relations for all nations and periods, add complexity incrementally to better reflect nation-specific and time-specific processes. For example, by using product terms to represent statistical interaction, the models can allow effects of variables to differ across nations and across time. In so doing, it can test for theoretically specified national and temporal differences in processes. In addition to selecting individual nations or individual time periods for separate examination with interaction terms, the analysis can also delete them one at a time to gauge the influence of outliers. This flexibility nicely balances the generality and simplicity of additive models for pooled data with the detail of 18 single-nation models.

Whether estimating additive or interactive models, including time-series data with the cross-sectional data requires statistical adjustments for four problems in ordinary least squares estimates: serial correlation, heteroscedasticity, cross-sectional correlation of residuals, and between-unit heterogeneity. Appendix A describes these problems and the estimation procedures to correct for them. In brief review, the models in appendix A present generalized least squares (GLS) estimates based on the work of Beck and Katz (1995) and often adjust for between-nation heterogeneity with fixed effects (FE-GLS) or dummy variables for each of the 18 nations minus one. Most important, the model coefficients and t-ratios reported in the tables with GLS results have the same interpretation as in ordinary regression but have been adjusted for problems stemming from the non-random structure of the data.

The estimation procedures offer a means of controlling for unmeasured influences on fertility. Rather than differencing the time series to model changes in fertility directly, the estimation proceeds in another way. In essence, GLS estimation differences the time series but by a factor equal to the autocorrelation coefficient rather than by one and provides more precise measures of over-time overlap in the time-series data. Differencing scores directly can overcorrect for the nonindependence of time series and can bias downward the effects of the independent variables.

CHAPTER 4

Relative Cohort Size and the Total Fertility Rate

Having presented theoretical arguments concerning the interactive relationships among cohort size, collectivism, and fertility, this chapter tests these arguments using the total fertility rate. To review the predictions from chapter 3, relative cohort size should have weaker negative effects on fertility in more recent years than in earlier years, in collectivist nations more than in other nations, and at high levels of female labor force participation more than at low levels. Testing these claims requires something more than the usual effort to examine the partial relationship between relative cohort size and fertility. If, as predicted, the relationship between relative cohort size and fertility varies across sociopolitical contexts, then typical analyses that assume constant or invariant relationships will not capture the crux of the arguments. The analyses thus focus on differences across contexts in the way that relative cohort size influences fertility.

In this chapter, I first describe cross-national and temporal patterns of the total fertility rate and then I examine the determinants of those patterns. I show that the small average relationship between relative cohort size and fertility varies substantially across nations, years, and levels of female labor force participation, which lends support to the basic thesis that institutional environments for social protection shape the meaning and consequences of relative cohort size for fertility. To make sense of the sometimes complex models, I summarize the implications of the statistical interactions by comparing coefficients across nations, time periods, and levels of female labor force participation, and I review, in nontechnical language in the conclusion, both the findings and the support they give to the theoretical claims of heterogeneity in relationships across sociopolitical contexts.

Cross-National Patterns

To begin, table 2 presents mean total fertility rates averaged across all years from 1951 to 1994 for each of the 18 nations. The mean total fertility rate varies from highs of 3.21 in Ireland and 2.89 in New Zealand to lows of 1.81 in Germany and 1.96 in Japan and Switzerland. Besides Ireland and New Zealand, other English-speaking (and individualist) nations such as the United States, Australia, and Canada have relatively high mean total fertility rates. At the other extreme, Italy, Sweden, Denmark, Austria, and Belgium have relatively low mean fertility rates.

In addition to the national differences in mean fertility, national differences exist in the variation around the mean. In table 2, variation around the mean reflects the degree of change over time in fertility rates within nations. The measures of temporal variation for each nation include the standard deviation, the minimum value, and the maximum value of the total fertility rate. As well as having the highest means, the English-

Table 2. Mean Total Fertility Rates and Related Characteristics by Nation and Time Period

Nation	Total Fertility Rate				Percent Catholic	Relative Cohort Size
	Mean	S.D.	Minimum	Maximum		
Australia	2.57	.63	1.85	3.54	24	.582
Austria	2.03	.48	1.44	2.81	86	.511
Belgium	2.04	.42	1.50	2.70	89	.495
Canada	2.47	.90	1.62	3.85	46	.626
Denmark	2.03	.45	1.37	2.63	1	.517
Finland	2.10	.52	1.50	3.06	0	.563
France	2.28	.43	1.65	2.87	86	.537
Germany	1.81	.46	1.24	2.53	39	.483
Ireland	3.21	.65	1.90	3.98	94	.609
Italy	1.99	.47	1.24	2.55	95	.544
Japan	1.96	.38	1.43	3.25	0	.620
Netherlands	2.27	.72	1.48	3.25	42	.596
New Zealand	2.89	.82	1.92	4.23	15	.628
Norway	2.29	.49	1.65	2.97	2	.516
Sweden	2.01	.25	1.60	2.47	1	.467
Switzerland	1.96	.43	1.49	2.85	44	.517
United Kingdom	2.23	.44	1.72	3.03	8	.497
United States	2.51	.73	1.77	3.71	26	.589
Total	2.25	.66	1.24	4.23	39	.550
1951–61	2.81	.55	1.95	4.23	39	.513
1962–72	2.63	.53	1.59	4.11	39	.561
1973–83	1.86	.42	1.34	3.82	39	.592
1984–94	1.72	.25	1.24	2.57	39	.532

speaking nations have the highest standard deviations and ranges. Canada has a standard deviation of 0.90, reflecting a low total fertility rate of 1.62 and a high total fertility rate of 3.85. New Zealand and the United States have the next two largest standard deviations. Fertility rates in these nations did not fall to the low levels of some European nations, but their maximum levels during the baby-boom years exceeded those of other nations (note especially the maximum value of 4.23 in New Zealand). In contrast, the standard deviation for Sweden equals only 0.25, largely because maximum fertility reached only 2.47. Several other European nations experienced relatively small increases, declines, and changes over time in fertility rates. Nearly all nations thus experienced rising fertility after World War II and declining fertility during the 1960s and 1970s, but English-speaking nations experienced the pattern much more intensely than did other high-income nations.

Across all nations, the grand mean of 2.25 exceeds the replacement rate of 2.1 but also masks wide swings over time. Based on the means grouped for four time periods in table 2, the total fertility rate of 2.81 during the baby-boom years of the 1950s falls during the 1960s to 2.63. By the late 1970s, the total fertility rate falls below the replacement rate. Across all nations, the total fertility rate peaks in 1963 at 2.93 and falls to its lowest level of 1.68 in 1994. After reaching a previous low level of 1.69 in 1985, the total fertility rate rose slightly until 1992. It then fell in 1993 and 1994 to a new low point.

The comparisons across nations demonstrate little in the way of religious differences in fertility. Column 5 of table 2 lists the mean percentage of Catholics for each nation. (The percentage of Catholics changes so little within nations that it is treated as a constant over time and only varies across nations.) The Catholic nations show wide variability in the total fertility rate. Ireland falls among the most fertile nations, Italy among the least, and France, Belgium, and Austria nearer the average. Among the Protestant nations, New Zealand has high fertility and Sweden has low fertility. Accordingly, the correlation between percentage of Catholics and the total fertility rate equals only $-.069$. Other national characteristics besides religion influence fertility.

Does relative cohort size vary across nations much as the total fertility rate varies? The last column of table 2 presents the mean of relative cohort size for each nation. Across all nations, the mean of 0.550 indicates that, on average, the nations contain 55 persons ages 15–29 for every 100 persons ages 30–64. The nation with the largest relative cohort size for young persons (when averaged across all years) is New Zealand, with 63 young persons for every 100 older persons. Also reflecting its large baby boom, the United States has a large mean relative cohort size of 0.59. At the other extreme, Sweden has the smallest mean relative cohort size, which reflects its small baby boom after World War II.

Although relative cohort size, like the total fertility rate, varies across nations, the two sets of means do not correspond closely. A correlation coefficient between the two sets of means essentially equals zero ($r = -.007$). To the extent that relative cohort size and the total fertility rate correspond, they do so over time within nations more than across nations. Accordingly, changes over time in relative cohort size should correspond to changes in fertility. Table 2 presents mean relative cohort size for four time periods. When averaged across all nations, relative cohort size in 1951–61 equals a low value 0.513 at the same time fertility reaches its high value of 2.81. As relative cohort size rises during the next two time periods, when the baby-boom generation reaches childbearing ages, fertility declines. Yet during the last time period, from 1984–94, the relative size of young persons falls as the baby-bust generation reaches young adulthood, but fertility continues to decline. As noted earlier, the aging of the baby-boom generation brings about a decline in fertility, but the fall in relative cohort size during the late 1980s and early 1990s elevates fertility only slightly.

To further illustrate the relationship, figure 1 plots relative cohort size

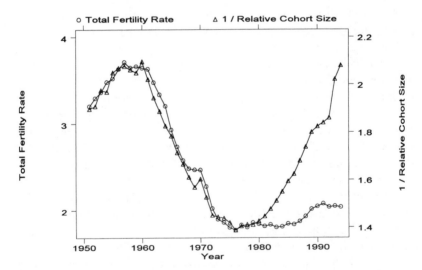

Figure 1. Fertility and Cohort Size Trends, United States

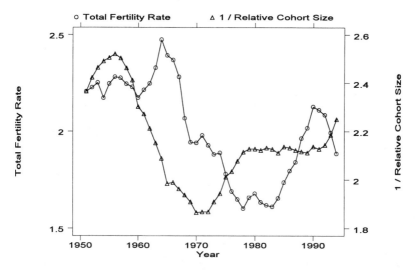

Figure 2. Fertility and Cohort Size Trends, Sweden

and the total fertility rate for the United States from 1951 to 1994. Although relative cohort size equals the ratio of the number of persons ages 15–29 to the number of persons ages 30–64, the graph presents the inverse of the ratio so that it changes in the same direction as the total fertility rate. Both measures increase in the early 1950s and decline from 1957 to 1980. However, the trends diverge in the 1980s—the total fertility rate increases only slightly while the inverse of relative cohort size increases more dramatically.

To illustrate the cross-national differences, figure 2 shows the trends in the inverse of relative cohort size and the total fertility rate for Sweden, a nation whose political and social institutions differ markedly from those in the United States. Despite some similarities, the trends in relative cohort size and fertility diverge notably compared to those for the United States. Like relative cohort size, the total fertility rate falls and then rises but only after a decade-long lag. The lack of correspondence in the trends suggests that factors other than cohort size produced the swings in fertility.

As a result of diversity in trends in fertility and relative cohort in other European nations, a graph of the two variables for all nations combined reveals a weak relationship. Figure 3 plots the mean total fertility rate and mean inverse of relative cohort size for all 18 nations for the period from 1951 to 1994. As for Sweden, relative cohort size and fertility both rise in the 1950s and decline in the late 1960s and 1970s. However, the decline

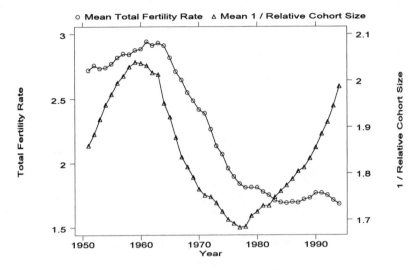

Figure 3. Fertility and Cohort Size Trends, 18-Nation Means

in relative cohort size substantially precedes the fertility decline. Moreover, the divergence in relative cohort size and fertility during the 1980s and 1990s appears here as it does in the United States. By averaging nations that support the relationship between relative cohort size and fertility and nations that do not, figure 3 masks much of the diversity in the relationship and highlights the need to consider national context.

National Differences in the Effect of Relative Cohort Size

To further explore the sources of the weak overall relationship between relative cohort size and fertility, the analysis can examine the bivariate relationship more precisely. It can then consider how the relative cohort size and fertility relationship varies across time, nations, and levels of female labor force participation. Using the pooled data for years and nations, a basic regression shows that relative cohort size—lagged 2 years to allow for the gap between fertility desires and births—affects fertility only modestly in this sample of countries and years (table 3 presents the detailed coefficients). The generalized least squares results without (GLS) and with (FE-GLS) controls for nation-specific dummy variables (or fixed effects) reveal a negative effect of relative cohort size on the total fertility rate of −1.22 and −1.25. If these coefficients alone have little meaning, it helps to note that both coefficients surpass their standard error by a factor of nearly 3. Perhaps more informatively, the corresponding standardized co-

Table 3. Unstandardized Coefficients for Regression of the Total
Fertility Rate on Relative Cohort Size—Additive Models

	Additive Models	
Independent Variable	GLS	FE-GLS
Constant	2.86	2.87
Relative cohort size$_{t-2}$	−1.22	−1.25
	(2.87)	(2.95)
R^2—OLS	.0053	.4091
df	790	773

Note. Numbers in parentheses are absolute values of t-ratios.

efficients for relative cohort size equal −0.157 and −0.161 and further
reflect the modest strength of the relationship. However, relative cohort
size alone explains less than 1% of the variance in total fertility rates (the
dummy variables for nation and relative cohort size explain 41% of the
variance).

To look at the result another way, the range of relative cohort size across
all nations and years goes from a minimum of 0.397 to a maximum of
0.848. When multiplied by the coefficient of −1.25, the range of 0.451
implies a maximum change in fertility due to relative cohort size of
−0.564. Without controls for other determinants of fertility, the calculated change in relative cohort size can account for a decline of one-half of
a child. Given a range of the total fertility rate, across all nations and years,
of 2.99 children (a low of 1.24 and a high of 4.23), relative cohort size can
at best account for only one-sixth of the change in fertility. All said, an
additive effect exists but not a strong one.

Because these models present the effect of relative cohort size averaged
across all nations, the small effect may hide large coefficients in some
nations and small coefficients in other nations. The nations under study
may, as suggested by the theoretical arguments in the last chapter, differ
substantially in the consequences of relative cohort size for their fertility
rates. To examine nation-specific effects of relative cohort size, the models
of fertility need to be expanded. One way to allow the effect of relative
cohort size to vary across countries involves including product terms between relative cohort size and each of the nation variables. From the resulting coefficients, one can compute the effect of relative cohort size for
each nation. Table 4 presents these nation-specific effects and notes which
deviate significantly from the average across all nations.

In brief, the nation-specific effects vary substantially around the average
effect. The negative coefficients for relative cohort size in column 1 are
largest for the United States, New Zealand, Australia, Belgium and Nor-

Table 4. Unstandardized Coefficients for Regression of the Total Fertility Rate on Relative Cohort Size—Nation-Specific Effects

Nation	FE-GLS Model Coefficients	Relative Cohort Size Effect	Relative Cohort Size Range	Maximum Relative Cohort Size Effect
Constant	2.22	. . .	. . .	. . .
Relative cohort size$_{t-2}$	−1.38**	. . .	. . .	. . .
Australia	−1.75	−3.13	.191	−0.60
Austria	−.120	−1.50	.136	−0.20
Belgium	−1.87**	−3.25	.161	−0.52
Canada	−1.45	−2.83	.288	−0.82
Denmark	1.96	.580	.134	0.08
Finland	.735	−.645	.258	−0.17
France	−.387	−1.77	.187	−0.33
Germany	2.50*	1.12	.116	0.13
Ireland	.804	−.576	.265	−0.15
Italy	.894	−.486	.142	0.07
Japan	2.10	.720	.415	0.30
Netherlands	−.888	−2.27	.185	−0.42
New Zealand	−1.87*	−3.25	.242	−0.79
Norway	−2.07**	−3.45	.187	−0.65
Sweden	1.59	.210	.139	0.03
Switzerland	3.11**	1.73	.185	0.32
United Kingdom	−1.53	−2.91	.156	−0.45
United States	−1.76**	−3.14	.244	−0.77
R^2—OLS	.6019	. . .	. . .	. . .
df	756	. . .	. . .	. . .

* $p > .05$.
** $p > .01$.

way—with the exceptions of Belgium and Norway, nations that also score low on the collectivism scale. The effect of relative cohort size becomes positive in the more collectivist nations of Japan, Switzerland, and Germany. The variance explained by the interactive model reaches 0.6019— a large increase from the variance explained of 0.4091 in the additive model. Of clear statistical significance, the increased variance explained further demonstrates the differences across nations in the effect of relative cohort size.

Along with having different coefficients for relative cohort size, the nations vary in the size of the changes in relative cohort size. As noted earlier, changes in relative cohort size reflect earlier swings in fertility, and those nations with the largest fluctuations in fertility show the largest changes in relative cohort size. Column 3 of table 4 lists the differences between the maximum and minimum values of relative cohort size for each nation. By far, the largest range appears in Japan. Otherwise, English-speaking nations with large baby booms in the 1950s, such as New Zealand, the United States, Ireland, and Canada, show large ranges in relative cohort size.

Some simple calculations further demonstrate differences across nations in the influence of relative cohort size on fertility. Multiplying the nation-specific ranges by the nation-specific coefficients for relative cohort size gives a measure of the maximum influence of relative cohort size within each nation. The range of 0.244 and coefficient for relative cohort size of −3.14 in the United States translate into a decline in fertility of 0.77 children. Other nations, such as New Zealand, Canada, and Australia, experience similarly large declines in the total fertility because of relative cohort size. Again, the English-speaking nations emerge as special. Some nations such as Sweden, Japan, Italy, and Switzerland show little change or even increases in the total fertility rate due to changes in relative cohort size.

Do these differences among countries in the consequences of relative cohort size for the total fertility rate relate meaningfully to contextual characteristics of the countries? The correlation between the effects of relative cohort size for countries in table 4 and the collectivism scale equals .346. The higher the collectivism, the higher (or less negative and closer to zero) the effect of relative cohort size. Further, a slightly stronger correlation of .425 emerges between the total change in fertility from relative cohort size and the collectivism scale. Interestingly, an inverse correlation exists between the range of relative cohort size and collectivism, indicating that differences in previous fertility also correlate with collectivism. Together, the range and effect of relative cohort size combine to have a moderate to strong relationship with collectivism. Thus, the total fertility rate responds more to relative cohort size in individualist nations than in collectivist nations.

As might be expected, the United States stands out in these tables. Having the lowest score on the collectivism scale, the United States also shows the third strongest negative effect of relative cohort size. Further, because of its large baby boom and baby bust, it has the fifth largest range in cohort size. Together, the strong effect and large range in the values of relative cohort size for the United States make for a strong maximum effect. The United States thus exhibits the influence of relative cohort size on fertility and highlights differences between the more collectivist European nations and the more individualist non-European nations.

Changes in the Effect of Relative Cohort Size over Time

These nation-specific results demonstrate diversity in the influence of relative cohort size but do not test claims about changes over time in the importance of that influence. Since institutional context can affect how the relationship between relative cohort size and fertility varies over time as well as across nations, the analysis needs to incorporate temporal contingency. Table 2 describes well-known trends in fertility, but additional analyses can examine how time affects the relationship between fertility and relative cohort size. Regression results in which time is treated as a set of dummy variables representing four 11-year time periods can address this issue (table 5). As they should, the coefficients show that fertility has declined steadily since the 1950s. The predicted period total fertility rates, controlling for relative cohort size, equal 2.63 for 1951–61, 2.52 for 1962–72, 2.27 for 1973–83, and 2.17 for 1984–94.

The coefficients also show that, with controls for time, relative cohort size has mixed effects, falling to below significance in one model but rising substantially in the other. At worst then, the effect of cohort size appears

Table 5. Unstandardized Coefficients for Regression of the Total Fertility Rate on Relative Cohort Size—Time-Specific Effects

Independent Variables	Additive Models		Interaction Models	
	GLS	FE-GLS	GLS	FE-GLS
Constant	2.63	3.36	2.63	3.11
Relative cohort size$_{t-2}$	−.280	−1.48	−.182	−.883
	(0.64)	(3.42)	(0.38)	(1.76)
1962–72	−.108	−.140	.355	.679
	(1.69)	(2.07)	(1.56)	(2.87)
1973–83	−.357	−.464	−.547	−.091
	(4.18)	(5.36)	(1.53)	(0.29)
1984–94	−.457	−.623	−1.01	−.481
	(4.56)	(6.36)	(2.17)	(1.19)
Relative cohort size$_{t-2}$				
× 1962–72	. . .	. . .	−.917	−1.60
			(2.12)	(3.43)
× 1973–83	. . .	. . .	.188	−.845
			(0.29)	(1.45)
× 1984–94	. . .	. . .	.815	−.458
			(0.97)	(0.61)
R^2—OLS	.5264	.8323	.5494	.8605
df	787	770	784	767

Note. Numbers in parentheses are absolute values of t-ratios.

Table 6. Unstandardized Coefficients for Regression of the Total Fertility Rate on Relative Cohort Size—Interaction Models

Independent Variables	Collectivism Interaction		Time Controls		Collectivism and Time Interactions	
	GLS	FE-GLS	GLS	FE-GLS	GLS	FE-GLS
Constant	2.80	2.81	2.75	3.26	2.79	3.08
Relative cohort size$_{t-2}$	−1.08	−1.12	−.565	−1.24	−.534	−.771
	(2.59)	(2.68)	(1.20)	(2.88)	(1.08)	(1.53)
1962–72	. . .	. . .	−.102	−.147	.253	.629
			(1.67)	(2.19)	(1.17)	(2.63)
1973–83	. . .	. . .	−.327	−.464	−.523	−.261
			(3.98)	(5.40)	(1.66)	(0.83)
1984–94	. . .	. . .	−.419	−.622	−.868	−.612
			(4.32)	(6.37)	(2.16)	(1.53)
Collectivism	−.638	. . .	−.580	. . .	−.621	. . .
	(2.72)		(4.12)		(4.48)	
Relative cohort size$_{t-2}$						
× Collectivism	.894	.891	.747	1.00	.832	1.01
	(3.22)	(3.24)	(2.97)	(3.96)	(3.35)	(4.19)
× 1962–72	. . .	. . .	. . .	. . .	−.687	−1.52
					(1.66)	(3.24)
× 1973–83	. . .	. . .	. . .	. . .	.277	−.547
					(0.49)	(0.94)
× 1984–94	. . .	. . .	. . .	. . .	.732	−.222
					(1.01)	(0.31)
R^2—OLS	.0941	.4155	.5847	.8396	.6037	.8637
df	788	772	785	769	782	766

Note. Numbers in parentheses are absolute values of t-ratios.

weak but persistently negative. More important, the additive effect of relative cohort size averages possibly different relationships over time. As in the analysis of nation-specific differences, the average size may hide substantial differences over time in the effect of relative cohort size.

To capture the changing influence of relative cohort size, the regression model can add product terms of the time dummy variables by relative cohort size (table 5). The results indeed reveal changes over time. To summarize the coefficients in these models, the figures that follow compare how the effect of relative cohort size changes across time periods. Based on the FE-GLS estimates, these effects equal: −0.883 for 1951–61, −2.483 for 1962–72, −1.728 for 1973–83, and −1.341 for 1984–94.[1] The effect of relative cohort size peaks in the late 1960s and early 1970s and falls afterward. By the late 1970s, the effect of relative cohort size does not differ significantly from the first time period and, thus, returns to a weak negative effect. (The coefficients in the GLS model, although less strong, also show a peak of relative cohort size in the second time period.) These results affirm the declining importance of relative cohort size in recent decades not just in the United States but also when averaged across all nations.

Modeling the Contingent Effect of Relative Cohort Size

The next step in the analysis can illustrate the importance of both national and temporal context for the effects of relative cohort size by formalizing the relationships between collectivism and the nation-specific effects of relative cohort size and by including the effect of time on the influence of relative cohort size. To do so, the regression equation can include relative cohort size, time, relative cohort size multiplied by collectivism, and relative cohort size multiplied by time (table 6). Consider first the interaction of relative cohort size and collectivism. The interaction terms have positive coefficients (0.894 and 0.891), which indicates that the negative effect of relative cohort size moves closer to zero as collectivism increases. As predicted, then, collectivist nations show a weaker influence of relative cohort size on fertility than individualist nations do.[2]

Using the estimates, I can translate the interaction coefficients into more concrete terms by calculating the effect of relative cohort size at selected levels of collectivism: low collectivism, −2.45; medium collectivism, −1.12; and high collectivism 0.216.[3] According to these results, the effect of relative cohort size differs substantially for nations with different scores on collectivism. When collectivism equals 0, the effect of relative cohort size equals −1.12—a coefficient in the predicted direction and similar in size to the coefficient averaged across all nations (the corresponding standardized coefficient equals −0.099).[4] At low levels of collectivism, such as for the United States, the effect of relative cohort size equals −2.45. At high levels of collectivism, such as for Sweden, relative cohort size has a positive and small coefficient of 0.216. With standardized coefficients of −0.292 and 0.094, the unstandardized coefficients for low- and high-collectivist nations highlight variation in the influence of relative cohort size.

These calculations do not directly match the actual relationships between relative cohort size and fertility for each of the countries described in table 4. They instead smooth and systematize national differences by allowing the effect of relative cohort size to vary with the collectivism scale.

Table 7. Effects of Relative Cohort Size on Fertility by Time and Collectivism

	1962–72	1984–94
Low collectivism	−3.81	−2.51
Medium collectivism	−2.29	−.993
High collectivism	−.775	.522

The match between collectivism and the effect of relative cohort size is not perfect since nations such as Norway and Belgium deviate from expectations. Still, collectivism seems to be a relevant underlying dimension that helps explain national variation in the influence of relative cohort size.

The interaction of collectivism and relative cohort size persists with controls for period changes in fertility (see cols. 3 and 4 in table 6). Further, it persists with the addition of interaction terms for time period by relative cohort size (see cols. 5 and 6 in table 6). Most important, combining the time-varying and nation-varying effects of relative cohort size identifies even stronger differences across contexts. Some calculations illustrate the contrasting effects (see table 7).[5] Relative cohort size has a strong and negative influence on fertility of −3.81 for low-collectivist nations during the 1960s but a weak and positive influence of 0.522 for high-collectivist nations during the 1980s. The difference between the maximum and minimum effect of relative cohort size is large indeed.

Reflecting the significance of the interaction coefficients, the interactions increase the explanatory power of the models. The ordinary least squares (OLS) variances explained without the interaction terms equal 0.5847 and 0.8396. The OLS variances explained with the collectivism and time interaction terms equal 0.6037 and 0.8637, respectively. The 2% increases due to the interaction terms prove statistically significant and helpful in explaining fertility patterns and trends. Together, the results demonstrate the predicted modification of the consequences of relative cohort size for fertility.[6]

In summary, substantial differences exist in the influence of relative cohort size across national and temporal contexts. The model captures national context with a measure of collectivism but relies on dummy variables to capture the effects of time. The next step requires the inclusion of time-varying variables that might better represent the effects of time and better describe contextual changes that shape the importance of relative cohort size. The next section considers several such determinants of fertility and how they interact with relative cohort size.

Other Influences on Fertility

Although they support the hypotheses, the initial analyses omit control variables in examining the relationship between relative cohort size and fertility. To improve these initial models, the analyses can add three dynamic measures for 1951–94—the female labor force participation rate, social security spending as a percent of GDP, and real GDP per capita (each lagged 1 year)[7]—along with relative cohort size and collectivism as additive determinants of fertility (table 8).[8]

These control variables have the expected effects on fertility. High relative cohort size, high female labor force participation, high social security spending, high national product, and high collectivism all significantly lower fertility. In terms of strength of effect, the variables do not differ greatly. In the FE-GLS model, national product has the largest standardized coefficient (−0.259), followed by female labor force participation (−0.217) and social security spending (−0.178). Collectivism in the GLS model has a similarly sized standardized coefficient of −0.177. Generous and relatively rich welfare states with high proportions of women in the labor force and with collectivist institutions, such as the Scandinavian nations, on average have the lowest fertility rates.

More important, the time-varying controls do not eliminate the additive influence of relative cohort size on fertility. It continues to have significant effects of a magnitude similar to those in previous models. In fact, the controls for female labor force participation provide a stringent test of the influence of relative cohort size on fertility. Since relative cohort size affects female labor force participation, its effect on fertility works indirectly through female labor force participation, and controls for female labor force participation have the potential to weaken substantially or to mediate the effect of relative cohort size. Perhaps because the measure of female labor force participation is not age-specific, it does not greatly reduce the effect of relative cohort size. Along with the other variables, however, female labor force participation raises the explanatory power of these additive models to 0.6103 without nation-specific dummy variable controls and to 0.8251 with such controls.[9]

Since the additive models ignore how contextual differences may modify the association between relative cohort size and fertility, they understate the importance of cohort change in some nations and time periods. To capture diversity in the effects, models can add interaction terms between relative cohort size and each of the other independent variables (see cols. 3

and 4 in table 8). The interaction terms show the change in the effect of relative cohort size for a one-unit change in the other interacting variable.[10]

In support of the predictions, the interaction term coefficients reveal that collectivism still moderates the negative effect of relative cohort size on fertility. As shown previously without controls, relative cohort size has

Table 8. Unstandardized Coefficients for Regression of the Total Fertility Rate on Cohort Size and Other Variables—Additive and Interaction Models

Independent Variables	Additive Model		Interaction Model		Interaction Model[a]	
	GLS	FE-GLS	GLS	FE-GLS	GLS	FE-GLS
Constant	3.68	4.10	2.25	2.26	2.37	2.37
Relative cohort size$_{t-2}$	−.999	−1.22	−.932	−1.26	−1.18	−1.78
	(2.60)	(3.23)	(2.50)	(3.49)	(3.05)	(5.30)
Female labor force participation$_{t-1}$	−.011	−.014	−.013	−.016	−.010	−.007
	(2.20)	(2.86)	(2.76)	(3.50)	(2.06)	(1.57)
Social Security spending$_{t-1}$	−.019	−.020	−.018	−.020	−.013	−.013
	(5.51)	(6.13)	(5.35)	(6.06)	(3.79)	(3.83)
Gross domestic product$_{t-1}$	−.032	−.049	−.032	−.048	−.066	−.087
	(2.84)	(4.62)	(2.78)	(4.58)	(4.72)	(7.44)
Collectivism scale	−.120	· · ·	−.098	· · ·	−.160	· · ·
	(1.95)		(1.74)		(2.87)	
Relative cohort size$_{t-2}$:						
× Collectivism	· · ·	· · ·	.685	.786	1.03	1.24
			(2.50)	(2.86)	(3.18)	(4.10)
× Female labor force participation$_{t-1}$	· · ·	· · ·	.067	.071	.037	.029
			(1.86)	(2.07)	(0.91)	(0.76)
× Social Security spending$_{t-1}$	· · ·	· · ·	−.023	−.048	−.023	−.066
			(0.66)	(1.40)	(0.58)	(1.77)
× Gross domestic product$_{t-1}$	· · ·	· · ·	−.067	−.142	.103	.004
			(0.80)	(1.78)	(0.96)	(0.04)
Unemployment rate$_{t-1}$	· · ·	· · ·	· · ·	· · ·	−.021	−.027
					(3.77)	(5.15)
Family allowance spending$_{t-1}$	· · ·	· · ·	· · ·	· · ·	.042	.052
					(2.66)	(3.24)
R^2—OLS	.6103	.8251	.6285	.8695	.6407	.8919
df	786	770	782	766	582	566

Note. Numbers in parentheses are absolute values of t-ratios.
[a] 1960–94.

Table 9. Effects of Relative Cohort Size on Fertility by Collectivism and Female Labor Force Participation

	Female Labor Force Participation		
	Low	Medium	High
Low collectivism	−3.50	−2.44	−1.37
Medium collectivism	−2.32	−1.26	−.195
High collectivism	−1.15	−.081	.984

weak effects on fertility in collectivist countries and strong effects in individualist countries. Further, measures of female labor force participation and social security spending overlap with the measure of collectivism but do not eliminate the collectivism and relative cohort size interaction. This interaction appears robust.

Only one other variable shows significant interactions with relative cohort size, and only in the FE-GLS model. A one-unit increase in female labor force participation weakens the negative effect of relative cohort size (i.e., moves it closer to zero) by 0.071. To explore the interaction of relative cohort size with both collectivism and female labor force participation implied by the FE-GLS estimates in column 4 of table 8, table 9 compares effects at the extremes.[11] The negative effect of relative cohort size appears strongest for low-collectivist nations with low female labor force participation. In contrast, relative cohort size has the largest positive effect for collectivist nations with high rates of female labor force participation. These results support claims that, by moderating the harm couples face from low male wages and work opportunities, high female labor force participation, like collectivism, reduces the harm of large cohort size for fertility. These results reaffirm the importance of social context for understanding the importance of cohort change.

The importance of female labor force participation would likely emerge more strongly with better data. Because of measurement problems, the analysis only crudely captures national and temporal differences in the roles of women. As a result, the interaction terms involving the female labor force participation rate are less robust than those for collectivism. Even so, they contribute to understanding changes in the effects of relative cohort size. Although the interaction terms involving collectivism explain only differences across nations, the interaction terms between relative cohort size and the female labor force participation rate explain the declining influence over time of relative cohort size on fertility and the recent divergence in trends in the United States.[12]

In contrast, interactions involving both social security spending and national product fail to reach statistical significance and strengthen rather than reduce or moderate the negative effect of relative cohort size net of other controls. The factor-based collectivism scale appears to capture the influence of social protection in reducing the influence of relative cohort size better than the measure of social security spending does. Perhaps the two income variables, social security spending and per capita GDP, reflect increases in aspirations that augment rather than mitigate the importance of relative cohort size. Alternatively, these results may reflect measurement problems. Social security benefits appear to reflect collectivism poorly. Without collectivist institutions to support universal distribution of benefits, social security spending does not lessen the effect of relative cohort size on fertility. Similarly, GDP per capita may not tap income changes of young persons making childbearing decisions.

Do these results reflect only the strong and unusual consequences of relative cohort size in the United States? Given its low score on the collectivism scale, the United States may strongly influence the interaction of relative cohort size and collectivism. Demonstrating a relationship among the other nations would strengthen the findings. A replication of models without the United States reduces, but does not eliminate, the interaction effect between relative cohort size and collectivism to below levels of statistical significance. The coefficients for collectivism by relative cohort size in the FE-GLS model equals 0.786; without the United States, the coefficient equals 0.702 ($t = 2.47$). The size of the interaction falls but remains positive and significant.

The same strategy can test for variation in the effect of relative cohort size on fertility among European nations. Canada, Australia, and New Zealand, and other non-European English-speaking countries, also score low on the collectivism scale and high on the effect of relative cohort size. Japan's unique cultural and political heritage also distinguishes it from the European nations.[13] Focusing only on European nations provides a stringent test of the interaction effects. With more than one-fourth of the countries deleted, the effect of the interaction between relative cohort size and collectivism declines to nonsignificance but remains positive. Most European nations do not show an effect of relative cohort size on fertility, and the high collectivism of European nations accounts for this result.

As a final test of the robustness of these interactions, the models add two other variables available only from 1960 to 1994: family allowance spending and the unemployment rate. Because these two variables do not have significant interaction effects, they are included in the equations as additive controls. The unemployment rate has a significant negative effect on fertility, while family allowance spending has a significant positive effect on fertility. Despite the shorter time span and the additional control variables, the interaction terms involving collectivism remain significant. However, the interaction terms involving the female labor force participation rate are no longer significant when excluding the unique period of the 1950s.

Conclusion

This chapter helps explain the discrepant findings in studies of Easterlin's hypothesis. While the relationship between changes in relative cohort size and swings in the total fertility rate in the post–World War II period appears in the United States and Canada, albeit not without some dispute, it seldom does in the European nations. Consistent with the general perspective offered in this book, I argue that social and institutional characteristics of nations affect the influence of relative cohort size on fertility. An institutional argument posits that national differences in collective responsibility for social protection shape the harmful impact of large cohort size on economic well-being. By moderating the consequences of an oversupply of labor, collectivist institutions can weaken the link between relative cohort size and fertility. European nations that advocate a collectivist ideology of social protection may thus show weak relationships between relative cohort size and fertility.

Similarly, evidence on the Easterlin effect in the United States shows a close correspondence over time between relative cohort size and fertility for the years from 1950 to 1980 but not afterward. Social change in institutions may contribute to the recent divergence in trends. The institutional argument also suggests that increases in female work and independence weaken the importance of cohort size for fertility.

To test these arguments, the analyses use the measure of collectivism to tap variations in universal and egalitarian policies of social protection. In addition to this time-invariant measure of national differences, the analyses use several dynamic measures of social conditions relevant to social protection. Social security spending and family allowance spending tap the generosity of benefits for social protection, while unemployment rates capture the success of national labor market policies in promoting full employment. To reflect changes in female independence and work that also may inhibit the influence of relative cohort size on fertility, the analyses use a measure of the female labor force participation rate.

Estimates averaged across all nations and years show a modest negative effect of relative cohort size on the total fertility rate. More important, the estimates produce evidence in support of the specifying influence of institutional factors. First, the effect of relative cohort size varies significantly across nations, having a strong effect on fertility in individualist nations such as the United States and a weak effect in more collectivist European nations. Second, the effect of relative cohort size also varies across time, with its influence peaking in the late 1960s and early 1970s. Third, changes over time in the effect of relative cohort size relate to increases in female labor force participation. The results thus explain the different effects of relative cohort size on fertility in the United States and Canada compared to Europe and the declining association between relative cohort size and fertility over time. The impact of relative cohort size emerges most strongly in the United States and Canada during the 1950s and 1960s—countries and years that also show the most pronounced fluctuations in the birth rate.

The results have implications for cross-national tests of Easterlin's theory. Measures of wages, earnings, or income alone may not fully reflect the financial situations of young couples. The degree of trust in the ability of governments to protect wage earners from fluctuations in the market relates to the importance of relative cohort size. Although trust and attitudes are difficult to measure, my reliance on less than ideal numerical measures of cohort size combined with nation-specific measures of collectivism nonetheless does suggest one way to examine the diverse impact of previous demographic change on current fertility. The context of economic decisions and demographic change varies systematically across nations in ways that are understandable and plausible. In turn, the institutional context shapes the meaning of cohort changes for individual decisions. The link between context and fertility combines political sociology, economic decision making, and demographic change.

CHAPTER 5

Female Labor Force Participation and the Total Fertility Rate

The theoretical arguments presented in chapter 3 suggest that sociopolitical context shapes the influence of female labor force participation on fertility much as it shapes the influence of relative cohort size on fertility. As in the previous chapter, testing this argument requires something more than the usual effort to examine the partial relationship between female work and fertility. Instead, it requires study of how the relationship between female work and fertility varies across contexts. According to the theoretical arguments, female work should have weaker negative effects on fertility in more recent years than in earlier years, in collectivist and women-friendly nations than in other nations, and at high levels of female work than at low levels of female work. The analyses thus focus on differences in effects across these contexts and how these contexts shape the way female work influences fertility.

As in the last chapter, in which I examined how relative cohort size combines with sociopolitical context in determining the total fertility rate, in this chapter I examine how female labor force participation combines with sociopolitical context in determining the total fertility rate. I begin by describing the relationship between female labor force participation and fertility across all time periods and nations and then I describe differences in the relationship across early and more recent years, across nations with individualist and collectivist institutions, and across nations with traditional and women-friendly institutions. I also examine how the relationship of female labor force participation and fertility changes as female work increases and modifies the context of fertility decision making. Even with controls for other economic determinants of fertility, such as national product, social security spending, unemployment, and family allowance spending, the effects of female work vary in ways predicted by the theoretical arguments and demonstrate the importance of institutional context in shaping the determinants of fertility.

Cross-National Patterns of Female Labor Force Participation

The measure of female labor force participation I have available for all nations and years suffers from several problems. It does not distinguish between work during and after childbearing ages, between full- and part-time work, and between employment in high- and low-status jobs. Further, it does not measure female wages relative to male wages—a crucial component of economic theories of fertility. Lacking detailed and cross-nationally comparable work and wage measures for the nations and years of this study, I must rely on a crude and incomplete measure.

Despite these weaknesses, the female labor force participation rate varies substantially across nations and years, and no doubt reflects something of importance in the changing opportunities and roles of women. It measures work directly but, more important, serves as a useful proxy closely related to unobserved changes in wages, education, gender roles, and values that are not measured comparably across a large number of nations and years. The measure should thus relate to fertility in expected ways and allow for a useful, if less than ideal, test of the theoretical arguments about the context of fertility.

Consider some of the national and temporal differences in the female participation rate. Table 10 lists the mean rate for each nation averaged across the 44 years from 1951 to 1994, as well as the average across all nations for four time periods. Across all nations and years, the mean equals 32.3, but substantial variation exists over time around this mean. Not unexpectedly, the female participation rate rose from a mean of 27.8 to a mean of 39.4 from the 1951–61 period to the 1984–94 period. These values understate the levels of participation for young and middle-aged women but likely reflect the same upward trend over time.

Also not unexpectedly, the female participation rate varies across nations. Ireland has the lowest mean rate of 21.8, and Finland has the highest mean rate of 42.5. More generally, the Scandinavian nations have high rates of participation, in large part because they make part-time work available to large numbers of women who are less willing to work full time. Several central and southern European nations—the Netherlands, Italy, Belgium—and several English-speaking nations—Ireland, Australia, New Zealand, and Canada—have relatively low participation rates.

Table 10. Mean Female Labor Force Participation Rates by Nation and Time Period

Nation	Female Participation Rate			
	Mean	S.D.	Minimum	Maximum
Australia	29.7	7.0	20.7	41.7
Austria	33.8	3.2	28.3	40.1
Belgium	27.2	4.5	20.8	34.9
Canada	30.4	10.9	16.3	45.5
Denmark	40.3	7.1	32.1	51.8
Finland	42.5	4.1	34.8	48.6
France	32.4	2.8	29.3	37.7
Germany	34.0	2.8	30.3	40.5
Ireland	21.8	2.1	19.3	28.6
Italy	25.7	2.8	21.7	31.3
Japan	38.1	2.0	34.3	42.3
Netherlands	23.2	6.6	17.2	38.0
New Zealand	26.4	8.2	17.8	41.8
Norway	32.7	8.5	23.0	45.8
Sweden	40.8	6.7	31.0	50.5
Switzerland	35.5	3.6	32.4	45.2
United Kingdom	34.1	4.2	28.8	41.6
United States	33.4	7.6	24.4	45.3
Total	32.3	8.2	16.3	51.8
1951–61	27.8	6.7	16.3	39.4
1962–72	28.9	6.5	18.1	41.0
1973–83	33.3	7.2	19.3	48.4
1984–94	39.4	6.9	21.8	51.8

Important differences also exist across nations in the trends in female participation rates. The last columns of table 10 list the standard deviations, minimum values, and maximum values of the female participation rate within each nation. Some nations such as Finland, Germany, Japan, and Switzerland show smaller variation than other nations because they begin and end the period of study with high rates. Other nations such as Italy, Ireland, Belgium, and Austria show small variation because they begin and end the period of study with low rates. Those nations that change the most include Canada, Norway, New Zealand, and the United States.

Based on the standard deviations across time periods, national differences in female participation rates appear not to have declined or converged. The standard deviation rises a bit during the 1973–83 period, as some pioneering nations moved ahead of others in their participation rates, but the standard deviation then drops during the 1984–94 period, as lagging nations begin to catch up. Convergence may yet occur as some nations approach maximum levels of participation and other lagging nations catch up further. Yet, for this time period, differences in participation remain and can continue to explain differences in fertility rates.

These national and temporal differences in the female labor force participation rate match those for the total fertility rate. The bivariate correlation coefficient between the two variables equals -0.609. A graph further illustrates the strong bivariate relationship over time (averaged across the 18 nations). Figure 4 depicts the inverse of the female labor force participation rate so that it changes in the same direction as the total fertility rate. Accordingly, both the inverse of the female participation rate and the total fertility rate begin falling in the 1960s. Nevertheless, some deviations exist between the two trends. Unlike fertility, the inverse female participation rate does not rise during the 1950s, fall as steeply in the 1960s and 1970s, and level off or increase during the 1980s. Rather it continues steadily downward (as the actual rate continues steadily upward). Consistent with the strong correlation coefficient, then, the general trends correspond closely, but the participation rate alone cannot explain the larger fluctuations in the total fertility rate.

If the theoretical arguments presented earlier hold true, the average trends mask diversity across nations. To illustrate variation across nations in the effect of female work, figures 5–7 graph the relationships for three illustrative nations—the United States, Sweden, and Italy, respectively.

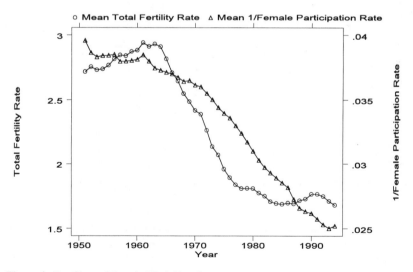

Figure 4. Fertility and Female Work Trends, 18-Nation Means

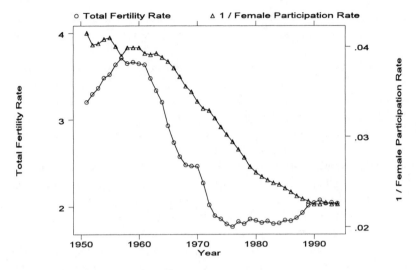

Figure 5. Fertility and Female Work Trends, United States

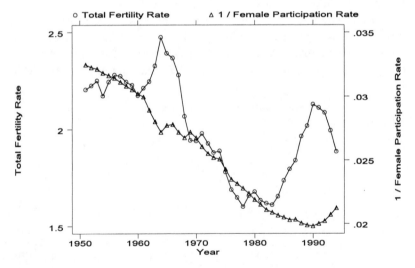

Figure 6. Fertility and Female Work Trends, Sweden

The United States shows a weaker correspondence between the two variables than the 18-nation average. In figure 5, fertility falls much faster than the inverse of the female participation rate. In both Sweden and Italy, the trends match more closely, except for two brief increases in fertility in Sweden, one in the early 1960s and the other in the 1980s. The relationship

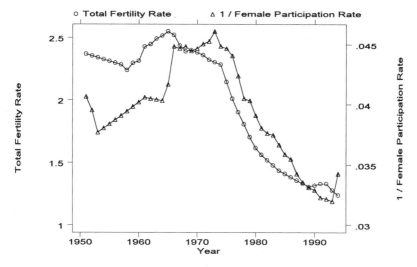

Figure 7. Fertility and Female Work Trends, Italy

between work and fertility appears strongest in Italy. The analyses need to model these national differences.

National Differences in the Effect of Female Labor Force Participation

To confirm the negative effect of the female labor force participation rate on fertility, table 11 presents a simple model with the female participation rate as the only independent variable. The estimates adjust for autocorrelation and heteroscedasticity, the nation dummy variables control for between-nation heterogeneity, and the model lags female participation 1 year to minimize problems of reverse causality. In both the GLS and FE-GLS models, the negative effect of the female participation rate easily reaches significance and explains substantial variance in the total fertility rate. The standardized coefficients equal −0.247 and −0.297—both larger than the coefficients for relative cohort size described in chapter 4. The statistical adjustments lower the crude bivariate correlation between the two variables but do not eliminate the relationship altogether. Despite the measurement weaknesses of the crude female participation rate that attenuate its relationship with fertility, the results emerge as expected.

Combined with the range in the female participation rate, these coefficients reflect a modest potential influence on the total fertility rate. The participation rate across all nations and years ranges from 16.3 to 51.8.

Table 11. Unstandardized Coefficients for Regression of the Total
Ferility Rate on the Female Labor Force Participation Rate—
Additive Models

Independent Variable	Additive Models	
	GLS	FE-GLS
Constant	2.88	3.02
Female participation rate$_{t-1}$	−.020	−.024
	(3.42)	(3.83)
R^2—OLS	.4259	.6581
df	790	773

Note. Numbers in parentheses are absolute values of t-ratios.

When multiplied by the coefficient of −0.020, the range of 35.5 implies a maximum change in fertility due to the female participation rate of 0.71. Compared to the range of the total fertility rate across all nations and all years of 2.99 children (a low of 1.24 and a high of 4.23), the female participation rate alone—like relative cohort size alone—could at best account for about one-quarter of the change in fertility.

These effects, however, represent an average across all nations and years when the effect of female labor force participation likely varies across contexts and may even reverse and become positive in some contexts. To examine nation-specific effects of the female participation rate, the FE-GLS model in table 12 includes product terms between the female participation rate and each of the dummy variables for nation. Using effect coding for the nation variables, the coefficients in column 1 for each nation equal the deviation in the effect of the female participation rate from the unweighted average effect of −0.031. Column 2 adds the coefficients to the average to obtain the nation-specific effect of the female labor force participation rate.

The comparisons across nations reveal substantial differences in the influence of female work on fertility. Although few coefficients differ significantly from the average, the coefficients vary markedly. The effect of −0.051 in the United States emerges much larger than the effect of −0.006 in Finland and −0.002 in Sweden. With a positive coefficient of 0.017, Austria differs even more from the United States and most other nations. Overall, Canada, the United States, and Ireland have stronger negative effects than the average, while Austria, Sweden, and Finland have effects that are either positive or close to zero. To some extent, individualist nations with institutions less supportive of women show greater fertility-inhibiting effects of female work than other nations. Similarly, the more traditional nations of Japan and Italy show relatively strong fertility-inhibiting effects of female labor force participation.

Table 12. Unstandardized Coefficients for Regression of the Total Fertility Rate on the Female Labor Force Participation Rate—Nation-Specific Effects

Nation	FE-GLS Model Coefficients	Female Participation Rate Effect
Constant	2.22	. . .
Female participation rate$_{t-1}$	−.031**	. . .
Australia	−.007	−.038
Austria	.048**	.017
Belgium	.001	−.030
Canada	−.032**	−.063
Denmark	−.005	−.036
Finland	.025	−.006
France	−.029	−.060
Germany	.001	−.030
Ireland	−.025	−.056
Italy	−.011	−.042
Japan	−.032	−.063
Netherlands	.009	−.022
New Zealand	.012	−.019
Norway	−.000	−.031
Sweden	.029**	−.002
Switzerland	.026*	−.005
United Kingdom	.010	−.021
United States	−.020	−.051
R^2—OLS	.7182	. . .
df	756	. . .

$^*p < .05.$
$^{**}p < .01.$

A positive correlation exists between collectivism and the effect of the female participation rate. The bivariate correlation coefficient of 0.551 indicates, as predicted, that collectivist nations have higher (or less negative) effects of female participation and that individualist nations have lower (or more negative) effects of female participation. This specifying effect of collectivism needs validation in more complete and appropriate statistical models but provides informative preliminary evidence. In addition, a similarly sized correlation exists between the scale of women-friendly institutions and the effect of female labor force participation. The correlation coefficient of 0.567 differs little in size from the correlation with collectivism.[1]

Based on these correlations, a simple test suggests that collectivist institutions have a stronger relationship than do women-friendly institutions with the effect of female labor force participation. Since the two scales of institutional characteristics are highly correlated, separating their unique influences creates difficulties. Still, a two-variable multiple regression predicting the nation-specific effect of the female labor force participation rate on fertility gives partial standardized coefficients of 0.436 and 0.220, respectively, for collectivist and women-friendly institutions. Recall that some conservative, central European nations with scores near the middle of the collectivism scale rank low on the women-friendly institutions scale; conversely, some individualist nations score higher than the conservative nations on the women-friendly institutions scale. The stronger effect of collectivism thus suggests that liberal, low-collectivist nations on average show a stronger inhibiting effect of female work than conservative, midrange-collectivist nations do (and both show an even stronger inhibiting effect of female work than social democratic, high-collectivist nations do). The collectivism scale, although focused generally on class equality, may perform better than a gender-specific measure in specifying the effect of female work on fertility.

Finally, the effect of the female participation rate correlates with the level of the participation rate. A positive coefficient of 0.173 suggests that the higher the participation rate and the less traditional the roles of women, the less harmful work is in terms of reducing fertility. It also suggests that, as the participation rate rose in more recent periods, the harm of work on fertility declined. The analysis needs to direct its attention to changes over time in the effect of labor force participation that complement the differences across nations.

Changes in the Effect of Female Labor Force Participation over Time

Along with differences across nations in the influence of female labor force participation, differences may also exist across time. The arguments about changing accommodation of institutions and public policy to female work suggest that the harm of labor force participation for fertility might decline over time. Table 13 examines the interaction between time and the female participation rate to describe the changing influence of women's work on fertility. The first two columns add three dummy variables to represent four time periods (1951–61, 1962–72, 1973–83, 1984–94). The coefficients again describe the well-known decline in fertility after the 1950s and early 1960s. Controls for time actually increase the effects of the female participation rate slightly compared to the effects in table 11.

Of more interest, the next two columns of table 13 consider changes in the effect of female participation. According to the hypotheses, the influ-

Table 13. Unstandardized Coefficients for Regression of the Total Fertility Rate on the Female Labor Force Participation Rate—Time-Specific Effects

Independent Variables	Additive Models		Interaction Models		Curvilinear Model	
	GLS	FE-GLS	GLS	FE-GLS	GLS	FE-GLS
Constant	3.33	3.55	3.77	3.99	5.16	5.47
Female participation rate$_{t-1}$	−.029	−.034	−.043	−.048	−.145	−.154
	(6.19)	(5.80)	(8.95)	(8.45)	(8.95)	(9.23)
Female participation rate$_{t-1}$ squared	...	...	...	...	.0018	.0018
					(7.13)	(7.95)
1962–72	−.071	−.100	−.159	−.129	−.072	−.104
	(1.30)	(1.71)	(1.19)	(0.96)	(1.33)	(1.80)
1973–83	−.261	−.349	−.608	−.666	−.273	−.384
	(3.56)	(4.56)	(3.26)	(3.54)	(3.79)	(5.14)
1984–94	−.303	−.402	−1.13	−1.33	−.332	−.457
	(3.47)	(4.43)	(5.06)	(5.89)	(3.88)	(5.18)
Female participation rate$_{t-1}$:						
× 1962–72	...	...	.003	.001	...	...
			(0.72)	(0.21)		
× 1973–83	...	...	.011	.009	...	...
			(2.03)	(1.86)		
× 1984–94	...	...	.023	.026	...	...
			(4.03)	(4.58)		
R^2—OLS	.6415	.8281	.7001	.8691	.7223	.8725
df	787	770	784	767	786	769

Note. Numbers in parentheses are absolute values of t-ratios.

ence should become less negative over time. The model adds three product terms of the time dummy variables by the female participation rate to identify how its influence changes over time. The female participation rate coefficients show a strong negative effect of the participation rate in the first time period ($b = -0.043$ and -0.048). During these baby-boom years, nations with high rates of female labor force participation had substantially lower fertility rates; similarly, as participation rates rose from 1951 to 1961, fertility fell.

To evaluate the changes over time, consider the coefficients for the product terms. The first product term for the 1962–72 dummy variables does not reach statistical significance. Thus, the effect of the female participation rate on fertility differs little in 1962–72 from the earlier period. Conditions still existed that made high participation especially harmful for fertility. After 1972, the negative effect of female labor force participation moderates. The coefficients for the product term for the 1984–94 period, in particular, are positive and relatively large (0.023 and 0.026) and reduce the negative effect in the first time period. The fertility consequences of female work thus decline substantially in the last decade compared to earlier decades.

To summarize the implications of the model, some simple calculations reveal the effect of the female labor force participation rate on the total fertility rate for four time periods.[2] Based on the GLS estimates, these effects equal −0.043 for 1951–61, −0.040 for 1962–72, −0.032 for 1973–83, and −0.020 for 1984–94. The coefficient in the last time period reaches only half the size of the coefficient in the first time period. The change supports the hypothesis positing the importance of temporal context for the influence of female work.

An alternative way to model the changing influence of the female participation rate, and to represent the institutional adjustment hypothesis, involves adding a quadratic term to the equation. The last columns of table 13 replace the time-participation interaction with a participation-squared term. Since the female participation rate increases over time, changes in its effect at high levels also represent the changes in its effect over time and eliminate the need to include the time and female participation rate interaction along with the curvilinear terms. To summarize the results briefly, the negative coefficient for the participation rate and the positive coefficient for the participation-rate squared fit the predictions. Initially, rising female participation lowers fertility, but this effect tends to level off at higher participation rates.[3] The implied relationship becomes positive only at relatively high levels of female participation but otherwise declines over the range of participation values.

To describe this curvilinear relationship in more detail, calculations can show the implied rate of change in the fertility rate for a unit change in the female labor force participation rate at various levels of the latter rate. The effects implied by the GLS model for female participation are −0.073 for 20%, −0.037 for 30%, −0.001 for 40%, and 0.035 for 50%.[4] These coefficients show strong negative effects at low levels of participation. When few women work, increases in participation substantially lower fertility. However, the harm of work on fertility declines steadily as participation rates increase. When female work reaches 40.3%, the effect on fertility becomes zero,[5] and as female work approaches its maximum of 51.8, it becomes positive. Like the comparisons over time, these comparisons demonstrate that the harm of female work for fertility declines as the participation rate reaches new highs. Both time periods and high levels of participation define contexts that modify the relationship between female work and fertility.

Collectivism and the Contingent Effect of Female Labor Force Participation

To make sense of national differences in the influence of female participation on fertility—along with the differences across time and levels of participation just described—the models focus first on collectivism. According to the theoretical arguments, collectivism likely has little direct influence on fertility but may modify the effect of female work on fertility. Thus, the first two columns of table 14 include an interaction term for collectivism by the female participation rate to demonstrate this contextual effect. As shown by the coefficients for the interaction term, the combined effect of the two variables significantly raises fertility ($b = 0.014$ and 0.012), thus demonstrating that collectivism moderates the harm of female work for fertility.[6] To illustrate the implications of these results, calculations from the GLS model can contrast the influence of female work on fertility across low- (-0.050), medium- (-0.029), and high-collectivist (-0.008) nations.[7] Thus, the effect in a high-collectivist nation such as Sweden differs little from zero, while the effect in a low-collectivist nation such as the United States remains strongly negative. Both nations deviate substantially from the average effect (i.e., when collectivism equals zero) of -0.029.

The results for the collectivism measure simplify the nation-specific results described in table 12 and, no doubt, fail to capture all national contextual differences in the effect of the female participation rate.[8] Some collectivist nations show strong negative effects of female labor force participation and some individualist nations show weak negative effects. Although the match between collectivism and the influence of female work is not perfect, a pattern appears that matches predictions and suggests the importance of this one component of national context.

Along with collectivism, time changes the influence of female labor force participation on fertility. The next two columns in table 14 also control for changes in the effect of the female participation rate over time. The interaction terms for the time dummy variables do not eliminate differences across nations in the effect of female participation but again demonstrate that the negative effect declines over time. As in previous tables, the positive interaction coefficients in table 14 for all three periods weaken the negative coefficients of -0.040 and -0.044 for the first time period. To summarize the combined influence of national and temporal context shown among the perhaps overwhelming sets of coefficients in the table, the effects for low-, medium-, and high-collectivist nations in the earliest and latest time periods can be found in table 15.[9] The influences of female work at the extremes differ greatly: low-collectivist nations such as

Table 14. Unstandardized Coefficients for Regression of the Total Fertility Rate on the Female Labor Force Participation Rate—Collectivism and Time Interaction Models

Independent Variables	Collectivism Interaction		Time Interaction		Curvilinear Interaction	
	GLS	FE-GLS	GLS	FE-GLS	GLS	FE-GLS
Constant	3.33	3.54	3.66	3.86	5.02	5.31
Female participation rate$_{t-1}$	−.029	−.033	−.040	−.044	−.141	−.149
	(6.44)	(5.89)	(8.69)	(8.04)	(8.45)	(9.00)
Female participation rate$_{t-1}$ squared	...	...	...	...	.0017	.0017
					(6.59)	(6.93)
1962–72	−.082	−.108	−.099	−.077	−.074	−.103
	(1.48)	(1.83)	(0.76)	(0.58)	(1.38)	(1.78)
1973–83	−.295	−.378	−.531	−.576	−.286	−.390
	(3.99)	(4.93)	(2.93)	(3.15)	(3.99)	(5.27)
1984–94	−.346	−.435	−1.08	−1.23	−.350	−.467
	(3.95)	(4.81)	(4.97)	(5.58)	(4.11)	(5.35)
Female participation rate$_{t-1}$:						
× 1962–72	...	...	.000	−.001	...	...
			(0.08)	(0.31)		
× 1973–83	...	...	.007	.006	...	...
			(1.35)	(1.19)		
× 1984–94	...	...	.020	.022	...	...
			(3.57)	(3.95)		
Collectivism	−.561	...	−.544	...	−1.25	...
	(6.84)		(7.18)		(5.04)	
× FLFP$_{t-1}$	.014	.012	.014	.011	.064	.057
	(5.55)	(5.53)	(5.82)	(5.08)	(4.12)	(3.61)
× FLFP$_{t-1}$ squared					−.0008	−.0007
					(3.54)	(3.18)
R^2—OLS	.7097	.8469	.7488	.8772	.7794	.8810
df	785	769	782	766	783	767

Note. Numbers in parentheses are absolute values of t-ratios. FLFP = female labor force participation.

the United States in the 1950s have a coefficient of −0.061 compared to a coefficient of 0.001 for high-collectivist nations such as Sweden in the 1980s. In standardized terms, the coefficients of −0.061 and 0.001 equal −0.748 and 0.025 and further highlight the diversity across nations.[10] Both collectivism and time thus dampen the negative effect of female work on fertility.

The logic of the separate collectivism and time interactions might fur-

Table 15. Effects of Female Labor Force Participation on Fertility by Time and Collectivism

	1951–61	1984–94
Low collectivism	−.061	−.041
Medium collectivism	−.040	−.020
High collectivism	−.019	.001

ther suggest more complex interactions: for instance, the modifying effect of collectivism on the female participation rate might change over time. This implies interaction among collectivism, time, and female participation in determining fertility and inclusion of three-way product terms. However, none of these interaction terms has a significant net effect on fertility. Collectivism modifies the effect of female participation and time modifies the effect of female participation, but time does not modify the interaction between collectivism and female participation. The national differences in the effect of female labor force participation remain pretty much the same over time. Similarly, the declining effect of female labor force participation over time does not differ significantly across collectivist and individualist nations.

The interactions with collectivism remain when the female participation–rate squared replaces the time interactions. The last columns in table 14 include each term of the quadratic and each term of the quadratic times collectivism. When collectivism equals zero, the coefficients for the participation rate are negative (−0.141 and −0.149) and the coefficients for the participation-rate squared are positive (0.0017 and 0.0017). Note, however, that collectivism moderates the negative effect of the participation rate with positive coefficients (0.064 and 0.057) and moderates the positive effect of the participation-rate squared with negative coefficients (−0.0008 and −0.0007). This shows that the initial harm of rising participation is smaller and the subsequent rebound less strong in collectivist nations than in individualist nations.[11]

To illustrate how the curvilinear effects vary across nations, figure 8 includes curves for high-, medium-, and low-collectivist nations. The figure shows that the curvilinear pattern emerges most strongly for individualist nations, rather than for collectivist nations. For individualist nations, fertility drops strongly at low levels of female participation but not at high levels of female participation. For collectivist nations, the effect of female work is generally less negative and, therefore, changes less at higher levels of female participation.

These results indicate multiple paths to a weakened negative effect of

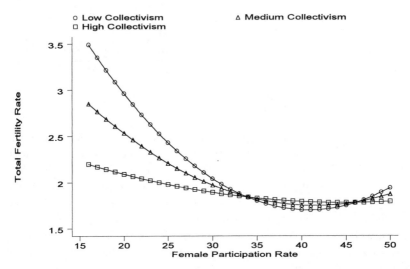

Figure 8. Female Labor Force Participation and Fertility, by Collectivism

female labor force participation. First, for collectivist nations, the institutional environment moderates the harm of female work on fertility at all levels of female work, and the weak effect of female work changes little as female work rises. Second, for individualist or low-collectivist nations, weak institutional support means that female work more strongly reduces fertility but also that high levels of female work bring about changes that reduce its effect on fertility. These two paths reveal a tendency toward convergence in effects between collectivist and individualist nations: the curves for the two types of nations move toward one another as levels of female participation increase. Collectivism proves more important in reducing the effect of female work at low levels of female work than at high levels. Movement toward weakened negative effects of female work takes longer to occur in individualist nations, but the harm of female work for fertility declines in all nations.

To summarize these complexities, then, both collectivism and levels of female work, according to table 14 and figure 8, serve as contexts that shape the influence of female work on fertility. The context of high female work reduces—but does not eliminate—the difference between collectivist and individualist nations, showing that high levels of female work partially counter the lack of collectivist institutions.

Do these results emerge from the unusual influence of one nation? To check, I examined Cook's D case-influence diagnostic measure. The largest values of 0.018 and 0.016 (values well below typical cut-points used to identify influential cases) occur for Australia and Japan. Replicating the equations in the last columns of table 14 with each of these nations deleted strengthens the interaction between female labor force participation and fertility. In addition, a model that deletes the United States—the most extreme individualist nation—does little to change the results. The coefficients for the interaction terms decrease only slightly without the United States and remain clearly significant. A single atypical nation does not appear to produce artificially the combined effect of female work and collectivism.

Do the results emerge from the unusual influence of a small set of years? Perhaps the atypical and unexpected fluctuations in fertility in the past decade exert a disproportional influence on the results. To check, I replicated models by successively deleting the years 1993–94, 1990–94, and 1987–94. The first two deletions leave the results virtually unchanged. Deleting the past 8 years slightly weakens the interaction coefficients but does not reduce them to below statistical significance. It makes sense that the ability to detect changes in the effect of female work would lessen when excluding years in which the largest contextual changes occurred. Yet the results do not depend wholly on the experiences of nations in the past 8 years.

Women-Friendly Institutions and the Effect of Female Labor Force Participation

Replicating the models in table 14 with the measure of women-friendly institutions substituted for the measure of collectivist institutions further demonstrates the contingent nature of the effects of female work on fertility. Table 16 presents these results. The first two columns consider the interaction between female work and gender equality with multiplicative product terms. When the gender scale equals zero, the effects of female labor force participation in the first time period equal -0.025 or -0.030. Yet the gender-based scale multiplied by the female labor force participation rate in columns 1 and 2 has positive coefficients. As the gender scale increases, the positive interaction terms of 0.022 and 0.016 balance the otherwise negative effects of female work on fertility. Conversely, as the gender scale decreases (i.e., falls below the mean of zero), it heightens the negative effects of female work.

A few calculations illustrate the varied effects of female work in the GLS

Table 16. Unstandardized Coefficients for Regression of the Total Fertility Rate on the Female Labor Force Participation Rate—Gender and Time Interaction Models

Independent Variables	Gender Interaction		Time Interaction		Curvilinear Interaction	
	GLS	FE-GLS	GLS	FE-GLS	GLS	FE-GLS
Constant	3.19	3.45	3.50	3.81	4.34	5.06
Female participation rate$_{t-1}$	−.025	−.030	−.035	−.042	−.104	−.132
	(5.72)	(5.28)	(7.73)	(7.63)	(6.59)	(8.63)
Female participation rate$_{t-1}$ squared	...	...	...	...	.0012	.0015
					(5.08)	(6.81)
1962–72	−.081	−.105	−.090	−.085	−.075	−.103
	(1.45)	(1.78)	(0.71)	(0.65)	(1.39)	(1.78)
1973–83	−.294	−.371	−.495	−.586	−.288	−.389
	(3.92)	(4.77)	(2.82)	(3.26)	(3.98)	(5.21)
1984–94	−.344	−.429	−1.03	−1.27	−.349	−.465
	(3.87)	(4.66)	(4.91)	(5.86)	(4.07)	(5.28)
Female participation rate$_{t-1}$						
× 1962–72	...	...	.000	.001	...	...
			(0.01)	(0.25)		
× 1973–83	...	...	.006	.006	...	...
			(1.18)	(1.23)		
× 1984–94	...	...	.019	.023	...	...
			(3.43)	(4.17)		
Gender	−.893	...	−.909	...	−2.27	...
	(7.09)		(7.83)		(5.88)	
×FLFP$_{t-1}$	.022	.016	.023	.016	.114	.079
	(6.11)	(4.57)	(6.82)	(4.66)	(5.03)	(3.72)
× FLFP$_{t-1}$ squared	...	...	...	...	−.0014	−.0010
					(4.34)	(3.32)
R^2—OLS	.7414	.8517	.7670	.8790	.7897	.8817
df	785	769	782	766	783	767

Note. Numbers in parentheses are absolute values of t-ratios. FLFP = female labor force participation.

model. Taking the highest score on the gender scale (France at 1.29), the lowest score (Japan at −1.22), and the mean of zero as illustrative cases, the model implies an effect of −0.052 for female work on fertility for women-unfriendly institutions, −0.025 for neutral institutions, and 0.003 for women-friendly institutions.[12] In standardized terms, the coefficient of −0.052 equals −0.273, and the coefficient of 0.004 equals 0.026.[13] The large difference across the measures of women-friendly institutions again demonstrates the importance of context in influencing the effect of female work on fertility. Thus, supportive institutions for women, like collectivist institutions more generally, reduce the negative influence of female work on fertility.

The additional models in table 16 confirm these results and conclusions. Adding interaction terms that allow the effects of female work to vary by period again show moderation in the harm of work on fertility in the latest time periods but do not otherwise change the influence of national differences in support of women on work-fertility relationships. The coefficients for the product of women-friendly institutions and female labor force participation equal 0.023 and 0.016—nearly identical to the coefficients in the previous models. The implications of the model are illustrated in table 17.[14] As with collectivism, these results reveal stark differences across national and temporal contexts. The strongest negative effect emerges in nations lacking women-friendly institutions in the 1950s, and a positive effect emerges in women-friendly nations in the 1980s. Both nation and time contexts shape the consequences of female work.

The nation interaction also remains when the female participation–rate squared replaces the time interactions. The last columns in table 16 include each term of the quadratic and each term of the quadratic times the gender scale. As in previous tables, the coefficients for the female participation rate are negative (-0.104 and -0.132) and the coefficients for the participation-rate squared are positive (0.0012 and 0.0015). Further, the gender scale moderates the negative effect of the participation rate with positive coefficients (0.114 and 0.079) and moderates the positive effect of the participation-rate squared with negative coefficients (-0.0014 and -0.0010). This shows that the initial harm for fertility of rising participation is smaller and that the subsequent rebound is less strong in nations with women-friendly institutions than in other nations.

Figure 9 compares the curvilinear effects of female work across nations grouped by the gender equality measure. The figure shows that nations

Table 17. Effects of Female Labor Force Participation on Fertility by Time and Gender Equality

Type of Nation	1951–61	1984–94
Women unfriendly	−.063	−.044
Neutral	−.035	−.016
Women friendly	−.005	.014

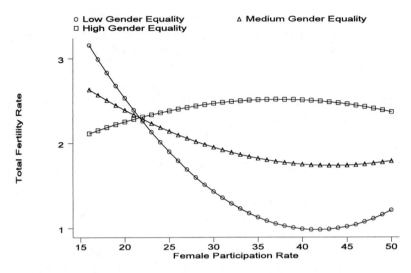

Figure 9. Female Labor Force Participation and Fertility, by Gender Equality

least supportive of women most strongly reflect the curvilinear pattern. Without public institutions highly supportive of women, the negative effect of female work does not reverse until reaching high levels of participation. Nations with women-friendly institutions show less change in fertility—perhaps even a small increase—with levels of female work. For these nations, a majority of working women need not be present to reduce the harm of female work for fertility. However, for other nations with less supportive institutions, the path to weaker negative effects of female work differs. In these nations, a near majority of working women is needed to reduce the harm of female work. All nations thus exhibit tendencies toward weaker effects of female work, but the tendency emerges more slowly in nations without supportive institutions.

Both measures of national context—collectivist and women-friendly institutions—modify the influence of female labor force participation in the fertility models. Since the two measures correlate with one another, the similar results for each are not surprising. Indeed, the overlap in the measures makes it difficult to demonstrate the superiority of one over the other in these models. Comparing tables 14 and 16, the *t*-values for the gender-scale interactions appear larger in the GLS models, but those for the collectivism interactions appear larger in the FE-GLS models. Further, if models include both scales and both interactions, the coefficients for the gender scale emerge dominant in the GLS model, but those for collectivism emerge dominant in the FE-GLS model.

The evidence favoring both types of national contexts suggests that each institutional feature contributes to changes in the processes determining fertility, albeit in different ways. Both class-based institutions and gender-based institutions provide social protection that makes work and childbearing more compatible. The class-based institutions do so indirectly and the gender-based institutions do so directly, but the effect of each makes it difficult to identify the influence of one independently of the other. It seems less important, then, to identify one measure as superior than to recognize multiple ways to support working parents. Those nations high on both scales do the most, those nations low on both scales do the least, and those nations high on one and low on the other fall somewhere between the extremes in helping women to combine work and family duties more easily.

Controls for other determinants of fertility do not change these conclusions. As in analyses in the previous chapter, the results with additional control variables (data not presented) show that national product and public spending both lower fertility. However, they do little to change the interaction involving female participation. The same holds true for models with unemployment and family allowance spending for the shorter time period: high unemployment lowers fertility and high family allowance spending raises fertility, but they leave the interaction effects of female work unchanged.

Perhaps these other determinants of fertility also shape the influence of female participation (much as they shaped the influence of relative cohort size). High national product, generous social security and family allowance spending, and low unemployment may reduce the negative effect of female work on fertility. I therefore examined the interactions between female labor force participation and national product, social security spending, unemployment, and family allowance spending. Without presenting more tables, I can summarize the results. The interaction terms of national product and social security spending (for the years 1951–94) and family allowance spending (for the years 1960–94) by the female labor force participation rate have the expected positive effect. That is, the higher the national income and spending on social protection in general or family support in particular, the less negative the impact of female labor force participation on fertility. To some extent, the income and spending measures reflect institutional contexts that shape the influence of female labor force participation.

Do these models fit some nations better than others? A check of mean residuals for each nation shows the largest positive prediction errors for Ireland, Austria, and the United Kingdom—nations that have higher fertility than expected under the model. The largest negative errors (i.e., lower fertility than expected) appear for Japan, Finland, and the Netherlands. The positive mean residual for the United States shows it has higher fertility than expected but does not deviate as widely from the predictions as other nations. Perhaps a better measure than the mean residual is the nation-specific standard deviation of the residuals, which reflects variation around the mean. The nations with the largest residual standard deviations are the Netherlands, New Zealand, Ireland, and the United States. The models on average capture fertility rates in these nations but do not fully capture the swings in fertility over time. They show predictions lower than expected in the 1950s and higher than expected in the 1970s. Beyond this, however, only one nation—Ireland, the lowest-income nation in the sample—stands out as poorly predicted according to both the mean and standard deviation of the residuals.

Conclusion

As in the chapter on relative cohort size, the information in this chapter helps explain discrepant findings in the consequences of female labor force participation for fertility. Both economic and sociological theories provide reasons to expect that female work—and the underlying changes in female wages and values of autonomy and independence that rising female work reflect—lowers fertility. Numerous microlevel and macrolevel studies confirm the expected negative relationship. However, several studies in recent years have noted exceptions that suggest that the consequences of female work for fertility vary with national and temporal institutional contexts.

Again consistent with the perspective offered in this book, I argue that institutional characteristics of nations, and changes over time in those characteristics, affect the relationship between female labor force participation and fertility. By moderating the conflict between work and family roles experienced by women, class-based collectivist institutions and gender-based women-friendly institutions may reduce the negative influence of female labor force participation on fertility. Further, the institutions should do more to reduce the negative influence in more recent periods than in earlier periods and at higher levels of participation than at lower levels.

To test these arguments, I used time-invariant scales for collectivist and women-friendly institutions to tap national contextual differences. In addition, I examined changes over time in the effects of female work and curvilinear effects of female work on fertility. These results thus tested arguments about institutional adjustment within nations that complement arguments about institutional differences across nations.

The findings reveal substantial differences across nations and time periods in the effects of female labor force participation. Averaged across all nations and years, female participation has a negative relationship with fertility that persists with controls for between-nation and between–time period heterogeneity but that also masks variation. Across nations, the inhibiting effects of female labor force participation are smaller in collectivist nations than in individualist nations and in nations with strong women-friendly institutions than in nations with weak women-friendly institutions. Policies in collectivist and women-friendly nations, more so than those in other nations, aid women in combining work and family roles and, therefore, reduce the downward pressure that female labor force participation exerts on fertility.

The context of the relationship between female participation and fertility also varies over time. Initial increases in female labor force participation strongly lower fertility, but continued increases in female labor force participation have a progressively less negative influence on fertility. Although it never becomes positive, the effect of female work on fertility nearly reaches a value in which increased female work no longer lowers fertility. Combined with the findings about national context, the results reveal the strongest influence of female participation in individualist, liberal nations during the 1950s—when and where the baby boom was largest. The weakest influence occurs in collectivist, women-friendly nations during the 1980s and 1990s—a result consistent with rising fertility in Sweden in recent years.

Combined with the additive and interactive effects of relative cohort size reported in chapter 4, the findings in this chapter affirm the importance of sociopolitical context in determining fertility. The effects of both relative cohort size and female participation (two variables closely related, according to Easterlin) differ across nations and time periods. Further, the effects remain with additive and interactive controls for national product, social security spending, unemployment, and family allowance spending.

Overall, the results emphasize the importance of sociopolitical institutions not for the levels of fertility but for the processes that determine levels of fertility. Variation in contexts across nations and time periods affects the decisions made by couples to work, have children, or do both.

A daunting problem in these analyses comes from the crude measure of female labor force participation. Measures that distinguish between rates by age, hours worked, and types of jobs would no doubt demonstrate stronger effects than the crude measure I must use. Further, female work can only indirectly tap changes in female wages and social values that contribute to low fertility. Despite these measurement problems, the results confirm the theoretical predictions. Nevertheless, direct measures of wages and values would likely make it easier to distinguish nation-specific and period-specific effects.

PART III

Mortality

CHAPTER 6

Cohort Size and Suicide and Homicide Mortality

Comparative studies of mortality often examine rates averaged across all causes, usually in the form of life expectancy at birth, or concentrate on death rates for the most common causes, such as heart disease and cancers. However, suicide and homicide—forms of mortality that involve violence and daily problems of living—deserve special study for several reasons. First, together they represent major causes of death in high-income nations, especially among younger persons. For those ages 15–24, homicide and suicide follow accidents as the second and third most common causes of death (Rockett 1998, 10; Singh and Yu 1996). Because homicide and suicide victimize otherwise healthy young people, these types of deaths are also among the leading causes of years of life lost before age 65 (Rockett and Smith 1989). Lethal violence occurs at older ages, but the rising incidence of degenerative diseases lowers its relative rank. Even so, suicide ranks eighth among causes of death of persons ages 45–64 (Rockett 1998, 10).

Second, violent mortality relates more directly to social conditions than do other causes of death and better reflects the immediate consequences of everyday behavior for persons of all ages. Social behaviors involving poor diet, alcohol abuse, inactivity, smoking, and stress promote heart disease, lung cancer, and liver cirrhosis but may take decades to produce a death. Mortality from degenerative diseases at the older ages results primarily from the long-term accumulation of the effects of unhealthy behaviors. Social behaviors also affect HIV infection and death from AIDS but, again, after a delay of a few years and often much longer. In contrast, social behaviors involving violence, crime, recklessness, self-destructiveness, and drug and alcohol abuse result more immediately in suicide and homicide. By spreading violent deaths across all ages rather than concentrating them at the oldest ages, this immediacy makes it possible to better isolate the consequences of social behavior for violent mortality than for other causes of death.

Third, although they both relate directly to social conditions, the two types of violent mortality differ in important and theoretically meaningful ways. Suicide and homicide both represent, to varying degrees, forms of self-inflicted mortality, with suicide the most overt and homicide the more subtle manifestation of self-destructive tendencies. Dating back to the 1950s (Henry and Short 1954), scholars have argued that suicide and homicide both relate to social conditions that produce violence but that suicide involves internalized aggression and homicide involves externalized aggression. Since suicide expresses intentional violence against self and homicide expresses intentional violence against others, each may respond in different ways to social and economic conditions that promote violence.

Fourth, violent mortality varies substantially across nations and time. Other causes of death treatable by medical care tend to change similarly across high-income nations that have adopted uniform medical techniques, drugs, and treatment procedures. Problems of suicide and homicide, although the object of public health campaigns in many nations, cannot be rectified by advances in medical care. Rather, cultural and social differences have a greater impact on violent mortality than they do on other forms of mortality. The varied national patterns appear, for example, in high homicide rates in the United States and high suicide rates in Germany and Japan (Rockett 1998, 7). Nations may differ even more in the trends over time in age-specific violent mortality rates. In the United States, suicide and homicide rates have increased, particularly at the younger ages. Given the cultural and social traits of their citizens, other nations no doubt have experienced special trends in each type of violent mortality.

Finally, the study of violent mortality raises special issues involving age structure and cohort size. Perhaps most obviously, societal homicide rates rise with a large youth population for the simple reason that crime in general and homicide in particular peak during youth (Hirschi and Gottfredson 1983). In terms of compositional arguments, the common form of the relationship between age and homicide implies through simple demographic accounting a macrolevel relationship between the percentage of the population prone to committing homicide and the national rate of homicide. When the rates of homicide soared in the United States in the late 1960s, scholars needed no grand theory to explain why an increase in the proportion of persons most at risk of offending would inflate the homicide rate. The change in age composition of the population directly affects the homicide rate given a constant relationship between age and homicide.

Although less important than for homicide, the compositional argument applies also to suicide. Suicide rates rise steadily over the life course and peak at the oldest ages. As a result, population aging can inflate overall suicide rates just as compositional changes in the size of the youth population inflate overall homicide rates.

Beyond these obvious compositional influences, age structure may have processual effects on violent mortality rates through cohort size. Population changes can affect the relationship between age and mortality such that the propensity of young persons to fall victim to homicide increases with a large youth population, and the propensity of old persons to commit suicide increases with a growing aged population. Younger persons may always be more prone to death from homicide than older persons, but especially prominent differences may emerge when young cohorts are particularly large. Older persons may always be more prone to suicide than younger persons, but especially prominent differences may emerge when older cohorts are particularly large. Alternatively, a large aged population with increasing economic resources and political power may result in lower suicide at the older ages. In either case, this reasoning suggests a focus on changes in age-specific rather than crude rates of violent mortality as a result of changes in cohort size.

Given the importance of the study of violent mortality, this chapter extends the logic of the study of fertility by considering the processual effects of cohort size on age-specific suicide and homicide rates. Following the theoretical arguments that this chapter presents, the next two chapters analyze the determinants of each type of lethal violence.

Competing Views of the Effects of Cohort Size

To review briefly, Richard Easterlin (1978, 1987a) argues that members of a large cohort face competition over increasingly scarce resources. They experience shortages of teachers and schools in childhood, labor market competition and unemployment in early adulthood, low pay and promotion in adulthood, and tight public retirement benefits in old age. If the cohorts of their parents were smaller, enjoyed economic success, and raised their children in affluence, members of large cohorts feel further deprived in comparison to their parents and childhood standard of living. Late marriage, low fertility, and high divorce result. Just the opposite occurs for smaller cohorts, whose members enjoy better economic success and a more stable and satisfying family life.

The consequences of cohort size and relative economic status relate to mortality. In psychological terms, limited prospects for economic success create pessimism, alienation, and mental stress among members of large cohorts, which in turn increase the propensity for destructive behaviors such as suicide and homicide. In structural terms, entrance of large cohorts into different stages of the life course creates friction and social disorganization, which also can increase suicide and homicide. Members of smaller cohorts face less stress, easier adjustment to age-based changes in status, and lower suicide and homicide than members of larger cohorts. Given these processes, Easterlin argues that suicide and homicide result from the relative economic and social well-being of age groups and, therefore, from cohort size.

In support of his arguments, Easterlin (1987a, 102) graphs the suicide and homicide rates of males ages 15–24 in the United States. From the late 1940s until the late 1960s, the rates declined or increased only slightly. However, as the members of the baby-boom generation reached their late teens and early twenties during the late 1960s and 1970s, both homicide and suicide rates increased dramatically. Consistent with Easterlin's claims about the importance of cohort size to mortality and fertility, suicide and homicide rates began rising at the same time birth rates began falling.

A competing viewpoint, however, predicts the opposite consequences of cohort size: large cohorts may enjoy advantages in political expression and economic power compared to small cohorts. Again, to review briefly, Preston (1984) argues that large cohorts have sufficient numbers to influence public policy and garner consumer resources. Because large cohorts represent potentially large voting blocs and purchasing segments, the political and economic concerns of large cohorts become societal concerns (Bouvier and DeVita 1991; Uhlenberg 1992). This increases their sense of group efficacy, the salience of their age identity, and their degree of social integration into age-based groups. Moreover, when smaller cohorts follow larger ones, the larger cohorts continue to dominate the economy and fill most of the jobs—even many that normally would go to younger people.

Like Easterlin, Preston (1984) applies his arguments to age differences in suicide and homicide mortality. In recent years, violent mortality among a shrinking adolescent population has increased, while violent mortality among an expanding aged population has decreased. Among young people in the United States, suicide continues to rise steadily and signifies increasing anomie, pessimism, and difficulty in fitting into society (Holden 1986). Trends in impoverishment, family breakup, and lessened government support of families may contribute to rising teen suicide rates. At the other end of the life cycle, suicide of the elderly exceeds that of the young (Girard 1993). Yet until recently declining rates among the elderly combined with rising rates among youth appeared to foreshadow a convergence.[1]

For homicide, victimization concentrates at the younger ages, but the trends over time appear, much as they do for suicide, to harm younger persons in smaller cohorts more than older persons in larger cohorts. In 1991, persons ages 15–29 represented 22.1% of the population but 46.5% of all homicide victims in the United States (U.S. Bureau of the Census 1994). Persons age 65 and over represented 12.6% of the population but only 4.7% of homicide victims. Further, the propensity for younger persons to be homicide victims has risen faster over time than for other groups. Homicide victimization rates in the United States have risen from 1955 to 1985 by 17% for persons ages 15–34, 12% for persons 35–54, and 6% for persons 55 and over. Despite declining cohort size among the young, the concentration of homicides at the youngest ages has increased over time.

Multivariate evidence for the United States, like the descriptive evidence of Easterlin and Preston, offers mixed support for the Easterlin effect. Studies of official arrest data (Maxim 1985; O'Brien 1989; O'Brien, Stockard, and Isaacson 1999; Smith 1986), self-reported delinquency (Menard 1992; Menard and Elliot 1990), homicide rates (Cutright and Briggs 1995), and suicide rates (Ahlburg and Schapiro 1984) demonstrate the predicted positive effects of cohort size. Other studies of arrest rates, however, do not find the expected effects (Steffensmeier, Striefel, and Harer 1987; Steffensmeier, Striefel, and Shihadeh 1992).

In any case, the competing views concerning age-based trends in suicide and homicide highlight the political implications of behaviors that most view as the result of special physiological and psychological problems experienced by persons at different stages of the life course. While age differences in violent mortality seem the natural consequence of human development, the varied integration of individuals at different ages into social groups, and biosocial changes in aggression and physicality, they may also stem from an age-based system of stratification that favors some age groups or generations over others. In the past, family ties and class identities once bonded members of different generations in common interests, but generational sharing has shifted in recent decades from families and classes to the public arena and formal bureaucracies. Currently, public institutions in high-income democracies may discourage close ties across generations and encourage political competition among age groups (Pampel 1994).

Thus, age patterns of suicide and homicide take on increasing importance as indicators of the economic and social well-being of age groups.

Divergence across Ages and Nations

A review of more sophisticated empirical evidence on the relationship between cohort size and suicide and homicide, evidence that considers age and national differences in the relationships, adds even more complexity to the issue. For suicide, a time-series study of the United States (Holinger, Offer, and Zola 1988) finds a positive correlation between cohort size and suicide among the young but finds a negative relationship among the old. McCall and Land (1994) find relative cohort size raises suicide among the young but lowers suicide among the old in the United States. With data on Japan, Lester (1991) reports that the correlation between cohort size and suicide rates varies remarkably from .63 to −.87 among different age groups. Further, Girard (1993) demonstrates that the age pattern of suicide differs for men and women and for developed and developing nations. The existing studies thus falsify any simple posited relationship between cohort size and suicide and reinforce the need to study age-specific rates (McCall and Land 1994).

For homicide, evidence on the effects of cohort size across ages and nations likewise appears complex. Time-series studies of the United States confirm empirically the expected relationship between age structure and homicide but fail to differentiate between the compositional and processual sources of the relationship. Cohen and Land (1987) find that the growth of the youth population from the entrance of large baby-boom cohorts into adolescence during the late 1960s increased homicide just as later declines in the youth population from entrance of small baby-bust cohorts into adolescence during the 1980s symmetrically reduced homicide. That increases in the proportion of youth in the population had similarly strong effects on homicide as decreases in the proportion of youth—albeit in the opposite direction—demonstrates the robustness of the relationship. However, studies that do not examine age-specific homicide rates cannot separate changes due to higher homicide rates from changes due to higher proportions of persons at homicide-prone ages.

Cross-national studies of homicide fail to find much of a relationship between age structure and homicide or fail to replicate findings for the United States. Although few studies compare differences across nations in the processual relationship between cohort size and age-specific homicide rates, less demanding comparative tests of compositional effects prove insightful. Gartner (1990) finds that across 18 high-income nations over a 30-year time span the percentage of the population that is ages 15–29 has no effect on homicide. She suggests the lack of an effect across all nations and time points may hide more complex, country-specific influences of age structure on homicide. For instance, the only three nations to show decreases in the percentage of the population that is ages 15–29—Japan, Italy, and West Germany—also show either a decline in homicide or a negligible increase. Gartner and Parker (1990) explore the possibility of nation-specific effects in detail by examining the impact of age structure separately for five nations. They find effects of the relative size of the young population only for Italy and the United States and only in the post–World War II period; no effects emerge for England and Wales, Scotland, or Japan. Cross-sectional analyses of high-income nations thus reveal little or no relationship between age structure and homicide, while time-series analyses demonstrate a relationship only for a few nations and only for a limited time period.

Only Cutright and Briggs (1995) offer support for processual arguments with evidence of a relationship between relative cohort size and age-specific homicide rates (that control for age composition of the population). They do not, however, search for differences in the size or direction of the relationship across nations.

A Contingent Relationship

The divergent findings concerning the relationships of cohort size with suicide and homicide imply that social context may influence the relationship. As shown in previous chapters, the European countries differ from the United States in their institutions for social protection and, therefore, might also differ in the associations they exhibit between cohort size and violent mortality. Analogously, time periods and age groups differ in ways that may also shape the influence of cohort size on suicide and homicide mortality rates. Yet most studies fail to examine the diversity in processes that determine mortality outcomes.

To make sense of the competing theories of Easterlin and Preston and the complex empirical findings about the advantages and disadvantages of cohort size, the effect of cohort size on suicide and homicide mortality needs to be treated as a variable amenable to explanation. Recognizing the contingency of the relationship offers a means to integrate ostensibly contrasting arguments. Where Easterlin emphasizes the harmful impact of large cohort size on success in private labor markets, Preston emphasizes how cohort size affects public and private transfers to those out of the labor force. The arguments emerge as compatible when considering the relative importance of state and market for group income. To summarize the basic thesis, the larger the role of transfers relative to the earnings of a group, or the larger the role of the government relative to the market, the greater the advantages of belonging to a large cohort; and the larger the role of earnings and the market, the greater the disadvantages of belonging to a large cohort. Four dimensions of the market/transfer distribution may shape the impact of cohort size on suicide and homicide: age, gender, nation, and time.

Age. The source of income varies with the current age of a cohort. Comparing prime age adults—ages 25–44—with those approaching and those entering old age suggests that age groups most attached to the labor force and most dependent on market earnings suffer more from membership in large cohorts. Labor force participation peaks among prime age males, begins falling after age 45, and reaches especially low levels during older, retirement ages (Organization for Economic Cooperation and Development 1996 and various years). Accordingly, a positive effect of cohort size should emerge during the prime ages but decline and become negative during old age. Identifying the specific age at which the relationship peaks or shifts directions proves difficult; the salience of work problems for psychological functioning may shift before actual rates of labor force participation change. Regardless, one may argue that the relationship between cohort size and violent mortality moves from positive to negative as a cohort goes from high rates of labor force participation and high levels of earnings during early and late middle age to low rates and levels during old age.

Young people should show a more strongly positive effect of cohort size on violent mortality than middle-aged adults. Those under age 25, even if not yet in the labor force, perceive their employment prospects and potential future earnings as crucial to their well-being. Despite similarly low levels of labor force participation, youth and the elderly interpret the meaning of their position differently. Young people depend little on public transfers, at least on those awarded universally or near-universally by virtue of one's age; governments seldom make student grants and loans or unemployment benefits universally available to youth in the way they do for pensions to the elderly. Moreover, compared to older persons, young people show lower rates of voting (U.S. Bureau of the Census 1994, 287) and political activity and exert less influence on government transfer poli-

cies. As a result, large numbers fail to provide the political benefit or economic advantage for young people that they do for older persons. Instead,
the crowding and competition in families, schools, and labor markets faced
by young members of large cohorts create impediments to reaching social and financial goals. Thus, large cohorts may increase violent mortality
among the young but reduce it among the old.

Gender. Gender relates to attachment to the labor force and market earnings independently of age. Traditionally, and to a lesser extent still today,
women have lower participation rates, hours worked, market earnings, and
attachment to the labor force than do men of the same age (Easterlin
1987a). Differences in sex role socialization of men and women mean that
poor employment prospects and large cohort size may exert more harm on
men than on women (Girard 1993; Ahlburg and Schapiro 1984). Further,
with respect to suicide, the stronger social integration of women (also a
result of sex role differences) protects them from suicidal impulses more
than men (Krull and Trovato 1994; Travis 1990). The relationships between age-specific cohort size and suicide for women should reflect the
same life-cycle pattern for men—the harm of cohort size declines with
age—but the overall impact and therefore the degree of decline will
emerge more weakly for women than for men. For homicide, gender differences may emerge less sharply because males often kill females. Since
male homicide victimization still exceeds female victimization, females will
likely experience the homicide consequences of cohort size less intensely
than men do.

Nation. The national context of welfare policy, by defining the link between individuals and the market, may influence the importance of cohort
size for violent mortality but in somewhat more complex ways than age
and gender do. By providing relatively high levels of social protection for
their citizens, governments can partially mitigate the financial harm of
membership in a large cohort. Thus, the impact of large cohort size would
emerge as smaller in nations that provide greater social protection for their
citizens. For example, national collectivism, taken as a stable characteristic
of nations during the post–World War II period, reflects the strength of
national institutions in sharing the risks of loss of market earning power
and limiting the impact of such loss. Similarly, social security spending and
general taxes to fund such spending, which vary across both time and nation, may affect the degree to which workers are freed from dependence
on market income. Finally, the strong commitment of nations to full em-

ployment can limit the impact of cohort oversupply. The effect of relative cohort size emerges when large numbers translate into poor opportunities for employment, wages, and promotion. By keeping unemployment at a minimum and guaranteeing jobs for those who desire them, government efforts toward full employment can moderate some of the harmful consequences of large cohort size. Full-employment policies also may increase the confidence of workers that fluctuations in the supply of labor force entrants will not threaten their future income.

Along with increasing social protection for vulnerable groups, such things as collectivist institutions, social security spending, and full-employment policies can also ease the transition of large cohorts into life-course stages and reduce common problems of adjustment. Strong ties to encompassing class groupings in collectivist nations can weaken age boundaries and age differences in suicide and homicide. Age transcendent bonds can mute the impact of changing cohort size. This argument builds on an underlying assumption that when biological characteristics and social positions of age groups coincide, when socially based age distinctions exacerbate the importance of biological differences, transitions from youth to adulthood and from adulthood to old age become more difficult. Under these conditions, age-role differences become well defined and generational conflict becomes more common. However, nations with collectivist institutions promote class solidarity that in part transcends age differences. Similarly, redistributive policies in collectivist nations tend to equalize differences not only across classes but also over the life cycle. Collectivist institutions and policies thus promote solidarity within classes and across age groups. When these institutions moderate generational differences, cohort size will prove less important for suicide and homicide.

In summary, the national context of institutional collectivism can shape the impact of cohort size on mortality through two mechanisms: it can ease the incorporation of large cohorts into the labor force with minimum dislocation, and it can reduce the harmful consequences of large cohort size by promoting identification with mobilizing class groups. Applying these arguments to homicide would suggest that individualist institutions magnify the impact of large cohort size on youth homicide. In contrast, collectivist institutions should minimize age-based boundaries and isolation of a youth culture and reduce the impact of cohort size on homicide. Applying these arguments to suicide and old age would suggest that social protection throughout the life course in collectivist nations moderates the contrast between stages of work and retirement: the shift from market dependence to state dependence is less abrupt and novel. As the harm of large cohort size during the working years is smaller, the benefits of large cohort size for suicide in old age is also smaller. Thus, the age and gender patterns of the influence of cohort size emerge strongest in nations whose citizens depend more on market income than in nations whose citizens depend less on market income, in noncollectivist nations than in collectivist nations, and in nations with low social security spending more than in those with high spending.

Time. One further contextual influence relating to social change may shape the importance of cohort size. Trends over time in the nature of work, the economy, and the state may change the impact of cohort size—including the differential impact by age—on suicide and homicide. Conditions most strongly promoted the Easterlin effect during the 1950s and 1960s. Relative to other periods, these decades showed a sharp division of labor in families between men and women, stable economic demand, and modest international immigration from low-income to high-income nations, all of which strengthened the link between relative cohort size and earnings (Oppenheimer 1982). Changing sexual norms, high female labor force participation, increased immigration, and slower economic growth in recent decades may limit the benefits of small cohort size. Similarly, the general expansion of the welfare state over time within both collectivist and individualist nations may reduce the effect of cohort size on a variety of consequences, including suicide and homicide. If, for these reasons, cohort size less strongly influences suicide and homicide in more recent times, it implies that age differences in the effect of cohort size will also decline. Cohort size will have fewer negative consequences for the young but also have fewer positive consequences for the old.[2]

Hypotheses. In review, the theoretical arguments specify first-order (additive), second-order (two-way interactive), and third-order (three-way interactive) conditions for violent mortality. The hypotheses take the following form:

   1. averaged across all ages, the greater the relative size of an age group or cohort, the higher the rates of violent mortality;
   2. the effect of age-group or cohort size on violent mortality will be strong and negative at the youngest ages, weak or near zero at the middle ages, and positive at the older ages;
   3. the varied effects across ages of age-group or cohort size on violent mortality will emerge more strongly for males than for females;
   4. the varied effects across ages of age-group or cohort size on violent

mortality will emerge more strongly in individualist nations than in collectivist nations; and

5. the varied effects across ages of age-group or cohort size on violent
mortality will emerge more strongly in earlier time periods than in later
time periods.

Although collectivism in these hypotheses has an interactive influence,
it may also have an additive effect on violent mortality—an effect averaged
across different ages, years, and cohort sizes. The same collective senti-
ments that protect citizens from loss of market income may protect citizens
from violence and risk taking. Collectivist values, to the extent that they
reflect social integration, may directly affect suicide. Similarly, the sense of
political solidarity reflected in collective institutions may likewise exist in
interpersonal relations and therefore directly reduce homicide.[3] Alternatively, collectivism may overlap with regional and cultural determinants of
suicide and homicide (Cutright and Fernquist 2000). The interaction argument does not require such reasoning, however: collectivism need not
independently affect the levels of violent mortality for it to condition the
effect of cohort size. Indeed, if an interactive relationship exists, the additive relationship between collectivism and violent mortality may misrepresent the processes, as would the additive relationship between cohort size
and suicide or homicide. One can better view collectivism and cohort size
as intertwined rather than separate.

Variation in Effects across Violent Types

The initial hypotheses make general statements about the determinants
of all types of lethal violence. Good reasons exist for treating suicide and
homicide similarly—they both respond to the social and economic problems present in a group, community, or nation, and they do so without a
long delay. Accordingly, Unnithan et al. (1994) suggest combining suicide
and homicide mortality into a single measure of lethal violence that relates
to social deprivation. Demographic studies that examine all causes of death
likewise group types of violent mortality together in a single category to
make contrasts with deaths from degenerative and infectious diseases. To
some degree, then, suicide and homicide should respond in predicted ways
to cohort size.

At the same time, however, the determinants and circumstances of suicide and homicide obviously differ. Noting that suicide reflects inward
direction of blame for social and economic problems, while homicide re-

flects outward direction of blame, Unnithan et al. (1994) suggest measuring the ratio of suicide to homicide. The ratio would reveal the importance of social and economic conditions that promote one type of blame and one type of lethal violence relative to the other type of blame and lethal violence. Following this logic, cohort size may produce more suicides than homicides in ages, genders, nations, and time periods prone to internal blame and more homicides than suicides in those prone to external blame.

In terms of hypotheses, high levels of suicide relative to homicide among age groups, genders, nations, and time periods would suggest the predominance of internal blame and produce larger effects of cohort size on suicide rather than homicide. High levels of homicide relative to suicide should produce the opposite—larger effects of cohort size on homicide than suicide. For example, cohort size would more strongly influence suicide than homicide among older persons and in northern European nations and more strongly influence homicide than suicide among younger persons and in nations like the United States with high levels of interpersonal violence.

Another difference between suicide and homicide mortality relates to the predictions about age differences. Arguments about cohort size emphasize the distribution of problem behaviors across age groups. For suicide, because the age of the victim and killer are the same, age-specific mortality rates identify the age of the killer. For homicide, however, the age of the victim and perpetrator can differ. To the extent that murderers and their victims come from the same age group, one can make inferences about homicide offenders with data on the ages of victims. Indeed, for many types of murder, victims and offenders have the same sociodemographic characteristics (Lauritsen, Sampson, and Laub 1991). However, cross–age group homicides limit the ability of victim data to isolate the effect of cohort size on the behavior of offenders. For example, the stress of large cohort size among young persons may result in the murder of younger and older persons. The potential for age mismatch of offenders and victims will make it harder to identify the effects of cohort size for age-specific homicide rates than for age-specific suicide rates.

Still, even without data on offenders, the study of age-specific homicide victimization can prove useful. Since older persons rarely murder younger persons, and younger persons usually murder other younger persons, the key discrepancy involves younger persons who murder older persons. This implies that large cohort size among the young will primarily affect homicide victimization among the young but will secondarily affect homicide victimization among older age groups. All this should attenuate the age differences in the effects of cohort size, producing results that may well support the interaction arguments but to a lesser degree than for suicide. Because suicide most clearly identifies the age of the offender, it may be most strongly affected by cohort size and most clearly demonstrate the interactions specified by the hypotheses.

Other Determinants

Given my theoretical concerns, the hypotheses concentrate on the varied effects of relative cohort size on suicide and homicide. Of course, other determinants affect spatial and temporal variation in suicide and homicide. I can briefly mention the importance of several control variables but do not give them the same attention I give to cohort size. More detailed summaries of the literatures and determinants of suicide and homicide can be found in Fernquist and Cutright (1998) and Cutright and Briggs (1995).

Following Durkheim's classic arguments, family and religious integration should relate closely to suicide (Breault 1986). Divorce reduces family ties and increases suicide, while marriage and childbearing have the opposite effect. A high female labor force participation rate may similarly reflect reduced family ties and increase suicide.[4] Again following Durkheim's classic arguments, Catholicism reflects the religious integration of a society; alternatively, it may reflect stigma associated with suicide (van Poppel and Day 1996) or high levels of family integration (Burr, McCall, and Powell-Griner 1997). In any case, a large Catholic population should reduce suicide rates. In a variation on the religious integration argument, Ellison, Burr, and McCall (1997) suggest that Catholic or Protestant religious beliefs mean less for suicide than does the degree of religious homogeneity. Social bonds and integrative ties emerge most easily among those who share the same faith and involve themselves in the same religious clubs, schools, and charities. If true, suicide might emerge lowest in primarily Catholic or primarily Protestant nations and highest in nations more evenly mixed between Catholics and Protestants.

Many of the same factors influencing suicide also influence homicide, although the theoretical arguments differ. For example, Cohen and Felson's (1979) routine-activities approach treats homicide rates as a function of the opportunities for victimization. Opportunities increase and homicides occur more often where people spend much time outside the home or away from family members (Gartner 1990). Rising divorce and female labor force participation therefore increase homicide, while high marriage and fertility should lower homicide. Unlike for suicide, however, little connection exists between religious composition and homicide.

Studies of homicide also identify determinants that vary across nations but change little over time. Differences across nations in income inequality, ethnic-linguistic heterogeneity, and economic discrimination increase homicide (Cutright and Briggs 1995). These national characteristics overlap substantially with collectivism and social security spending; universal sociopolitical institutions for social protection and generous levels of public spending reduce inequality, discrimination, and group conflict. Checks for the additive and interactive influence of these other national characteristics would complement the analysis of collectivism. Similarly, Archer and Gartner (1984) find that homicide rates rise with cultural support for legitimate violence in the form of deaths from government executions (i.e., the death penalty) and battle casualties in war. These characteristics differ substantially across nations and may affect homicide rates directly or may serve as additional contextual characteristics that modify the determinants of homicide.

Both suicide and homicide respond to fluctuations in unemployment and economic growth. High unemployment and low economic growth exacerbate problems of inequality that produce feelings of deprivation, unfairness, social strain, and failure. As noted by Henry and Short (1954) and Unnithan et al. (1994), these feelings may produce either suicide or homicide, depending on whether people attribute blame to themselves or others. Many studies demonstrate a rise in both forms of violence during periods of high unemployment (e.g., Hammarström 1994).

These determinants of suicide and homicide often overlap with cohort size. In particular, family changes and economic opportunities that affect suicide and homicide often occur in response to the problems brought on by membership in large cohorts. Easterlin (1987a) notes that members of large cohorts compensate for the financial stress they face by delaying marriage, reducing fertility, and maintaining dual incomes. They also experience higher unemployment and divorce. Thus, even as cohort size directly increases suicide and homicide through low relative income and feelings of deprivation, it also indirectly increases them through changes in family life and labor force status. By lowering levels of childbearing, raising divorce rates and rates of labor force participation among wives, and increasing risks of unemployment, large cohort size contributes doubly to high suicide and homicide. To identify both direct and indirect effects of cohort size on suicide and homicide, models need to examine the effects of cohort size without and with controls for these compensating mechanisms (Ahl-burg and Schapiro 1984; McCall and Land 1994). The effects of cohort size alone will include both direct and indirect effects, the effects of cohort size with controls will include only the direct effects, and the difference in the effects without and with controls will include the indirect effects.

Measurement Problems

The figures on national differences in suicide and homicide rates needed to test the arguments about the varied effects of relative cohort size as well as the direct influence of other control variables immediately raise concerns over measurement error. Critics of official statistics claim that sympathetic physicians classify some suicides as accidents or homicides to protect the families and friends of the victim from embarrassment. Indeed, circum-stances of violent mortality do not always make it clear if a death was in-tentional or accidental or involved one person or two (Day 1987). Both unintentional and intentional errors would tend to understate suicide rates and overstate homicide rates.

Van Poppel and Day (1996) identify a religious dimension of bias in suicide statistics. They find that the difference in suicide rates between Catholics and Protestants in the Netherlands during the early 1900s re-sulted from the large number of Catholic deaths included in the categories of "sudden deaths" and "cause of death unknown or unspecified," both of which the authors consider as alternative classifications of suicide. Com-bining suicide with these residual categories reverses or eliminates the de-nominational gap and offers evidence that religious differentials in suicide result not from social integration but from measurement error.[5] Similar sorts of misclassifications may bias more recent comparisons of suicide rates across nations with diverse religious compositions. Even modern death registration systems include a category labeled "signs, symptoms, and other ill-defined conditions" that may serve as a location for disguised suicides and bias the officially reported suicide rates. The use of the cate-gory may occur more commonly in Catholic than in Protestant nations.

Assuming that misclassified suicides show up as accidents or ill-defined conditions, one means to evaluate bias due to misreporting involves the study of suicide with controls for these other types of mortality. The ap-proach can help adjust for classification errors in ways not possible from the study of just one type of death (Pescosolido and Mendelsohn 1986). If measurement bias removes deaths from the suicide category and places them in the accident or unknown categories, negative partial relationships should, with appropriate control variables, emerge between the other types of mortality and suicide. Further, the models can more accurately identify the effects of cohort size, family integration, and economic opportunities on suicide after adjusting for levels of the other types of mortality. In fact, Pescosolido and Mendelsohn's (1986) study of counties in the United States finds that the social determinants of suicide become stronger with controls for misreporting—in other words, measurement error masks rather than spuriously overstates relationships.

Following this strategy, cross-national models of suicide should be replicated with controls for accident and ill-defined mortality rates. If the results change greatly, it may reflect spuriousness due to measurement bias; if the results change little, it will demonstrate the robustness of the models and findings. However, controls for other types of mortality no doubt overcorrect for measurement error. Even with perfect classification of deaths, suicide and homicide would correlate because they respond similarly to social conditions. Pescosolido and Mendelsohn (1986) deal with this problem by using predicted measures of the other types of mortality rather than actual measures. With proper specification, using instrumental variables to predict accident and unknown mortality and then using the predicted values for these two types of mortality to determine suicide can help capture overlap due to measurement error without also overcorrecting for common social determinants. The strategy should produce more accurate estimates of the effects of cohort size on suicide and homicide.

Data and Measures

The tests of the hypotheses use aggregate data on the same 18 high-income nations as the previous chapters but for a slightly shorter time span. The World Health Organization (1996 and various years) reports consistent mortality rates for these nations from 1955 to 1994 (rather than from 1951 to 1994 as for the fertility rates). That provides for 18 × 40, or 720 cases. In addition, the World Health Organization (1996 and various years) reports male and female suicide and homicide rates for seven 10-year adult age groups: 15–24, 25–34, 35–44, 45–54, 55–64, 65–74, and 75 and over.[6] It also reports the population size of each sex-age group, which the next chapter uses to measure age-specific relative cohort size.

Chapters 7 and 8 analyze the data and measures by combining nations, years, and ages. Rather than analyzing models of mortality separately for each age group, I pool all three dimensions of variation. Pooling ages with nations and years creates a sample size of 720 × 7, or 5,040 cases, incor-

porates another source of variation in mortality rates, and maximizes the
degrees of freedom in the multivariate analyses. The basic estimates for
data pooled on the three dimensions need to control for the age, nation,
and time characteristics of the units with dummy variables or polynomials
but otherwise summarize relationships averaged across all ages, nations,
and years. Because simple pooled models ignore diversity across ages as
well as nations and time periods, and the hypotheses specify different
relationships across ages, nations, and years, the additivity assumption
must be relaxed. By using product terms to represent statistical interaction, the models can allow the effects of variables to differ across nations,
across time periods, and across ages. In so doing, they can test for theoretically specified contextual differences in processes determining mortality
outcomes.

Whether estimating additive or interactive models, pooling time-series
data with cross-sectional data requires statistical adjustments for serial correlation, heteroscedasticity, and between-unit heterogeneity. Appendix B
extends previous material on estimation in appendix A by describing how
the procedures correct for violations of the ordinary least squares (OLS)
assumptions in data pooled by age as well as nation and time. Despite the
additional dimension of age, the models again use generalized least squares
(GLS) estimates based on the work of Beck and Katz (1995) and typically
adjust for between-nation heterogeneity with fixed effects or dummy variables for age and nation. Most important, the model coefficients and
t-ratios reported in the tables have the same interpretation as in ordinary
regression but reflect adjustments for problems stemming from the non-
random structure of the data.

In contrast to the mortality and relative cohort size variables, the other
variables in the analyses are not available separately by age. The female
labor force participation rate, social security spending as a percentage of
GDP, real GDP per capita, the unemployment rate, and the total fertility
rate are measured as in the previous chapters. Two other variables, the
crude marriage rate and the crude divorce rate, both available from the
United Nations' *Demographic Yearbook* (1996 and various years), measure
the number of marriages or divorces per 1,000 population. These measures
also differ only by nations and years and are treated identically for all age
groups—an undesirable but necessary procedure given data limitations.
To measure stable contextual differences across nations, I again focus on
the measures of collectivist and women-friendly institutions defined in
chapter 2. In addition, a stable measure of percentage of Catholics (Barrett
1982) supplements the institutional measures in the study of suicide, and

several measures of inequality, group conflict, and legitimate violence supplement the institutional measures in the study of homicide.

Conclusion

By virtue of their prevalence at both younger and older ages and their immediate connections to social conditions, suicide and homicide mortality rates prove ideal for studying variation in the effects of cohort size across ages, genders, nations, and time periods. Extending the perspective presented in previous chapters on fertility, I have applied, in this chapter, arguments about the sociopolitical and institutional context to suicide and homicide mortality. To help make sense of the competing arguments about—and mixed empirical evidence on—cohort size as presented by Easterlin and Preston, I have specified conditions that strengthen or weaken the effects of cohort size. The hypotheses thus predict stronger effects at younger than older ages, among men than among women, in individualist nations than in collectivist nations, and in earlier time periods than in more recent time periods. The nature of the two types of lethal violence lead further to predictions that the hypotheses will be more strongly supported for suicide than for homicide mortality. Other determinants of violent mortality, such as family integration and economic opportunity, may also stem from changes in cohort size and therefore mediate the relationship between cohort size and violent mortality outcomes. The next two chapters test the hypotheses, with controls for these other determinants and for measurement bias in mortality classifications.

CHAPTER 7

Age-Specific Suicide Rates

The relationship between cohort size and suicide entails considerable complexity. Demographic theories posit both harmful effects (Easterlin 1987a) and beneficial effects (Preston 1984) of large cohort size, and empirical studies find that the relationship varies in both its direction and strength. Given the complexity, considerable debate has emerged in the United States over the contribution of age-group size to recent increases in suicide among the young relative to the elderly. Consideration of differences in the effects of cohort size on suicide across nations outside the United States further complicates the issues. The previous chapter attempted to make sense of the diverse theories and findings by arguing that suicide has a contingent relationship with cohort size. The theoretical framework presented in chapter 6 suggests that the direction and magnitude of the influence of cohort size depend on the relative roles of market and transfer income in the economic support of groups and individuals. Based on the contingent argument, Easterlin's claims about the harm of cohort size should fit those groups most dependent on market earnings, while Preston's claims about the benefits of cohort size should fit those groups most dependent on public and private transfers. In this chapter, I test the hypothesis that the relationship of cohort size and suicide varies across social and economic conditions by examining the contextual influences of four factors related to the relative importance of state and market: age, gender, national context, and time period.

Measuring Suicide and Cohort Size

I measure the male and female suicide rates of seven 10-year adult age groups (15–24, 25–34, 35–44, 45–54, 55–64, 65–74, and 75 and over) for 18 high-income democracies from 1955 to 1994. The sex- and age-specific rates equal the number of suicides per 100,000 population of the specified sex and age group. Although the international scheme for classifying causes of death has changed over the past several decades, the rules for placement of deaths in the suicide category have remained relatively constant. The study of high-income nations—all of which have instituted reliable death registration systems—also limits problems of measurement error. Still, the potential for systematic bias discussed in chapter 6 remains and requires some special tests later in the analyses.

Given the age-specific rates of suicide, the analyses need measures of cohort size for the same age groups. The suicide rate of persons ages 15–24, for example, needs to match a measure of cohort size also specific to persons ages 15–24. Accordingly, cohort size for each combination of nation and year is based on the number of males and females in each of the seven age groups. Since years comprise the units of analysis rather than the cohorts themselves, the measures do not follow individual cohorts through time. Rather, the larger the size of the age group in any single year, the larger the cohorts that make up the age group.

The choice of the denominator for relative cohort size presents more problems. A straightforward measure takes cohort size as a percentage of the total population for each nation and year. This measure corresponds to Preston's analysis of age-group size but not to Easterlin's conceptualization. Easterlin's arguments dictate a measure that compares the size of a cohort (or age group) to the size of the cohort's parental generation. The larger the ratio of the number of persons ages 15–24 to the number of persons 10–40 years older—ages 35–54, in other words—the larger the relative cohort size of young people. Similar ratios of persons 25–34 to 45–64, of 35–44 to 55–74, and of 45–54 to 65 and over would reflect the same concept. For older cohorts, however, mortality has nearly eliminated the parental generation. Ahlburg and Schapiro's work (1984) suggests measuring cohort size of older age groups as the inverse of cohort size for younger age groups: an advantage in relative cohort size of the young corresponds to a disadvantage of older cohorts, and a disadvantage in relative cohort size of the young corresponds to an advantage of older cohorts. Therefore, as relative cohort size of persons ages 15–24, 25–34, 35–44, and 45–54 is measured relative to cohorts 10–40 years older, relative cohort size of persons 55–64, 65–74, and 75 and over is measured relative to persons 10–40 years younger.

For the seven age groups, then, relative cohort size takes the following form:

Age Group	Relative Cohort Size Measure
1. 15–24	(15–24)/(35–54)
2. 25–34	(25–34)/(45–64)
3. 35–44	(35–44)/(55–74)
4. 45–54	(45–54)/(65+)
5. 55–64	(55–64)/(25–44)
6. 65–74	(65–74)/(35–54)
7. 75+	(75+)/(45–64)

All measures thus compare child and parental cohorts, except that the first four take the ratio of child to parental generation and the last three take the ratio of parent to child generation. Thus, the seven indicators tap cohort size of a 10-year age group relative to a 20-year age group (excepting the open-ended category of 75 and over). The mean across all age groups equals 0.444, indicating that the 10-year age groups in the numerator on average are only 44% as large as the comparison groups in the denominator. The metric differs substantially from cohort size as a percentage of the population, which has a mean of 10.9.

To provide an overview of the measures, the analysis begins with a description of the mean male suicide rates, female suicide rates, and population percentages for each of the nations. Table 18 displays these figures for each nation, averaged over the 1955–94 time period. To simplify the presentation, I combine the seven age groups into three: young (15–24, 25–34), middle age (35–44, 45–54, 55–64), and old (65–74, 75+). For all nations combined (listed in the row labeled "total"), the means are highest among males and older persons. The lowest mean across all nations and years equals 6.5 female suicides per 100,000 population at ages 15–34; the highest mean equals 46.0 male suicides per 100,00 population at ages 65 and over. At each age, male suicide rates are two to three times larger than female suicide rates; and for both males and females, suicide rates at the oldest ages are two to three times larger than suicide rates at the youngest ages.

Across nations, the figures show additional variation. The lowest male suicide rate (6.0) appears for young persons in Italy, and the highest male suicide rate (76.7) appears for older persons in Austria. The lowest female suicide rate (2.3) appears for young persons in Ireland, and the highest female suicide rate (50.0) appears for older persons in Japan. More generally, the Nordic and middle European (West Germany, Austria, and Switzerland) nations have high rates among youth and adults. Among the elderly, Belgium and France also show high suicide rates. Interestingly, Ja-

Table 18. Mean Male and Female Suicide Rates and Age Group Size by Nation, Time Period, and Age Group

Nation	Young (15–34)			Middle Aged (35–64)			Old (65+)		
	MSR	FSR	% Pop.	MSR	FSR	% Pop.	MSR	FSR	% Pop.
Australia	19.4	6.1	31.0	27.2	12.3	32.9	33.5	9.5	9.4
Austria	28.9	8.7	28.9	51.0	19.4	35.9	76.7	28.1	14.0
Belgium	15.9	6.0	28.6	33.1	16.1	36.5	71.9	22.6	13.5
Canada	20.4	5.4	32.1	26.4	9.6	31.7	26.8	6.3	9.0
Denmark	21.4	9.1	29.3	49.6	28.4	35.9	57.5	27.3	13.1
Finland	39.2	8.9	30.9	62.0	16.6	35.1	59.8	11.3	10.3
France	17.2	6.0	29.3	39.5	13.8	34.6	75.4	21.3	13.3
Germany	22.4	7.9	29.3	38.3	18.2	37.6	57.8	24.3	13.5
Ireland	9.0	2.3	28.5	12.1	4.8	30.5	10.2	2.8	11.0
Italy	6.0	2.5	30.1	13.6	5.4	36.0	· 30.5	8.2	11.8
Japan	23.3	13.9	32.6	30.6	15.8	34.8	65.2	50.0	8.4
Netherlands	8.4	4.4	31.4	16.4	10.9	33.3	31.8	14.2	10.8
New Zealand	17.3	5.3	30.8	23.2	10.7	31.0	31.3	9.8	9.4
Norway	15.7	4.2	28.4	24.5	9.2	35.1	22.3	6.5	13.6
Sweden	21.4	8.9	27.6	40.9	16.1	37.3	47.1	13.4	14.8
Switzerland	28.5	9.3	30.2	43.6	17.5	36.1	64.0	20.3	12.4
United Kingdom	9.8	3.7	28.2	17.5	10.1	36.3	24.1	11.7	13.7
United States	18.3	5.2	30.7	26.4	9.5	32.6	42.2	7.2	10.6
Total	19.0	6.5	29.9	32.0	13.6	34.6	46.0	16.3	11.8
1955–64	15.0	6.2	28.2	32.7	12.9	35.0	47.0	15.8	9.9
1965–74	15.7	6.3	29.4	31.6	14.0	33.8	44.2	16.4	11.0
1975–84	21.8	7.2	31.3	32.5	14.9	33.6	46.0	17.5	12.6
1985–94	23.6	6.4	30.6	31.2	12.6	36.1	46.8	15.7	13.8

Note. MSR = male suicide rate of specified age group; FSR = female suicide rate of specified age group; and % Pop. = population percentage of specified age group.

pan shows strikingly high rates of suicide among the young and elderly but not among other adults. Gender comparisons demonstrate substantially lower rates of suicide for women in all nations. Only in Japan do female rates approach even half those of men. Otherwise, female rates, as for male rates, emerge highest for the Nordic and middle European nations.

Despite some exceptions, nations high on suicide at one age tend to have high rates at other ages. The similarity shows in the correlations over all 18 nations and 40 years between the suicide rates for each of the age groups. The higher the correlation, the more similar the national and temporal patterns across ages. For the male suicide rate, the average correlation among the seven age groups equals .686, with the smallest and largest correlations equaling .392 (between men 15–24 and 75+) and .917 (between men 35–44 and 45–54), respectively. Similarly, large and positive

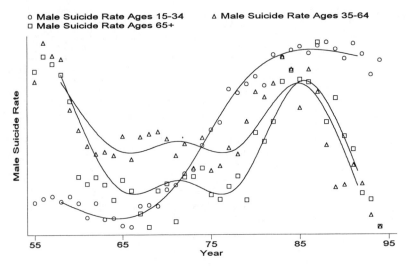

Figure 10. Male Suicide Rate Trends, 18-Nation Means

correlations emerge among female age-specific suicide rates. Thus, forces exist within countries and over time that affect suicide at all ages similarly. The correlations identify the need to control for these general tendencies in analyzing age-specific suicide rates. However, because the correlations fall far from unity, they indicate the potential for differences across ages in the determinants of suicide and the need to examine age-specific rather than crude rates.

The last four rows of table 18 describe the means by time period. For young persons, male suicide rates clearly trend upward. For middle age and older persons, male suicide rates fall from the early to the middle time period but rise again in the latest period. This suggests curvilinearity in the male suicide trend. For female suicide, the trends reveal steady increases for all age groups until the latest time period. To describe these trends more precisely, figures 10 and 11 plot the yearly male and female suicide rates averaged across all nations for the three age groups. Since suicide rates fluctuate considerably from year to year, the graphs smooth the curves using a moving-average and spline function.[1] For male rates in figure 10, the trend for youth suicide differs from the trends for suicide at older ages. Young males show a huge increase from the late 1960s to the mid-1980s. Rates for the older age groups also increase during this time period but then fall relative to the youngest age groups during the late 1980s and early 1990s. In contrast, the trends for women appear similar at all ages: after slight declines during the 1950s, they rise during the 1960s and 1970s and fall during the 1980s and 1990s. Rates among young males deviate most from the general pattern in their failure to decline with other age groups and women in recent years.

Table 18 also presents the percentage of each nation's population in the three age groups. Averaged across all years, non-European nations have, in general, the youngest populations, where western and northern European nations have the oldest populations. For example, Australia, New Zealand, Japan, and the United States have among the highest, and Sweden, Norway, Belgium, and Austria have among the lowest percentages of their population ages 15–34. Conversely, across the full time period, Sweden has the largest (14.8) and Canada (9.0) and Japan (8.4) have the smallest elderly populations. For these postwar years, the patterns reflect the relatively larger baby booms in the non-European nations.

The time trends in age structures demonstrate expected patterns (see table 18, bottom four rows). The size of the youth population rises until the 1980s, reflecting aging of the baby boomers into young adulthood. The size of the middle-aged population first falls and then increases as the baby boomers reach middle age during the 1980s. The size of the elderly population rises steadily, reflecting population aging. The temporal patterns of age-group size thus reflect movement of cohorts of different size through the life course.

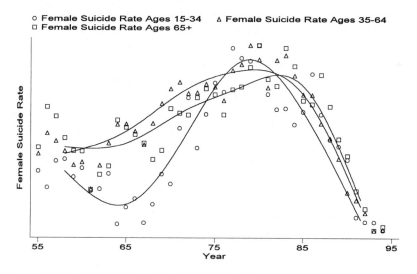

Figure 11. Female Suicide Rate Trends, 18-Nation Means

Cohort Size and Suicide: Relationships by Age and Sex

To connect suicide rates and cohort size, I can begin with some simple correlations. Averaged across all ages, nations, and years, the correlation between the male suicide rate and the population percentage implausibly equals −.445, and the correlation between the male suicide rate and relative cohort size equals −.475. The same two correlations for the female suicide rate equal −.336 and −.357, respectively. These negative relationships indicate that large cohort size lowers suicide—just the opposite of expectations. Yet, the direction of the relationships may make little sense because the coefficients mix diverse, even counterbalancing relationships at different ages.[2] A more appropriate analysis would compute correlations within each age group. Each of the seven age groups has its own suicide rate for males and females and its own measure of the population percentage and relative cohort size. Large age-group size should increase suicide at the younger ages but reduce suicide at the older ages.

Bivariate correlations between suicide rates and cohort size done separately for each of the seven age groups and for males and females do indeed produce the expected age pattern. Table 19 presents bivariate relationships within each of the seven age groups. While only preliminary to the multivariate statistical estimation to follow, the correlations offer a first look at the plausibility of the hypotheses. The first column correlates the suicide rate of males for each age group with its population size, and the second column presents the same correlations for females. Within each age group, then, the correlations describe the extent to which suicide rates and age-group or cohort sizes covary across nations and years.

Although not large, the bivariate associations in the top panel of table 19 between cohort size as a percentage of the total population and suicide rates roughly follow the predicted pattern. The correlations prove strongest for males 25–34 (.388) and weakest for females 75+ (−.008). Although considerable fluctuation occurs across ages and sex in the correlations, they show some decline from youth to old age.

The results appear less strong in the bottom panel of the first two columns of table 19. These correlations employ measures based on each age group's size relative to the size of the parental generation (or child generation, as appropriate) instead of to the total population. Here, the correlations for the youngest age groups are slightly stronger than the correlations for the oldest ages groups, but the weakest correlations occur for middle-aged persons. Rather than declining steadily from youth to old age, the correlations decline from youth to middle age and then rise from middle

Table 19. Correlation Coefficients of Suicide Rates and Cohort Size by Age and Sex

	Bivariate		Net Country		Net Time	
Age Group	Male	Female	Male	Female	Male	Female
Population percentage:						
15–24	.207	.262	.233	.309	.217	.315
25–34	.388	.286	.343	.146	.274	.370
35–44	.226	.105	.107	−.075	.256	.229
45–54	.267	.187	.023	−.125	.311	.273
55–64	.309	.263	.041	−.082	.316	.263
65–74	.139	.098	−.246	−.096	.238	.131
75+	.243	−.008	.129	.038	.361	−.060
Relative cohort size:						
15–24	.118	.193	.219	.389	.161	.237
25–34	.225	.189	.388	.276	.088	.172
35–44	−.086	−.137	.026	−.105	−.083	−.090
45–54	−.004	−.082	.046	−.032	−.045	−.108
55–64	.199	.152	.121	.011	.181	.135
65–74	.028	−.013	−.122	.014	.085	−.046
75+	.137	−.083	.126	.060	.169	−.304

age to old age. This unexpected pattern results in part from weaknesses in the measures of relative cohort size for persons 35–54. The denominators for the measures include age groups 65 and over that have been reduced in size by mortality and, therefore, may overstate relative cohort size.[3] More generally, since relative cohort size at other ages also has smaller correlations with suicide than the population percentage, cohort size appears best measured relative to the total population rather than to parental generations.

The next two columns examine relationships net of dummy variable controls for each country. Regression models with the country dummies in essence take scores for both suicide and cohort size as deviations from national means, and the partial standardized coefficients reflect association over time within nations.[4] The coefficients for males demonstrate the contingent effects of cohort size for both measures: they are positive for young people, near zero for middle-aged adults, and negative for persons 65–74. The coefficients for females less clearly support the predicted pattern but do show a decline in the size of the correlations after ages 25–34. The supportive results emphasize the importance of controlling for between-nation heterogeneity in isolating the age-specific effects of cohort size.

The last two columns examine relationships net of time, time squared, and time cubed. Regression models with the time polynomials in essence take scores for both suicide and cohort size as deviations from the average trend, and the partial standardized coefficients reflect average cross-sectional relationships. The correlations net of time generally reveal stronger effects for the population percentage than for relative cohort size, for males than for females, and for younger age groups than for older age groups.

The 84 coefficients in table 19 make it hard to reach a straightforward conclusion about the varied effects of cohort size across ages. The multivariate results, which follow in the next section, will do more to simplify the diversity of these results, but some additional efforts to organize these coefficients can highlight important findings. Across both measures of cohort size and all three models, the correlation between age and the coefficients for men equals −.396.[5] This correlation implies that, when comparing youth with older persons, the correlation of relative cohort size and suicide falls. Despite many exceptions, then, the results, on average, support the prediction that the positive effect of cohort size will decline over the life course. Similarly, across seven age groups, two cohort size measures, and three models, the correlation −.311 is .085 lower for women than for men, again supporting the predictions about sex differences. Although modest, the evidence for the contingent hypothesis appears in these preliminary results.

Multivariate Results

More than these preliminary correlations, multivariate analyses can provide precise tests of the contextual influences of age and sex on the relationship between cohort size and suicide. They can also provide additional tests of the contextual influences of nation and time on the relationship. The multivariate models use a single suicide measure and a single cohort size measure for data pooled by nation, year, and age (see app. B for a discussion of the statistical methodology). In addition to the influence of cohort size, the additive models include variables representing age, nation, and time that control for the diverse sources of suicide in the pooled data. The interaction models add multiplicative terms of cohort size by age to test the hypothesis that the impact of cohort size on suicide varies by age. Similar sorts of models also allow the effects of age to vary by nation and year.

I take the natural log of suicide (plus 1) as the dependent variable to reduce positive skew and focus on percentage change in suicide rates due to changes in the independent variables. With data pooled by nation, year, and age, the coefficients for the additive models have a straightforward interpretation: they show the change in the logged suicide rate for a one-unit change in the independent variables averaged across all nations, years, and ages. The coefficients for the interaction terms, however, allow the effects of cohort size to differ by age, nation, and year.

Additive Relationships. First, consider age differences in suicide rates. With the log of suicide as the dependent variable, and the units of analysis defined in part by age, it is easy to construct dummy variables that identify the age group to which the observation, suicide rate, and cohort size apply. The coefficients for the dummy variables for each age group (with the middle category of those 45–54 omitted) presented in columns 1 and 2 of table 20 reveal a pattern for males and females that matches well-known life-course changes. Suicide rates rise steadily (almost linearly), with teens having the lowest rate and the elderly the highest rate. For example, in the first equation, males ages 15–24 have a logged suicide rate lower by 0.889 than males ages 45–54 when averaged across all nations and years. Males ages 75 and over have a logged suicide rate 0.590 higher than males ages 45–54. The age pattern of female suicide resembles that for males, except that, with lower levels of suicide rates, females exhibit a smaller gap than males between suicide rates of the young and old.

Next, the results describe the trends over time in suicide rates (averaged across all nations and ages). Rather than include a set of dummy variables for each year, I again capture the general trend with three polynomial terms. In the male equation, the negative coefficient for time shows an initial decline in suicide, the positive coefficient for time squared shows an increase in suicide after the initial decline, and the negative coefficient for time cubed shows another decline in suicide in more recent periods. The pattern described by the coefficients matches figure 10.[6] For females, the coefficients have the same signs, but the initial decline represented by the negative coefficient for time does not reach statistical significance. Little change occurs in the female suicide rate during the earliest years, but then the rate rises and declines in later years.

The models also control for between-nation heterogeneity with dummy variables for each nation. The country effects show tendencies for suicide among all age groups within a country and generally reflect the patterns presented by table 18. (Because the coefficients for the nation dummy variables add little new information, I omit them from the table.)

Table 20. Unstandardized Coefficients for Regression of Age-Specific Suicide Rates on Cohort Size—Age Interaction Models

	Population Percentage				Relative Cohort Size			
	Additive		Interactive		Additive		Interactive	
Independent Variables	Male	Female	Male	Female	Male	Female	Male	Female
Age:								
15–24	−.889	−1.05	−1.96	−2.34	−.920	−1.10	−1.37	−1.66
	(13.5)	(25.3)	(5.89)	(6.74)	(14.0)	(25.1)	(4.21)	(5.00)
25–34	−.439	−.587	−.807	−1.01	−.462	−.627	−.688	−.979
	(9.18)	(14.7)	(2.51)	(2.83)	(9.70)	(15.8)	(2.26)	(2.64)
35–44	−.250	−.322	−.194	−.296	−.260	−.341	−.322	−.475
	(6.12)	(7.65)	(0.62)	(0.77)	(6.36)	(8.06)	(0.81)	(0.92)
55–64	.157	.118	.100	−.048	.170	.142	.124	.067
	(4.26)	(4.25)	(0.41)	(0.19)	(4.57)	(5.04)	(0.43)	(0.22)
65–74	.291	.156	.652	−.106	.322	.215	.696	.254
	(6.56)	(3.66)	(2.78)	(0.44)	(7.06)	(5.04)	(2.53)	(0.87)
75+	.590	.055	.521	−.559	.642	.151	.817	−.110
	(8.41)	(0.75)	(2.51)	(2.11)	(8.95)	(2.09)	(3.18)	(0.35)
Time	−.021	−.0005	−.021	−.002	−.023	−.002	−.022	−.001
	(3.53)	(0.06)	(3.43)	(0.21)	(3.73)	(0.29)	(3.52)	(0.13)
Time^2	.002	.001	.002	.001	.002	.001	.002	.001
	(4.84)	(2.15)	(4.62)	(2.01)	(4.60)	(2.05)	(4.58)	(1.90)

Time[3]	−.00003	−.00002	−.00003	−.00002	−.00003	−.00002	−.00003	−.00002
	(5.03)	(3.38)	(4.63)	(3.05)	(4.46)	(3.01)	(4.47)	(2.87)
Size	.025	.021	.006	−.020	.798	.842	.529	.211
	(3.67)	(2.72)	(0.40)	(1.16)	(4.20)	(4.31)	(1.09)	(0.36)
× 15–24	...	...	.075	.094	...	...	.790	1.05
			(3.33)	(3.75)			(1.30)	(1.61)
× 25–34	...	...	.029	.036	...	...	.438	.724
			(1.26)	(1.38)			(0.74)	(1.00)
× 35–44	...	...	−.002	.002	...	...	.146	.322
			(0.09)	(0.08)			(0.19)	(0.32)
× 55–64	...	...	.002	.009	...	...	.064	.072
			(0.10)	(0.41)			(0.10)	(0.11)
× 65–74	...	...	−.061	.011	...	...	−1.44	−.516
			(2.44)	(0.47)			(2.02)	(0.74)
× 75+	...	...	−.016	.072	...	...	−1.41	.434
			(0.60)	(2.25)			(1.84)	(0.49)
Constant	3.06	2.16	3.25	2.63	2.99	2.02	3.07	2.29
df	5,012	5,012	5,006	5,006	5,012	5,012	5,006	5,006
R²—OLS	.7827	.7395	.7935	.7474	.7887	.7457	.7956	.7484

Note. Numbers in parentheses are absolute values of *t*-ratios.

To review, Finland, Austria, and Switzerland have the highest male suicide rates, while Italy, Ireland, and the Netherlands have the lowest rates. For women, national differences prove much smaller than for males, but the ranking of nations changes little. Women in Japan have by far the highest suicide rates, and women in Ireland have by far the lowest suicide rates.

Finally, the first two columns of table 20 reveal the influence of cohort size when measured as the population percentage for each age group on suicide averaged across all ages, nations, and years. Examining the effect of cohort size while controlling for time and age suggests an age-period-cohort analysis. However, rather than distinguish cohorts with dummy variables, which introduces problems of identification, I simply measure cohort size directly. As shown by the additive results, cohort size, when taken net of the other variables, does indeed increase suicide. The coefficient for males shows that, averaged across all nations, years, and ages, a 1% increase in age-group size raises the log of suicide by 0.025 (or the actual suicide rate by about 2.53%). Column 5 shows that a one-unit increase in relative cohort size raises the male log of the suicide rate by 0.798 (or the actual suicide rate by about 122.1%). As predicted, the additive effect is not large: the standardized coefficients of the population percentage for males and females equal 0.147 and 0.126, respectively. The standardized coefficients of relative cohort size emerge somewhat larger: 0.195 and 0.204, respectively, for males and females.

Cohort Size–Age Interactions. Given this background information from the additive models, tests of one hypothesis come from adding interaction terms of cohort size by age. Accordingly, the remaining equations of table 20 add these terms. In these equations, the coefficient for cohort size represents the effect for the omitted age group of persons 45–54. The coefficients for the product terms of cohort size by each of the dummy age variables represent age differences relative to the omitted group in the effect of cohort size on suicide rates. In this way, the interaction terms test the hypothesis that the influence of cohort size changes across ages.

The coefficients for the interaction terms fit the hypothesis. Based on the coefficients of column 3 of table 20, some simple calculations illustrate age differences in effects of cohort size as a percentage of the population for each age group. The effects equal 0.081 for ages 15–24, 0.035 for 25–34, 0.004 for 35–44, 0.006 for 45–54, 0.008 for 55–64, −0.055 for 65–74, and −0.010 for 75+.[7] The positive effect for the youngest age group contrasts with the near-zero effect for middle-aged groups and the negative effect for the oldest age groups. Cohort size thus raises suicide among the young but reduces suicide among the old. The predicted effects add only slightly to the explained variance but make theoretical sense.[8] Overall, the additive effect masks opposite signed coefficients, while the interactive effects support the idea that groups having recently entered the labor force experience the most problems in social well-being from large cohort size and that the weaker ties of older age groups to the labor force bring benefits of large cohort size for suicide.

The equation for males in table 20 with relative cohort size in column 7 provides weaker support for the expected age patterns of effects. The coefficients demonstrate positive effects for the young, near-zero effects for the middle-aged, and negative effects for the old, but only one of the coefficients differs significantly from the coefficient for the omitted group. Although in the predicted direction, the effects do not emerge as strongly as for the percentage measure.

The results for females, unlike those for males, demonstrate little in the way of age differences in the relationship between cohort size and suicide rates. The effects of both measures of cohort size on suicide among women for the omitted group do not differ significantly from zero, and the effects of cohort size for most age groups do not differ statistically from this zero effect. The effects of women ages 15–24 and 75+ become significantly positive for the percentage measure but do not produce the expected differences in signs.

The results thus far provide modest support for the hypothesis that age shapes the relationship between cohort size and suicide rates. Only for males using the population percentage measure do the coefficients emerge significant and in the predicted direction. However, the comparison of effects across ages does not consider contextual influences of nation and time on the relationship. The hypotheses also predict that cohort size will have stronger effects in individualist nations than in collectivist nations and in earlier time periods than in later time periods. Since age differences should appear most strongly in individualist nations and in early time periods, examining age differences across all nations and years may weaken the results.[9] The analysis considers next how the effect of cohort size and age differences in the effect of cohort size vary across nations and years.

Nation and Time Interactions. Testing hypotheses about differences in cohort size across nations and time involves estimating models of male suicide for two groups of nations and two time periods.[10] Table 21 presents truncated versions of these models: the coefficients calculated from the

Table 21. Unstandardized Coefficients for Regression of Age-Specific Male Suicide Rates on Cohort Size—Age, Nation, and Time Interaction Models

	% Pop.		RCS		% Pop.		RCS	
	Collectivism				Time Period			
Age Group	Low	High	Low	High	Early	Late	Early	Late
15–24	.113**	.015	1.65	.266	.110**	.040	2.18	.749
25–34	.034	.038	1.13	.485	−.027**	.019	.380	.666
35–44	−.010	.026	.301	.882	−.063**	.013	−1.23**	1.01
45–54	−.006	.004	.291	.500	.029	.005	1.49*	.189
55–64	−.009	.025	.383	.733	.018	.020	.290**	.858
65–74	−.088**	−.048	−1.77	−.472	−.012**	.022	.420**	.654
75+	−.070	.018	−3.15**	.287	−.011	.086**	−.750**	.485
Range	.201	.086	4.80	1.36	.173	.081	3.67	.821

Note. % Pop. = cohort size as a percentage of the population; RCS = relative cohort size.
* Omitted category coefficient differs significantly ($t > 2.0$) from zero.
** Dummy variable coefficient differs significantly ($t > 2.0$) from omitted category.

interaction terms describe the effect of cohort size (with controls for age, time, and nation) on suicide for each age group. The table divides the nations into those with collectivism scores below the mean (i.e., individualist nations) and those with collectivism scores above the mean and divides the sample into the years 1955–74 and 1975–94. Comparing the coefficients across equations indicates how national and temporal contexts modify the determinants of suicide.[11] For example, the coefficient of 0.113 in the first column exhibits the effect of population percentage on the male suicide rate for persons ages 15–24 in low-collectivist nations. The corresponding coefficient for collectivist nations equals 0.015.

The results in table 21 indicate smaller age differences in the effects of cohort size in the collectivist nations. Few of the coefficients reach statistical significance, but the pattern of effects supports the predictions of weaker age differences in collectivist nations than in individualist nations. For cohort size as a percentage of the population, low-collectivist nations show effects of cohort size equal to 0.113 and −0.088 for the youngest and next to oldest age groups, respectively. The range of coefficients equals 0.201. For collectivist nations, the coefficients do not deviate significantly from the near-zero effect of cohort size for the omitted ages 45–54. The effects of cohort size for these nations vary only from 0.038 to −0.048 and have a range less than half that for individualist nations. Similar results arise for the relative cohort measure. The range of effects of cohort size across ages in low-collectivist nations exceeds the range in high-collectivist nations by a factor of more than three.

The separate models for time periods also reveal differences in effects consistent with the hypothesis. As predicted, the early years more strongly indicate the interactive effects of age and cohort size on suicide. In the early period, the positive effects of both measures at ages 15–24 become negative at older ages. For example, in the early time period, the coefficient for relative cohort size for persons 15–24 equals 2.18 and the coefficient for persons 75 and over equals −0.750. For the later time period, only one coefficient reaches statistical significance, and no evidence appears of a shift from positive to negative effects of cohort size. Further, the range of effects proves much larger for the early time period than for the later time period.

Interpreting together the results by nation and time suggests that cohort size proves less influential in collectivist nations in recent time periods. Cohort size has positive effects at the youngest ages and negative effects at the oldest ages most clearly in individualist nations in early time periods. Given the diversity of influences on suicide and the difficulties in capturing the contextual influences with aggregate-level data, the results, for the most part, demonstrate effects of relative cohort size near zero. Still, within specific contexts, coefficients become more positive at younger ages and more negative at older ages.

Control Variables. The models so far support the predictions about the varied influence of cohort size across age, gender, nation, and time but do not control for other determinants of suicide that may overlap with relative cohort size. For instance, changes in cohort size affect female labor force participation, marriage and divorce, fertility, income growth, and unemployment, which in turn affect social integration and regulation and may mediate the influence of cohort size on suicide.[12] To examine the effects of these variables on suicide and on the relationship between cohort size and suicide, I include them in the equations for male and female suicide rates in table 22. Models with these controls offer a more severe test of the influence of relative cohort size as well as a more complete set of determinants of suicide.

These control variables show little influence on male suicide rates. The negative coefficients for the marriage rate and national product indicate that family ties and higher income reduce suicide, but they barely reach statistical significance. In contrast, the control variables more strongly influence female suicide rates. Female labor force participation rates raise suicide for women, while high marriage and fertility lower suicide. Otherwise, the divorce rate unexpectedly shows negative effects.[13] Finally, Catholic nations also show lower suicide rates for males and females, net of all

Table 22. Unstandardized Coefficients and t-Ratios for Regression of Age-Specific Suicide Rates on Cohort Size and Other Variables—Age Interaction Models

Independent Variable	Male		Female		Male[a]	
	b	t	b	t	b	t
Age:						
15–24	−1.97	−6.30	−2.30	−6.70	−1.69	−5.39
25–34	−.766	−2.47	−.972	−2.89	−.881	−2.94
35–44	−.183	−0.60	−.313	−0.94	−.167	−0.56
55–64	.108	0.38	−.067	−0.22	−.018	−0.07
65–74	.662	2.55	−.121	−0.43	.554	2.16
75+	.523	2.25	−.581	−2.31	.441	1.91
Time	−.015	−2.46	.006	0.89	−.031	−3.00
Time²	.001	3.33	.0003	0.57	.002	3.75
Time³	−.00002	−3.44	−.00001	−1.71	−.00003	−3.61
Size	.007	0.39	−.020	−1.02	.006	0.33
× 15–24	.075	3.19	.091	3.53	.059	2.52
× 25–34	.026	1.10	.034	1.33	.036	1.57
× 35–44	−.003	−0.13	.004	0.14	−.003	−0.11
× 55–64	.002	0.06	.011	0.40	.013	0.50
× 65–74	−.062	−2.28	.013	0.46	−048	−1.80
× 75+	−.014	−0.52	.076	2.63	.001	0.05
FLFP	.004	1.71	.007	2.41	.003	1.14
Divorce rate	−.009	−0.65	−.060	−3.38	−.020	−1.42
Marriage rate	−.018	−2.06	−.022	−2.09	−.011	−1.29
Total fertility rate	−.047	−1.74	−.128	−4.07	−.069	−2.56
Gross domestic product	−.125	−2.04	−.008	−1.03	−.016	−0.23
Unemployment	...	...	...	...	.008	2.44
Constant	3.52		3.19		3.60	
df	5,001		5,001		4,496	
R^2—OLS	.8036		.7600		.8046	

Note. FLFP = female labor force participation.
[a] For years 1959–94.

variables. Summing the coefficients for the nation dummy variables (not presented) for the primarily Catholic nations yields lower logged suicide rates than for non-Catholic countries. The low suicide rates come primarily from Italy and Ireland; Austria, Belgium, and France, despite a high percentage of Catholics, have net suicide rates above the mean.

The unemployment rate may also directly raise suicide among males and females. Lacking data before 1959 for unemployment, the model including this variable requires separate analysis for a truncated time span. The last two columns of table 22 indicate that unemployment raises suicide rates among males. A similar equation for females reveals no influence of unemployment on suicide (results not presented). Note also that deleting the first 4 years reduces the effect of the marriage rate on the male suicide rate to insignificance and raises the effect of the total fertility rate to above significance.

The crucial point from table 22, however, concerns the effects of cohort size and age on suicide. The interaction found for males between cohort size and age remains even with the controls for the other variables. For males, large cohort size continues to raise suicide rates at ages 15–24 and to lower suicide rates at ages 65–74. This provides further evidence of the robustness of the interactive effects of relative cohort size specified by the contingent hypotheses.

Measurement Error

Do these results stem from errors inherent in official suicide statistics? On the surface, it seems unlikely. Measurement bias may inflate the comparisons across Catholic and non-Catholic nations in table 18, but the essential results relate only tangentially to religious differences. They center, instead, on how the effects of cohort size differ across ages, sexes, nations, and time periods. To explain away the results, measurement error would have to vary systematically with cohort size and age. Yet few reasons exist to suppose that measurement error inflates the suicide rate for young people in large cohorts but deflates the bias for old people in large cohorts; that it inflates suicides of males in large cohorts but not females in large cohorts; and that it inflates suicide rates for persons in large cohorts in individualist nations and for early time periods but not in collectivist nations and for later time points. The complexity of the results of the analysis limits the likelihood that the results could spuriously stem from measurement bias.

Still, some simple tests can help demonstrate the robustness of the empirical results in the face of measurement error. Aggregate data do not allow for a precise adjustment of the error—if it did I would have corrected the dependent variable from the start—but do allow for three simple tests. First, if the false classification of many suicide deaths as accidents or as death from unknown causes spuriously produces relationships between cohort size and suicide rates, then controlling for accident and unknown mortality as independent variables should eliminate the additive and interactive effects of cohort size. Second, controlling for accident and unknown mortality by adding them to the dependent suicide rate variable should do the same. Third, controls for accidents without adjustment may overcorrect for measurement bias. Since common forces affect both suicide and accident mortality, the overlap between the two types of mortality involves more than measurement error. An instrumental variable solution uses deaths from unknown causes—a measure of the quality of death registration systems—to predict accidental deaths and then uses predicted accident mortality as a determinant of suicide rates. If these three means of adjustment for measurement error eliminate the varied effects of cohort size, it will cast doubt on the findings; if they do not, it will increase confidence in the robustness of the results.

The final set of analyses in this chapter replicate the models in table 22 but with the controls for accident and unknown deaths. To get immediately to the point, and avoid another table of coefficients, the results can be summarized simply: they offer no evidence of spurious cohort effects. To begin with, controls for both accident and unknown mortality make the age interaction results a bit stronger than before. Both accident and unknown mortality have modest positive influences on the suicide rate but do not substantially change the coefficients for other variables. Also, the model for the dependent variable combining suicide, accident, and unknown mortality creates changes in the coefficients for the substantive variables, but the interaction terms still show positive effects of cohort size at young ages and negative effects at older ages. The substantive variables affect accident and unknown mortality differently than they affect suicide mortality, but cohort size does not. Finally, the coefficients net of the predicted accident mortality variable differ little from the coefficients without the control. In short, then, measurement error does not appear to have produced the findings in support of the contingent hypothesis presented in this chapter.

Conclusion

Using data from 1955–94 on suicide and age-group size for seven age groups and 18 nations, the analyses support the hypotheses specifying the contingent effects of cohort size. In general, the effect of cohort size proves positive for young age groups and negative for old age groups. Further, both the effect of cohort size and the varied impact of cohort size by age prove stronger for males than for females. The results also suggest some differences across nations and time periods. Although the differences are not large, the age pattern of the effects of cohort size emerges more distinctly in individualist nations than in collectivist nations and in earlier decades than in more recent decades. The varied effects by age, gender, national context, and time period support the thesis that reliance on public transfer income moderates the positive effect of cohort size on suicide found among groups dependent on market income.

Debates over generational equity can profit from the contingent viewpoint offered by these results. Population aging may improve the well-being of the elderly relative to young people in certain contexts such as the United States. Given the contrasting effects of cohort size for the youngest and oldest age groups, the concomitant growth of the young population from the baby boom and of the elderly population from high past fertility and lower mortality created rising suicide among the young relative to the elderly. The diverse effects of cohort size for the young and the old thus contribute to trends beneficial to the elderly. In other national contexts, however, changes in cohort size may have little influence on age-group well-being and suicide.

The larger implications of these results highlight the contingent nature of demographic forces on social outcomes. Rather than debating whether cohort size emerges as important relative to other less demographic social forces on outcomes such as suicide, scholars need to recognize that demographic and nondemographic forces combine to influence the outcomes. Rather than competing perspectives in which one emerges as supported and the other one as rejected, demographic and nondemographic factors should both be viewed as contributing relatively more or less within different contexts. The integrative theoretical perspective, and the associated strategy of interactive analysis of macrosociological data, bring clear benefits to our understanding of suicide mortality.

CHAPTER 8

Age-Specific Homicide Rates

Although it differs in important ways from suicide mortality, homicide mortality may respond similarly to cohort size. Going beyond claims that large cohort size and the problems it brings increase homicide, the hypotheses predict that the strength of the relationship varies across contexts. As it does for suicide, cohort size may increase homicide at younger ages but reduce homicide at older ages. These age differences in homicide victimization might also appear more strongly for men than for women, for individualist nations than for collectivist nations, and for earlier post–World War II decades than for later decades. The study of homicide victimization can thus provide additional evidence for the contingent influence of cohort size and for a theory that integrates the ostensibly competing arguments about the negative effects of cohort size in Easterlin and the positive effects of cohort size in Preston.

The relationship between cohort size and homicide victimization, however, may be attenuated by differences between the age and cohort size of homicide offenders and victims. The lack of comparable cross-national data on age of homicide offenders makes it hard to identify the cohort size of those who cause rather than fall victim to murder. Even so, since victims and offenders typically have the same demographic characteristics, the study of homicide mortality reflects the cohort-based actions of offenders and offers another test of the theoretical arguments concerning contextual influences on cohort processes.

Despite this measurement problem, homicide mortality brings several advantages to the study of lethal violence and cohort size. One such advantage is that homicide victimization, more so than suicide, reflects problems of youth. Whereas older persons have the highest suicide rates, younger persons have the highest rates of homicide victimization. When, as it often does, the harm of large cohort size among young people takes the form of violence against others rather than against self, it makes homicide a crucial object of investigation. Another advantage of the study of homicide is that it relates to social conditions of inequality and conflict. Discrimi-

nation, deprivation, and heterogeneity increase homicide more than suicide. Where suicide occurs more commonly in egalitarian Scandinavian
nations, homicide occurs more often in less egalitarian nations like the
United States and Italy. Many other social conditions besides inequality
affect homicide rates, but homicide raises special issues of social conflict
not present in suicide rates.

With these problems and advantages in mind, in this chapter I again
test the argument that cohort size will have positive effects on homicide
deaths among groups that depend on market earnings and will have negative effects on homicide deaths among groups that depend more on public
and private transfers. I do so by examining how the relationship of cohort
size and homicide mortality varies with age, gender, national context, and
time period. I also give special attention to national characteristics related
to collectivism, such as inequality, discrimination, and heterogeneity, that
may contribute to group conflict and high homicide rates. And, finally, I
compare the similarities and differences between suicide and homicide victimization across ages, nations, and years.

Measuring Homicide and Cohort Size

I measure the homicide victimization rate—defined as the number of
homicides per 100,000 population of the specified age and sex group—
for the same 18 nations, 40 years, and seven 10-year adult age groups of
males and females used to measure suicide. The source of the homicide
data, the World Health Organization (1996 and various years), defines
homicide as deaths due to injury purposely inflicted by others. Because the
WHO relies on medical certification, their figures on cross-national homicide victimization data do not contain the reporting errors common in
figures from criminal justice organizations. Some problems exist in the
treatment of war deaths and police killings but likely do not greatly bias
the results (Gartner 1990). Some difficulty in distinguishing homicides
from suicides and accidents may also exist, but the problems of identifying
homicides seem less serious than those involved in distinguishing between
suicides and accidents. Thus, these homicide data show high levels of reliability across both nations and years (Bennett and Lynch 1990).[1]

I use both male and female homicide victimization rates as dependent
variables. The most diverse component of the homicide rate (both over
time and across nations) comes from the killing of unrelated young males
by other males. Since nations differ less in domestic or primary group
homicides than they do in male-male killings, the cross-national relation-

ship between cohort size and homicide should emerge more strongly for male killings. Killings involving females, in part because they most often occur within primary groups, have a flatter age curve (Gartner and Parker 1990). For this reason, and despite a correlation of .806 between male and female homicide rates, the analysis examines mortality for each sex separately.[2]

As in the previous chapter, cohort size for each nation-year is based on the number of males and females in each age group. One measure takes cohort (or age group) size as a percentage of the total population. This measure corresponds to Preston's (1984) treatment of age group size. Easterlin's (1987a) measure compares the size of a cohort (or age group) to the size of the cohort's parental generation. These two measures replicate those described in chapter 7, with higher values indicating larger cohort size for each of the age groups.

In examining the influence of cohort size on age-specific homicide rates of men and women, the models use the same control variables as the models for suicide. The divorce, marriage, and total fertility rates relate to family integration. Family breakup and a high female labor force participation rate may have effects in either direction: they may reflect reduced family ties and lost protection from stranger and acquaintance violence or they may reflect women leaving violent and life-threatening intimate relationships. Real gross domestic product per capita reflects the standard of living, and the unemployment rate reflects short-term fluctuations in the economy along with the economic consequences of cohort supply. The scale of collectivism measures sociopolitical context.

Descriptive Results

Mean male and female homicide rates within each of the 18 countries for the period from 1955 to 1994 show considerable variation. Table 23 displays mean homicide rates for each nation and three combined age groups: young (15–24, 25–34), middle aged (35–44, 45–54, 55–64), and old (65–74, 75+). For all nations combined (listed in the row labeled "total"), the means are highest among males and younger persons. The lowest mean in the row equals 0.88 female homicides per 100,000 population at ages 65 and over; the highest mean equals 3.00 male homicides per 100,000 population at ages 15–34.

Across nations, the United States has homicide rates that greatly exceed those of any other nation. For example, among younger males the rate for the United States of 21.4 reaches levels more than five times higher than

Table 23. Mean Male and Female Homicide Rates and Age Group Sizes by Nation, Time Period, and Age Group

Nation	Young (15–34)			Middle Aged (35–64)			Old (65+)		
	MHR	FHR	% Pop.	MHR	FHR	% Pop.	MHR	FHR	% Pop.
Australia	2.63	1.76	31.0	2.75	1.38	32.9	1.50	.92	9.4
Austria	1.70	1.15	28.9	1.56	1.06	35.9	1.40	1.16	14.0
Belgium	1.60	1.05	28.6	1.59	1.16	36.5	1.37	1.26	13.5
Canada	3.29	1.77	32.1	2.98	1.42	31.7	2.27	.98	9.0
Denmark	1.02	.98	29.3	.77	.82	35.9	.59	.62	13.1
Finland	4.15	1.68	30.9	5.93	1.86	35.1	3.38	1.13	10.3
France	2.08	.71	29.3	1.89	.77	34.6	1.06	.83	13.3
Germany	1.46	1.17	29.3	1.46	.80	37.6	1.19	.85	13.5
Ireland	1.23	.45	28.5	.86	.30	30.5	.80	.49	11.0
Italy	3.22	.75	30.1	2.88	.68	36.0	1.63	.69	11.8
Japan	1.79	.67	32.6	1.47	.72	34.8	1.12	.92	8.4
Netherlands	1.23	.56	31.4	1.02	.39	33.3	.71	.48	10.8
New Zealand	2.27	1.30	30.8	1.69	.79	31.0	1.00	.75	9.4
Norway	1.14	.64	28.4	1.40	.69	35.1	.96	.50	13.6
Sweden	1.41	1.01	27.6	1.62	.85	37.3	.93	.53	14.8
Switzerland	1.01	1.05	30.2	1.05	.84	36.1	1.05	.71	12.4
United Kingdom	1.54	.81	28.2	1.08	.58	36.3	.62	.59	13.7
United States	21.40	5.45	30.7	13.80	3.60	32.6	6.08	2.49	10.6
Total	3.00	1.28	29.9	2.55	1.04	34.6	1.54	.88	11.8
1955–64	2.05	.92	28.2	1.88	.81	35.0	1.33	.72	9.9
1965–74	2.69	1.17	29.4	2.46	.98	33.8	1.54	.84	11.0
1975–84	3.44	1.49	31.3	3.01	1.16	33.6	1.78	1.01	12.6
1985–94	3.85	1.53	30.6	2.84	1.21	36.1	1.49	.97	13.8

Note. MHR = male homicide rate of specified age group; FHR = female homicide rate of specified age group; and % Pop. = population percentage of specified age group.

the next highest nation, Finland. Other nations with generally high male homicide rates include Italy and Canada. Those nations with particularly low homicide rates for particular age and sex groups include Denmark, Ireland, the Netherlands, and the United Kingdom. The range of male homicide mortality rates thus extends from 21.4 for young males in the United States to 0.59 for older males in Denmark.

Female homicide victimization falls considerably below male victimization, particularly among the young and middle aged. For persons ages 15–34, rates are 134% higher for men than for women; and for persons ages 35–64, rates are 145% higher for men than for women. At the oldest ages, when homicide rates for both males and females fall, male rates are 75% higher than female rates. Just as for men, the gap between the United States and the other nations appears among women. Although they experience lower homicide rates than men, female victimization in the United

States substantially exceeds rates for others nations. Rankings on male homicide generally match rankings on female homicide, but some exceptions exist. Italy and Japan, for example, have high male victimization rates but relatively low female victimization rates.

Across ages, homicide victimization is slightly lower among men and women of middle age than younger ages, and substantially lower for the elderly than for both younger groups. The trends over time also differ somewhat for the three age groups. For young persons, male and female homicide rates clearly trend upward but with greater growth during the 1960s and 1970s than later. For middle-aged men and older persons, male and female homicide rates rise more steadily until the 1985–94 period, when they decline. The trend for middle-aged women, however, resembles that for younger persons—it does not decline in the last time period.

To describe these trends more precisely, figures 12 and 13 plot the yearly male and female homicide rates averaged across all nations for the three age groups. Since rates fluctuate considerably from year to year, the graphs smooth the curves using a moving-average and spline function.[3] For males in figure 12, rates for all ages rise sharply from 1965 to 1975 but decline thereafter. During the late 1980s and early 1990s, however, the trend for youth homicide diverges from the trends for older age groups. While rates for older males continue to decline, or at least remain steady, rates for young males rise again. The trends for women depicted in figure 13 fluc-

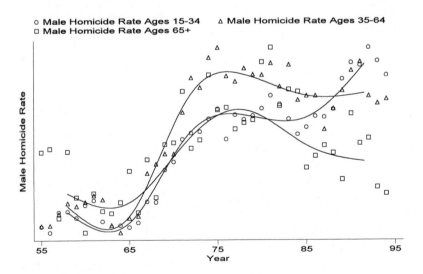

Figure 12. Male Homicide Rate Trends, 18-Nation Means

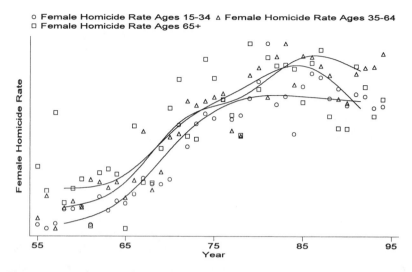

Figure 13. Female Homicide Rate Trends, 18-Nation Means

tuate less than those for men. Female homicide mortality rates neither increase as sharply as male rates during the 1960s and 1970s nor decline as much during the 1980s.

The trends over time for homicide mortality reveal both similarities and differences from those for suicide mortality. Like suicide rates, homicide rates rose in the 1960s and 1970s and fell during the 1980s and 1990s. The cycle for homicide rates, however, appears less striking than for suicide rates. Suicide rates both rose and fell faster than homicide rates. Further, the divergence between young and old during recent years appears stronger for suicide. General forces of change seem to affect both types of lethal violence but lead to greater fluctuations in suicide than in homicide.

Despite some exceptions, nations with high homicide rates at one age tend to have high rates at other ages. Across the 18 nations and 40 years, bivariate correlations among the age-specific homicide rates demonstrate the degree of similarity. For the male homicide rate, the average correlation across the nations and years for the seven age groups equals .830, with the largest and smallest correlations equaling .966 and .650, respectively. Somewhat smaller but still positive correlations exist among female age-specific homicide rates. Forces within countries that increase homicide similarly among all ages require controls for national or societal tendencies for homicide common to all age groups.

Table 23 also presents the percentage of each nation's population in each of the age groups from chapter 7. To review, non-European nations have the youngest populations, whereas western and northern European nations have the oldest populations. For these post–World War II years, the pattern reflects the relatively larger baby booms in the non-European nations. Over time and across all nations, the size of the youth population rises, reflecting the aging of the baby boomers into young adulthood, and the size of the elderly population rises, as well, reflecting population aging. In contrast, the size of the middle-aged population falls.

Cohort Size and Homicide: Relationships by Age and Sex

To connect homicide rates to cohort size, I can begin with some simple correlations. Averaged across all ages, nations, and years, the correlation between the male homicide rate and the population percentage equals .156, and the correlation between the male homicide rate and relative cohort size equals .190. The same two correlations for the female homicide rate equal .164 and .187. Yet the weak relationships mix diverse, even counterbalancing, relationships at different ages. The more appropriate analysis of correlations within each age group provides more sensible results.

According to the hypotheses, the relationship between cohort size and homicide should shift from positive at the youngest ages to negative at the oldest ages. Table 24 presents bivariate relationships within each of the seven age groups. While only preliminary to the multivariate statistical estimates to follow, the correlations offer a first look at the plausibility of the hypotheses. The first column correlates the homicide rate of males for each age group with its cohort size, and the second column presents the same correlations for females. Within each age group, then, the correlations describe the extent to which homicide rates and age group or cohort sizes covary across nations and years.

Although not large, the bivariate associations in the top panel of table 24 between cohort size as a percentage of the total population and homicide rates follow the predicted pattern. The correlations prove positive for young males and young females, but negative for most groups of older males and females. For example, the correlation for males 25–34 equals .181 and the correlation for males 65–74 equals −.213. The results in the bottom panel, which use relative cohort size rather than the population percentage, demonstrate the same age pattern of correlations. For males ages 25–34, the correlation equals .267, while for males ages 65–74 the correlation equals −.137. In contrast to the results for suicide rates, the results for homicide rates prove similar for both measures of cohort size.

Table 24. Correlation Coefficients of Homicide Rates and Cohort Size by Age and Sex

Age Group	Bivariate		Net Country		Net Time	
	Male	Female	Male	Female	Male	Female
Population percentage:						
15–24	.160	.196	.074	.130	.190	.189
25–34	.181	.253	.136	.203	.185	.224
35–44	−.053	.049	−.053	.034	−.115	.002
45–54	−.187	−.174	−.067	−.110	−.166	−.157
55–64	−.200	−.129	.004	−.081	−.203	−.130
65–74	−.213	−.110	−.009	.114	−.293	−.204
75+	−.122	.059	.044	.178	−.347	−.118
Relative cohort size:						
15–24	.178	.206	.067	.133	.255	.238
25–34	.267	.324	.151	.233	.271	.295
35–44	.107	.167	−.141	.003	.139	.206
45–54	.018	−.027	−.155	−.213	.241	.203
55–64	−.207	−.203	−.020	−.154	−.222	−.188
65–74	−.137	−.053	−.098	.180	−.239	−.161
75+	−.059	.111	.055	.194	−.316	−.058

Also in contrast to results for suicide rates, the correlations for women appear as strong as the correlations for men.

The next two columns examine relationships net of dummy variable controls for each country. Regression models with the country dummies in essence take scores for both homicide and cohort size as deviations from nation means, and the partial standardized coefficients reflect association over time within nations. The partial coefficients substantially weaken the age pattern of results, which suggests that national differences in the relationship between cohort size and homicide rates contribute substantially to the correlations in the first two columns.

The last two columns examine relationships net of time, time squared, and time cubed. Regression models with the time polynomials in essence take scores for both homicide and cohort size as deviations from the average trend, and the partial standardized coefficients reflect average cross-sectional relationships. The coefficients net of time again reveal the expected age pattern. The positive coefficients at younger ages for both males and females and for both measures of cohort size shift to negative at older ages.

To summarize the 84 coefficients in table 24, I treat each correlation as a separate case and then correlate the coefficients with age, sex, measure, and type of model. The correlation between age and the size of the coefficient in table 24 equals −.595.[4] Even more strongly than for suicide rates, the effect of cohort size on homicide rates changes over the life course from positive to negative. In contrast to the results for suicide, the correlations emerge higher for females than males and for relative cohort size than for the population percentage. These findings need confirmation from multivariate analysis but may well indicate a crucial difference between suicide and homicide. Where large cohort size affects male suicide more strongly than female suicide, large cohort size affects female homicide victimization at least as strongly as male victimization. Assuming that homicide mortality results primarily from male murderers, the results suggest that males in large cohorts kill themselves, other men, and other women.

Multivariate Results

The next step in testing the hypotheses uses data pooled by nation, year, and age, thus replicating the analyses presented in the last part of the previous chapter. Again, I take the natural log of homicide (plus 1) as the dependent variable to reduce positive skew (due especially to the rates for the United States) and focus on percentage change in homicide rates in response to changes in the independent variables. Table 25 examines the influence of both cohort size measures on age-specific homicide rates with controls for age, nation, and time; it also adds multiplicative interaction terms of cohort size by age to test the hypothesis that the impact of cohort size on homicide rates varies by age.

Additive Relationships. To control for well-known age-based variation in homicide, the model includes dummy variables for each age group (with the middle category of those 45–54 omitted). The resulting pattern for males shows the highest rates among persons from ages 25–34; rates are lower among persons 15–24 and over age 54. The resulting pattern for females is similar, except that the age differences are smaller than for males.

The equations include polynomial terms to capture the general trend in homicide rates. The coefficients prove similar for both males and females. The negative coefficient for the time term does not reach statistical significance, but the time squared term has a significant positive coefficient and the time cubed term has a significant negative coefficient. The signs of the coefficients indicate that after a period of little change, homicide rates increase and then decrease (figs. 12 and 13 illustrate the shape of the curves implied by the polynomial term coefficients).

The models also control for between-nation heterogeneity with varying intercepts. The country effects show tendencies for homicide among all age groups within a country and generally reflect the pattern indicated by table 23, only in this case the differences control for age structure. As before, homicide rates appear highest in English-speaking nations: the United States by far has the highest rates, and after Italy and Finland, Canada and Australia rank fourth and fifth highest. The United Kingdom and Ireland, however, have among the lowest homicide rates, as do Denmark, Sweden, and Japan. As the nation coefficients present little new information, I omit them from the table.

Cohort size in table 25 increases homicide rates net of controls for time, age, and nation. Measured as the percentage of the population, cohort size has a stronger effect on female homicide mortality than on male homicide mortality. Measured as relative cohort size, it has a stronger effect on males than on females. Comparing the two measures, relative cohort size does better than population percentage in the models. The standardized coefficients for relative cohort size equal .211 for males and .203 for females, while the same coefficients for the population percentage equal .058 and .145. These standardized coefficients are similar in size to those for the suicide rate.

Cohort Size–Age Interactions. Given this background information from the additive models, tests of the hypothesis come from adding interaction terms of cohort size by age. Based on the contextual arguments, cohort size should have positive effects at the younger ages, near-zero effects at the middle ages, and negative effects at the older ages. Accordingly, the remaining equations of table 25 add these terms. The first set of size × age interaction coefficients reflects the differences in the effect of cohort size (as a percentage of the population for each age group) from the insignificant effects of −0.026 and −0.011 for the omitted groups of males and females aged 45–54.

To summarize these interactions, table 26 shows the results when adding each of the interaction coefficients to the coefficients of −0.026 and −0.011. For men, the two youngest groups (15–24 and 25–34) differ significantly from the comparison group. The coefficients of 0.043 and 0.058 suggest that large cohort size raises homicide victimization among young males. The remaining coefficients for the interaction terms do not differ significantly from the near-zero coefficient for the omitted group. Although cohort size increases homicide at the younger ages, it has little or no effect at older ages; even if it brings no protection at the older ages, cohort size does no special harm. The failure to find the positive effects of cohort size among older age groups as specified by the hypothesis may

Table 25. Unstandardized Coefficients for Regression of Age-Specific Homicide Rates on Cohort Size—Age Interaction Models

Independent Variables	Population Percentage				Relative Cohort Size			
	Additive		Interactive		Additive		Interactive	
	Male	Female	Male	Female	Male	Female	Male	Female
Age:								
15–24	−.134	−.023	−1.07	−.431	−.227	−.049	−.750	−.512
	(5.37)	(1.16)	(3.43)	(2.38)	(8.40)	(2.55)	(2.38)	(2.72)
25–34	.096	.102	−1.02	−.473	.029	.083	−.968	−.635
	(3.99)	(4.88)	(3.88)	(2.65)	(1.15)	(4.10)	(3.01)	(3.12)
35–44	.061	.084	.078	−.160	.028	.076	−.142	−.703
	(2.62)	(4.93)	(0.31)	(1.02)	(1.17)	(4.43)	(0.30)	(2.59)
55–64	−.147	−.093	−.377	−.293	−.109	−.083	−.315	−.402
	(5.52)	(5.89)	(1.72)	(2.30)	(4.11)	(5.40)	(1.15)	(2.34)
65–74	−.242	−.054	−.398	−.180	−.143	−.029	−.299	−.395
	(5.40)	(2.09)	(2.00)	(1.48)	(3.14)	(1.15)	(1.05)	(2.21)
75+	−.214	.065	−.446	−.258	−.050	.107	−.180	−.399
	(4.26)	(1.94)	(2.34)	(2.14)	(0.97)	(3.36)	(0.64)	(2.34)
Time	−.007	−.001	−.005	−.0002	−.009	−.003	−.006	−.001
	(0.93)	(0.28)	(0.72)	(0.05)	(1.14)	(0.56)	(0.76)	(0.14)
Time^2	.001	.001	.001	.001	.001	.001	.001	.001
	(3.12)	(2.72)	(2.77)	(2.35)	(2.92)	(2.63)	(2.63)	(2.14)

	(1)	(2)	(3)	(4)	(5)	(6)	(7)	(8)
Time³ (× 100)	−.002 (3.65)	−.001 (3.42)	−.002 (3.17)	−.001 (3.00)	−.002 (3.19)	−.001 (3.04)	−.002 (2.92)	−.001 (2.61)
Size	.009 (1.88)	.014 (3.65)	−.026 (1.77)	−.011 (1.15)	.795 (6.39)	.491 (6.59)	−.077 (0.13)	−.522 (1.49)
× 15–24	...	...	.069 (2.99)	.033 (2.39)	...	...	1.05 (1.67)	.991 (2.60)
× 25–34	...	...	.084 (4.24)	.045 (3.33)	...	...	1.87 (2.90)	1.42 (3.50)
× 35–44	...	...	.003 (0.13)	.021 (1.72)	...	...	.419 (0.45)	1.58 (2.93)
× 55–64	...	...	.017 (0.87)	.016 (1.38)	...	...	.363 (0.61)	.621 (1.65)
× 65–74	...	...	.000 (0.01)	.003 (0.21)	...	...	.012 (0.02)	.638 (1.49)
× 75+	...	...	−.005 (0.19)	.033 (2.27)	...	...	−.671 (0.86)	1.17 (2.68)
Constant	.96	.54	1.35	.82	.73	.48	1.09	.95
df	5,012	5,012	5,006	5,006	5,012	5,012	5,006	5,006
R²—OLS	.6964	.5567	.7025	.5596	.7028	.5604	.7081	.5633

Note. Numbers in parentheses are absolute values of t-ratios.

Table 26. Age-Specific Effects on Homicide Rates
of Population Percentage

| | Population Percentage | |
Age Group	Males	Females
15–24	.043	.022
25–34	.058	.034
35–44	−.023	.010
45–54	−.026	−.011
55–64	−.009	.005
65–74	−.026	−.008
75+	−.031	.022

Table 27. Age-Specific Effects on Homicide Rates
of Relative Cohort Size

| | Relative Cohort Size | |
Age Group	Males	Females
15–24	.973	.469
25–34	1.79	.898
35–44	.342	1.06
45–54	−.077	−.522
55–64	.286	.099
65–74	−.065	−.116
75+	−.748	.648

result from age differences between victims and offenders. If large cohort size increases homicide offending among the young, some of the homicide victims of young offenders may belong to the older age groups. The cross-age homicides may counter the benefits of large cohort size at older ages.

For females, the interaction results replicate the age patterns for men. Large cohort size increases homicide among women from ages 15–34, but with the exception of women age 75 and over, has little effect on homicide at older ages. The positive effect of cohort size for the oldest women likely reflects the large number of elderly females vulnerable to crime by the young. Otherwise, the results for both men and women support claims that large cohort size harms younger age groups more than it does older age groups.

The equations in table 25 that use relative cohort size present similar evidence of age differences in the effects. Adding the interaction coefficients to the coefficients of −0.077 and −0.522 for the omitted groups produces the age-specific effects shown in table 27. For both men and women, the coefficients again demonstrate positive effects for the young and near-zero or negative effects for ages afterward. The interactive effects again support the idea that the closer the ties of an age group to the labor force, the greater the harm of large cohort size for homicide, and that the weaker the ties of an age group to the labor force, the less the harm of large cohort size for homicide.

Nation and Time Interactions. Along with differences by age and sex, the hypotheses predict stronger influence of cohort size among more individualist nations than among more collectivist nations and in earlier time periods than in more recent ones. Testing these hypotheses involves estimating models of homicide rates for two groups of nations, two time periods, and two measures of cohort size. Table 28 presents truncated versions of these models: the coefficients calculated from the interaction terms describe the effect of cohort size (with controls for age, time, and nation) on homicide rates for each age group. The table divides the nations into those with collectivism scores below the mean (i.e., individualist nations)

Table 28. Unstandardized Coefficients for Regression of Age-Specific Homicide Rates on Cohort Size—Sex, Age, Nation, and Time Interaction Models

Age Group	% Pop.		RCS		% Pop.		RCS	
	Collectivism				Time Period			
	Low	High	Low	High	Early	Late	Early	Late
Males:								
15–24	.071**	−.020	1.22	−.047	.011	.026	.550	.743
25–34	.059**	.050**	2.02	.995**	.023	.042	1.40	.912
35–44	−.055	.016	−1.06	.895	−.071**	.013	−1.01**	.171
45–54	−.038	−.020	.715	−.565	.012	.014	1.78*	.075
55–64	−.042	.002	.019	.405	.022	.026	.741	.209
65–74	−.066	−.060	−.575	−.473	.030	.015	.660	.512
75+	−.041	−.073	−.475	−1.90	.110	−.001	1.80	−.504
Range	.137	.124	3.08	2.90	.181	.043	2.79	1.42
Females:								
15–24	.043**	−.011	.715	−.120	.004	.016	.236	.396
25–34	.036**	.029	1.15**	.436**	−.005	.034	.163	.818
35–44	−.015	.040**	.463	1.57**	−.010	.020	.417	.748
45–54	−.027*	−.000	−.434	−.594	−.004	.015	.074	−.332
55–64	.000	−.000	.294	−.085	.025**	.019	.635	.045
65–74	.012**	−.039	.695**	−.307	.026**	−.001	.832	.174
75+	.026**	.017	.755**	.586	.068**	.028	1.61**	.594
Range	.070	.079	1.58	2.16	.078	.035	1.54	1.15

Note. % Pop. = cohort size as a percentage of the population; RCS = relative cohort size.
* Omitted category coefficient differs significantly ($t > 2.0$) from zero.
** Dummy variable coefficient differs significantly ($t > 2.0$) from omitted category.

and those with collectivism scores above the mean and divides the sample into the years 1955–74 and 1975–94. Comparing the coefficients across equations indicates how national and temporal contexts modify the determinants of homicide. For example, the coefficient of 0.071 in the first column equals the effect of the population percentage on the log of the male homicide mortality rate for persons ages 15–24 in low-collectivist nations. The corresponding coefficient for collectivist nations equals −0.020.

In opposition to the hypothesis, the results for males in table 28 exhibit few differences between individualist and collectivist nations. After age 35, the effects of the measures of cohort size do not significantly differ from zero in all nations. For ages 25–34, the effects of cohort size appear positive for all nations. Only at ages 15–25 do the results differ: large cohort size increases homicide mortality among males in individualist nations but not in collectivist nations. As indicated by the results in the bottom panel of table 28, the results for females identify more differences across nations at the youngest ages. Yet few consistent differences emerge across the nations at the oldest ages. As a result, the ranges of coefficients across ages do not differ greatly for the two groups of nations. At best, collectivism moderates the harm of cohort size only at the youngest ages.

The separate models for time periods also provide inconsistent evidence for the hypothesis that the effects of cohort size would decline in recent time periods. For both men and women, few age differences exist in the effects of cohort size within periods. Although the range of coefficients emerges larger in early time periods than in later periods, the lack of statistically significant coefficients suggests that randomness may contribute to the temporal differences. These results contrast with those for suicide and suggest different processes occur for the two types of violent mortality. The early years most strongly reveal the interactive effects of age and cohort size on suicide but not on homicide.

Reasons may exist for the different results across time periods for suicide and homicide rates. Although the general guiding principle is that the influence of cohort size has declined in recent decades, homicide rates may have characteristics that lead to increases in its influence. Gartner and Parker (1990) argue that age structure most influences homicide rates where interpersonal barriers to violence are weakest. In the absence of opportunities for homicide, an increasingly young population may have little impact on the homicide rate. With exceedingly low homicide rates, strong informal social controls, and few opportunities for homicide, the size of the youth population can have little influence, regardless of the context. With more tolerant views of interpersonal violence, and greater opportunities for crime, homicide rates will respond more directly to changes in age structure. This implies that the rise over time in social freedom, anonymity, and the breakup of traditional controls of community and kin may contribute to a growing importance of cohort size as a determinant of homicide. Such forces may otherwise counter those reducing the importance of cohort size in more recent time periods.

Control Variables. Changes in cohort size affect female labor force participation, marriage and divorce, fertility, income levels, and unemployment, which in turn might mediate the effect of cohort size on homicide. To examine the influence of these variables on homicide and on the relationship between cohort size and homicide, I include them in the equations for male and female homicide rates in table 29. Before reviewing the effects of these control variables, however, note the effects of cohort size and age. The relatively strong effects of cohort size at ages 25–34 and the near-zero effects at older ages remain even with the controls for the other variables and provide further empirical support for the contextual hypothesis.

The coefficients of the control variables differ for male and female homicide rates. Among males, female labor force participation raises, and the total fertility rate lowers, homicide mortality. Although coefficients for neither the divorce rate nor the marriage rate reach statistical significance, the results for female labor force participation and the total fertility rate suggest the importance of family ties for male homicide victimization. Male deaths from homicide typically involve conflict among strangers or acquaintances that occurs outside the family. To the extent that high female labor force participation and low fertility reflect peripheral ties of males to wives and family, these variables would affect the likelihood of male-to-male violence and male homicide victimization. Males involved fully in family life are less likely to become victims of homicide.

For female homicide victimization, female labor force participation and the total fertility rate have insignificant effects, but the divorce rate has a positive effect. The divergent results for men and women likely reflect their different positions in families. Female labor force participation alone does not influence female homicide victimization, but the breakup of intimate relationships increases the likelihood of homicide victimization. Since women often fall victim to male partners, their involvement with men through marriage or divorce increases homicide. Interestingly, the total fertility rate reduces male victimization but not female victimization. Family involvement thus benefits men more than it does women.

Table 29. Unstandardized Coefficients and *t*-Ratios for Regression of Age-Specific Homicide Rates on Cohort Size and Other Variables—Age Interaction Models

Independent Variables	Male		Female		Male[a]		Female[a]	
	b	*t*	*b*	*t*	*b*	*t*	*b*	*t*
Age:								
15–24	−.666	2.31	−.264	1.47	−.385	1.25	−.100	0.52
25–34	−.678	2.88	−.307	1.78	−.475	2.03	−.208	1.15
35–44	.091	0.39	−.161	1.06	.146	0.59	−.090	0.56
55–64	−.298	1.47	−.256	2.05	−.167	0.76	−.191	1.37
65–74	−.320	1.69	−.138	1.14	−.258	1.21	−.133	1.00
75+	−.344	1.91	−.208	1.73	−.241	1.24	−.167	1.28
Time	.011	1.40	.009	1.84	.005	0.36	.008	0.89
Time^2	.001	1.07	.000	0.57	.001	1.05	.000	0.42
Time^3 (× 100)	−.001	1.61	.000	1.14	−.002	1.42	.000	0.89
Size (% Pop.)	−.014	1.00	−.005	0.52	.002	0.11	.002	0.21
× 15–24	.040	1.87	.020	1.50	.018	0.77	.008	0.57
× 25–34	.058	3.26	.032	2.47	.041	2.29	.024	1.76
× 35–44	.000	0.01	.021	1.73	−.006	0.29	.015	1.17
× 55–64	.011	0.62	.013	1.17	−.000	0.01	.008	0.63
× 65–74	−.003	0.14	.000	0.02	−.005	0.21	.003	0.23
× 75+	−.008	0.31	.031	2.16	−.011	0.44	.032	2.08
FLFP	.011	3.77	.001	0.53	.009	2.71	.001	0.61
Divorce rate	.029	1.21	.059	3.46	.024	0.97	.052	2.91
Marriage rate	.013	1.12	.001	0.07	.019	1.54	.006	0.69
Total fertility rate	−.084	2.49	−.027	1.09	−.126	3.48	−.029	1.05
Gross domestic product	−.502	4.76	−.257	3.95	−.508	4.07	−.224	3.03
Unemployment	. . .	. . .	. . .	. . .	−.007	1.46	−.000	0.11
Constant	1.10		.688		1.11		.551	
df	5,001		5,001		4,496		4,496	
R^2—OLS	.7187		.5680		.7247		.5785	

[a]For years 1959–94.

Economic conditions may affect homicide rates as well. Gross domestic product consistently lowers male and female homicide rates, net of the other variables. With controls for the general upward trend in homicide, high-income nations generally have lower homicide rates than low-income nations do (the United States being the obvious exception). Unexpectedly, however, unemployment has few consequences for homicide of men and women in the models. Lacking data before 1959 for unemployment, the model including this variable requires separate analysis of the truncated time span. In the last columns of table 29, neither coefficient for unemployment reaches significance, and the negative signs of the coefficients indicate that homicide declines with unemployment. Otherwise, the results do not substantially change the interaction effects of cohort size or the additive effects of the control variables.

Any study of cross-national patterns of homicide must take account of the particularly high rates in the United States relative to other nations. The previous models control in part for the high levels with nation-specific dummy variables—the large and positive coefficient for the U.S. dummy variable reflects its number one ranking on homicide. However, the exceptionally high homicide rates in the United States may also stem from idiosyncrasies that greatly influence the model estimates. To check for this possibility, I replicate the models in table 29 with the United States deleted. As evidence of the robustness of the results, the coefficients for the age interaction terms change little in terms of size or significance. For example, the effect of the population percentage for males ages 25–34 equals 0.058 ($t = 3.76$) for all nations and 0.049 ($t = 3.44$) for all nations except the United States. Further, the control variables have nearly identical effects on male homicide without the United States. For women, deletion of the outlying nation similarly leaves the results unchanged. Without presenting a new set of coefficients in the table, the results demonstrate that the inclusion of the United States does not produce a misleading description of the determinants of male and female homicide rates.

Other National Influences. Unlike the literature on suicide, the literature on homicide has given much attention to national context. Studies of homicide have not considered the influence of collectivist institutions but have offered evidence of the influence of income inequality, ethnic-linguistic heterogeneity, economic discrimination, war deaths, and the death penalty—all characteristics that vary across nations more than they vary across time. In fact, measures of all five national characteristics correlate with collectivism. Collectivist nations have lower income inequality ($r = -.627$), lower ethnic-linguistic heterogeneity ($r = -.481$), lower economic discrimination ($r = -.158$), fewer war deaths ($r = -.189$), and no death penalty ($r = -.619$).[5] However, as determinants of male homicide rates (with controls for age, time, and relative cohort size), collectivism has the strongest effect, followed by ethnic-linguistic heterogeneity, the death penalty, and income inequality.

Could the alternative measures of national context do better than collectivism in specifying the influence of cohort size on homicide? Previous tables in fact demonstrate few differences between individualist and collectivist nations in the interactive relationship between cohort size and age.

Table 30. Regression Coefficients and *t*-Ratios for Regression of Age-Specific Homicide Rates on Cohort Size and National Context Measures—Nation Interaction Models

National Context Variables	Variable × Population Percentage			Variable × Relative Cohort Size		
	b	beta	*t*	*b*	beta	*t*
Collectivism	−.015	−.273	6.02	−.335	−.251	5.74
Income inequality	.0016	.418	1.92	.054	.582	2.77
Ethnic-linguistic heterogeneity	.0003	.130	3.13	.004	.072	1.91
Economic discrimination	.012	.026	0.72	−.250	−.002	0.66
War deaths	.029	−.102	2.83	−.321	−.045	1.28
Death penalty	.008	.076	1.64	.242	.096	2.34

Yet, ignoring the cohort size–age interaction, collectivism still may modify the average effect of cohort size and provide a reference to which the effects of other national characteristics can be compared.

To begin, we need a summary measure of how collectivism shapes the effects of cohort size across all ages. I add interaction terms of collectivism by cohort size to the models with controls for age, time, nation, and cohort size. As might be expected, the interaction terms are both negative and significant. The higher the collectivism score, the weaker the harm of cohort size for homicide rates. I further computed similar interaction terms for other measures of national characteristics. Table 30 lists the unstandardized, standardized, and *t* coefficients for interaction terms based on both the population percentage and relative cohort size. Of the interactions, only those involving collectivism are significant for both measures of cohort size. Further, collectivism has larger specifying effects than four of the other variables. The standardized coefficients for income inequality are larger than those for collectivism but do not always reach statistical significance. Although smaller in standard units, the coefficients involving collectivism appear more reliable than those for inequality. Based on the results for both the additive and interactive influence of the national-level variables, collectivism performs better than other alternatives.

Comparisons to Suicide Mortality

Although both are forms of lethal violence as well as indicators of social pathology, suicide and homicide mortality differ in the target of the violence—that is, self versus others, respectively. This has led some to suggest that certain social conditions increase both forms of lethal violence but that other social conditions lead to the predominance of one form over the other (Unnithan et al. 1994). The arguments suggest creating two additional mortality measures. One combines suicide and homicide mortality rates into a single measure of lethal violence, and another divides the homicide rate by the suicide rate to measure the relative importance of each form of lethal violence. As a final step in the analyses, I consider these alternate measures and their implications for understanding the effects of cohort size.

To begin, suicide and homicide rates do not have much of an association. The bivariate correlation coefficients equal .069 for male rates and .064 for female rates. However, these correlations do not control for age, nation, and time period heterogeneity. With such controls, the standardized coefficients relating suicide to homicide equal 0.129 for males and 0.225 for females. Some similarity exists between patterns of homicide and suicide rates for these ages, nations, and years, but it is not large. The coefficients do not demonstrate an inverse relationship, as might be expected from claims that homicide and suicide represent alternative forms of violence. In any case, examining the alternative dependent variables allows exploration of the relationship in more detail.

Table 31 lists coefficients for models of (1) a measure of lethal violence that sums homicide and suicide rates and (2) a measure of the homicide rate as a ratio to the suicide rate. The equations use the population percentage measure of cohort size, but the relative cohort size measure gives similar results. They otherwise include the variables used in previous tables.

The coefficients for the male combined lethal violence rate differ little in the broad outlines from the separate results for suicide and homicide rates. Cohort size has positive effects at the youngest ages but negative effects at the oldest ages. The female labor force participation rate raises lethal violence, but its coefficient does not reach statistical significance. The total fertility rate and national income lower lethal violence. The coefficients for females demonstrate the positive effect of cohort size at younger ages but not the negative effect at older ages; to the contrary, cohort size has positive effects for women ages 75 and over. Female labor force participation raises lethal violence against women, while the divorce rate, the marriage rate, the total fertility rate, and national product do the opposite. As an average of the results for suicide and homicide (with the more common suicide rates getting a larger weight in the sum), the results in table 31 present little new information. Social conditions that affect either suicide or homicide rates generally affect the combined measure of lethal violence.

The coefficients for homicide rates as a ratio to suicide rates in the last

Table 31. Unstandardized Coefficients and *t*-Ratios for Regression of Combined Age-Specific Homicide and Suicide Rates on Cohort Size and Other Variables—Age Interaction Models

Independent Variables	Homicide Rate + Suicide Rate				Homicide Rate / Suicide Rate			
	Male		Female		Male		Female	
	b	*t*	*b*	*t*	*b*	*t*	*b*	*t*
Age:								
15–24	−1.84	5.53	−2.12	6.25	.163	2.36	.459	6.82
25–34	−.730	2.30	−.945	2.71	−.018	0.29	.156	2.39
35–44	−.076	0.26	−.294	0.83	.049	0.77	.012	0.18
55–64	.039	0.17	−.125	0.52	−.104	1.94	−.047	1.02
65–74	.579	2.63	−.113	0.51	−.145	3.00	.036	0.74
75+	.471	2.41	−.507	2.05	−.117	2.57	.127	2.37
Time	−.015	2.30	.007	0.94	.004	2.10	.002	1.21
Time²	.001	3.04	.000	0.56	.000	0.09	−.000	0.72
Time³ (× 100)	−.002	3.19	.001	1.55	−.000	0.68	.000	0.84
Size	.007	0.51	−.017	1.02	−.003	0.74	.008	2.18
× 15–24	.071	3.13	.086	3.52	−.005	0.90	−.020	4.03
× 25–34	.027	1.21	.037	1.43	.007	1.52	−.004	0.79
× 35–44	−.009	0.40	.005	0.18	−.000	0.04	.004	0.72
× 55–64	.006	0.29	.016	0.73	.005	1.08	.002	0.50
× 65–74	−.056	2.37	.013	0.56	.007	1.47	−.004	0.94
× 75+	−.013	0.52	.067	2.32	.001	0.15	−.010	1.67
FLFP	.004	1.26	.006	1.64	.002	2.72	−.001	0.93
Divorce rate	−.000	0.01	−.037	1.68	.018	3.04	.053	6.71
Marriage rate	−.014	1.31	−.021	1.78	.005	1.57	−.001	0.31
Total fertility rate	−.051	1.33	−.118	3.02	.001	0.16	.033	2.61
Gross domestic product	−.123	1.84	−.110	1.34	−.098	3.77	−.049	2.01
Constant	3.57		3.19		.406		.264	
df	5,001		5,001		5,001		5,001	
R²—OLS	.7903		.7336		.7069		.6326	

columns of table 31 highlight the differences rather than the similarities between homicide and suicide rates. Some of the coefficients reveal well-known differences: because homicide occurs more often among the young and less often among the old than suicide does, the age coefficients are positive for the youngest age group and negative for the oldest age group. The time coefficient shows that homicide relative to suicide has risen linearly. The coefficients for the nation dummy variables (not presented in the table) indicate that the United States and Italy have high relative homicide rates, and Denmark, Switzerland, and Austria have high relative suicide rates. Otherwise, the female labor force participation and divorce rates raise, and national income lowers, male homicide rates relative to suicide rates; the divorce and the total fertility rates raise, and national income lowers, female homicide rates relative to suicide rates. No differences exist between homicide and suicide rates in the interaction between age and relative cohort size. Cohort size raises both suicide and homicide similarly at the youngest ages.

Conclusion

As in the study of fertility and suicide, the comparative study of homicide can benefit from a contextual perspective that recognizes the importance of relatively stable institutional structures as facilitating or inhibiting forces. The homicide literature sometimes refers to contextual influences as culture or ideology but has done little to incorporate context systematically into comparative quantitative studies. Claims have been tested, in this chapter, that the effect of cohort size on homicide depends on age, sex, national institutional structures, and temporal changes that moderate the economic harm and political benefits of large cohorts. Older age groups, female status, collectivist institutions, and more recent time periods should minimize the harm of large cohort size for homicide victimization.

The analyses generally, if not always, support the arguments. With respect to age, clear evidence of the harm of cohort size for homicide victimization exists among younger cohorts of both men and women. Although seldom themselves killers, young women may experience the consequences of low male relative economic status. The tendency of males to kill females as well as other males implies a stronger effect of cohort size on female homicide than on female suicide. Weaker evidence exists for the benefits of cohort size for homicide victimization at the older ages. The low rate of offending among older persons and the potential of older persons in cohorts of any size to become homicide victims of younger men attenuate the potential benefits of cohort size. Despite limitations in measures of age-specific victimization rates relative to age-specific offending rates, the analysis of homicide provides some interesting and meaningful results that complement and support those for suicide.

With respect to national differences, a collectivist orientation toward social protection relates to the average effect of cohort size on age-specific homicide rates. More reliably than other national characteristics, collectivism reduces the positive influence of cohort size on homicide. However, collectivism does little to change the interaction between cohort size and age. Thus, cohort size interacts with age and interacts with collectivism but does not interact simultaneously with age and collectivism (the same point also holds for the effects of time on the cohort size and age interaction).

Still, by identifying systematically which ages and nations respond most directly to changes in cohort size, the analysis helps account for diverse findings of the importance of age structure in comparative studies of homicide rates. They further provide partial if not complete support for the hypothesis that contextual factors shape the size and direction of the influence relative cohort size has on homicide. If not as strong as for suicide, the evidence for homicide rates nonetheless adds to that overall in favor of the contextual perspective. Indeed, the fact that similar support occurs for sometimes divergent types of social problems adds to the robustness of the results.

PART IV

Sex Differences in Mortality

Sex Differences in Suicide and Homicide Mortality

The connection between gender equality and mortality has gained much attention and generated much debate in the past several decades. The issue stems from a continued and steady increase in the life expectancy of women relative to men since the turn of the century and an acceleration of the increase since the 1950s. Given the inverse relationship between women's status and their mortality advantage, a causal connection might exist such that improvements in women's status and the equalization of gender roles will eventually eliminate that advantage. Yet the continued growth of the sex differential in death rates during the 1970s and 1980s—a period of improved status—has challenged these predictions. Scholars instead argue that gender equality does nothing to harm, and might actually expand, the mortality benefits enjoyed by women and that life expectancy will continue to increase faster for women than for men (Nathanson 1995). Perhaps women even have biological advantages in their resistance to degenerative diseases that become more important as social roles become more similar (Vallin 1993, 1995).

During the 1990s, however, a shift in the trends has occurred: after decades in which the female advantage in life expectancy widened, the gap has begun to narrow in some nations. Since women have already reached a long life expectancy, one might expect a narrowing for the simple reason that they have less room to improve; a more rapid increase in life expectancy among men can occur because they are farther from the maximum life expectancy. Perhaps more important, faster growth of lung cancer among women than men has contributed to a greater narrowing of death rates at ages 25–59 than at the oldest ages (Trovato and Lalu 1996, 1998). Further, the narrowing has occurred in the highest-income nations with the greatest gender equality. Given a lag in the consequences of gender equality for mortality, the recent changes appear consistent with claims that status improvements among women will eventually eliminate their mortality advantage and suggest that controversy over the relationship between gender equality and mortality will continue.

Although debates over the sex differential often focus on principal causes of death such as heart disease and lung cancer, they also apply to violence-related mortality. Indeed, much as they do for the study of cohort size, deaths from suicide and homicide have several characteristics that make them particularly appropriate for the study of gender equality. These types of deaths result from daily problems of living and personal distress, involve risky behaviors and lifestyles, and reflect social integration and support.[1] Whereas deaths from degenerative diseases at the older ages arise primarily from the long-term accumulation of the effects of certain behaviors, deaths from intentional violence respond more immediately to social circumstances, emerge as important at younger ages as well as older ages, and do not require decade-long lags to gauge the effects of changing gender roles.[2] Even if violent mortality represents a small portion of the differential between men and women, it proves especially important at younger ages and to issues of gender equality. Finally, rates of male and female mortality from violence vary across ages, nations, and time periods in ways that make them suitable for macrolevel study.

Linking the study of sex differences in suicide and homicide to changes in gender equality also has an advantage over other macrolevel approaches to the relative well-being of men and women. Objective indicators of women's position in the labor force, family, educational system, or political arena are in some ways unsatisfactory measures of improvements in gender equality. Indicators such as higher labor force participation, fewer children, more solo households, higher educational attainment, and more elected women officials provide limited information on the benefits these changes bring to women or on the meaning they have in their lives. However, assuming that suicide and homicide victimization reflect, to some degree, the well-being of groups, studying the varied impacts of changes in the objective indicators on sex differences in suicide and homicide can highlight the social consequences of gender equality.[3]

Since the study of mortality from suicide and homicide—or any other cause of death for that matter—can easily separate outcomes for males and females, the preceding several chapters have already made comparisons across genders relevant to sex differentials. In brief, results by gender reveal stronger effects of relative cohort size for males than for females. The lower levels of violence among women than men make it more difficult to find relationships with relative cohort size. Additionally, the weaker results for females match Easterlin's arguments that, because women have weaker attachments to the labor force than men, they experience less harm from cohort oversupply. Based on similar reasoning, women also experience fewer benefits than men do from large cohort size later in life.

However, these initial and incomplete conclusions about gender differences in the determinants of suicide and homicide mortality would benefit from more exact comparisons of relative male and female age-specific rates. Because male and female rates of lethal violence, at least to some degree, vary independently of each other, the gap in the two rates will capture aspects of mortality not apparent from the separate analysis of the rates. We know from previous results that male suicide and homicide mortality rates greatly exceed female rates. In the United States, for example, male suicide rates are three to six times higher than female rates, and male homicide victimization rates are two to four times higher than female rates. Yet, the exact size of the gap between males and females will vary with social conditions that differ across time, ages, and nations. Although not always apparent from the description of absolute mortality rates in the preceding several chapters, the gap likely differs between earlier prefeminist decades and recent decades, between more reckless and dangerous younger ages and older ages, and between collectivist and individualist nations.

Given their variation across time and space, relative rates of male and female violent mortality allow one to evaluate arguments about the consequences of changes in male and female social and economic roles. Like the gap in mortality between men and women, the gap between the social and economic positions of men and women varies across time, ages, and nations. Connecting variation in relative mortality to variation in gender equality can answer the question, "Do changes in work and related family roles of women reduce or increase their traditional advantage in suicide and homicide mortality?" The separate study of male and female violent mortality may allow for appropriate tests of Easterlin's arguments about cohort size, but the combined study of male and female violent mortality in the form of relative rates can test theories of the mortality consequences of gender change.[4]

In this chapter and in chapters 10 and 11, I therefore examine gender equality and relative levels of violent mortality. My focus in this and the next chapters is on how differences in female labor force participation affect sex differences in suicide and homicide mortality across ages, nations, and time periods, but I also consider the consequences of family changes involving marriage, divorce, and childbearing that relate closely to women's work. As the study of fertility in part 2 considered both cohort size and female work, this part of the book supplements part 3 by extending studies of cohort size and mortality to consider female work and mortality. In this chapter, I give the theoretical arguments concerning gender equality and sex differentials in suicide and homicide mortality, and in the next two chapters, I present the analyses that test the arguments.

Lethal Violence and Gender

In contrast to the usual benefits of status for mortality, gender comparisons demonstrate the well-known fact that lower levels of income, power, and prestige among women traditionally coexisted and currently coexist with lower levels of mortality. Yet, the relationship is consistent with two competing interpretations. On the one hand, the gender gap in both status and mortality suggests a causal relationship such that reducing the status differential would reduce the mortality advantage of women. On the other hand, if forces other than status differences produce the sex differential, then gender equality will not produce mortality convergence—it may instead widen the differential as women come to enjoy the benefits of equality.

Because the sex differential in mortality predates the extensive and more recent changes in women's roles, family forms, and labor force composition, trends in the differentials have theoretical significance. Assuming that social changes in recent decades have at least to some extent equalized the social experiences of men and women, then the relationship between these changes and relative rates of mortality can help evaluate arguments about the sources of the differential.[5] Similarly, considerable differences exist across the economically similar high-income nations in both the status of women (Lewis 1997) and the relative levels of mortality (Rockett and Smith 1989; Trovato and Lalu 1998; Waldron 1993). Like the time trends, national comparisons can tell us much about the influence of gender equality on sex differences in mortality.

Reduction in Protection. Applied to variation in the sex differential in violent mortality, arguments make straightforward predictions about convergence and divergence in male and female mortality. According to a "reduction in protection" argument, movement toward gender equality increases the mortality of women relative to men. In relation to suicide, one strand of Durkheim's writings ([1897] 1966) argues that the less intense involvement of women in social life outside the family protects them from egoistic suicide. By tightly integrating women, family life and particularly the presence of children lower the risk of suicide. Social change that brings women into the world of work, politics, and social life would end that family protection and promote convergence over time in male and female deaths from suicide. Durkheim's arguments reflect common assumptions of the time that females, being inferior to men except in their reproductive roles and expression of motherly love, require protection from the competitiveness of the male world.

More modern arguments make much the same prediction as Durkheim—without the explicitly sexist assumptions—by drawing out the implications of the concepts of status and role strain for suicide. Concerning status, Henry and Short (1954) develop a framework to explain its inverse relationship with suicide: higher-status persons commit suicide more often because they generally have weaker relational systems of external restraint. Those groups occupying subordinate statuses are more subject to social constraints and forces of conformity. Since women occupy lower-status positions than men and face greater external restraints, they will exhibit lower suicide rates than men. Their lower status may also isolate them from the loss of status experienced by men during downturns in the business cycle—another factor in high male suicide rates (Henry and Short 1954). However, improvements in women's status will weaken the special constrains they have faced, subject them to the same forces faced by men, and increase their suicide rates relative to those of men.

Concerning role strain, a hypothesis suggests that the more roles a person occupies, the greater the potential for poor performance because time constraints force attention to one role at the expense of another (Goode 1960). Trying to manage multiple role responsibilities often results in problems of physical and mental health and may increase the risk of suicide. Further, when the combination of roles occurs rarely in society, incumbents face low status integration, few sources of social support, and high suicide rates (Gibbs and Martin 1964). High role strain and low status integration can affect both men and women, but the entrance of women into the labor force heightens strain and integration problems. Even as they come to hold full-time jobs, women still keep primary duties for child care, cooking, cleaning, and family relationships and, therefore, confront enormous time and energy pressures. The low levels of support women receive in meeting these pressures increase their suicide rates relative to men.

A related version of the protection argument focuses less on motivations for suicide and more on access to the most lethal means of suicide and on differential classification of deaths. Male experience with firearms, for instance, may produce higher rates of suicide among men than women even if desires or attempts to commit suicide do not differ by sex (Kushner 1985, 1995). Since the lack of female access to lethal weapons relates directly to issues of gender equality, social changes that equalize the roles of men and women should reduce the differential access and the sex differential in suicide. Similarly, greater stigma of suicide for women may lead family members and sympathetic physicians more often to classify ambiguous deaths as accidents for females and as suicides for males. Again, however, changes in gender equality should reduce this stigma, moderate any measurement bias in the suicide rate of women relative to men, and contribute to convergence in male and female suicide rates.

In relation to homicide, female victimization likely involves increased exposure to male violence rather than increased exposure to female violence. In the United States, for example, 90% of those arrested for murder and nonnegligent manslaughter in 1992 were male (U.S. Bureau of the Census 1994, 206)—a percentage that has risen rather than declined over the previous decades. Reduction of protection explanations of female homicide victimization therefore focus primarily on the exposure of women to male offenders, and several theories suggest that changes in female status will increase their vulnerability to male lethal violence.

Power control theory posits that traditional families socialize women to avoid risk, thereby reducing their participation in social conflict (Hagan, Simpson, and Gillis 1987). When family arrangements are highly gender stratified and patriarchal, when women are socialized to be passive and subservient, female victimization is low (Curtis 1974). Egalitarian families, in contrast, allow more risk taking among women. Raising boys and girls similarly and removing women from the constraining but protective traditional family environment increases their potential to become involved in conflict and to become victims of lethal violence (Adler 1975; Simon 1975).

Similarly, routine activities theory posits that changes in lifestyles expose women to greater risks of criminal victimization (Cohen and Felson 1979). The theory notes that criminal acts require convergence in time and space of motivated offenders, suitable targets, and the absence of capable guardians. When more routine activities take place outside the home, it can increase the number of offenses without changes in the motivations of offenders. As sex roles become less differentiated and sexual barriers become less rigid, women increasingly participate in the same activities, lifestyles, and situations as men do (Hindelang, Gottfredson, and Garofalo 1978).

The increasingly similar lifestyles and routine activities equalize proximity of both men and women to offenders and risky situations and make risks of homicide victimization of men and women more similar (Kruttschnitt 1995; Miethe and Meier 1994). Social changes in women's work activities, autonomy from family members, and freedom to move about make it more likely for women to appear in sex-integrated public places, away from guardian family members and around strangers. They are therefore exposed to greater risks of violence than in the past.

Along with these changes in opportunities to victimize women, motivations for violence against women may increase with gender equality. Women's improved status and independence may threaten traditional status hierarchies, challenge male dominance over resources, and provoke a backlash against women (Gartner and McCarthy 1991; Kruttschnitt 1996). Particularly in intimate relationships, some men may respond with deadly violence to the threat and competition brought on by their partner's independence or desire to leave the relationship (Browne and Williams 1993).

Reduction in Inequality. According to a "reduction in inequality" argument, the unequal benefits of marriage for men and women and the limited roles reserved for women have in the past moderated the potential female advantage in mortality. Social change toward gender equality would thus lead to further divergence in men's and women's mortality. For suicide, another strand of Durkheim's work suggests that, in some ways, the conjugal unit actually may harm women.[6] In Durkheim's terms, men gain more protection from egoistic and anomic suicide with marriage than women do. Suicide thus emerges more highly among single men than among single women. More generally, because traditional marriage and family roles benefit men more than they do women, changes in those roles harm men more than women. The end result of the reduction in gender inequality is divergence in mortality rates.

A variation on this argument concerning gender differences in suicide suggests that men suffer more from recent social changes than women do because men rarely find social integration and emotional support outside the family (Almgren et al. 1998; Krull and Trovato 1994). Since male ties in the work world tend to emphasize competition, autonomy, and individualism, family changes that sever the ties between men and family roles raise the risks of suicide for men. In contrast, women respond to declining traditional family roles by developing close emotional ties outside the family. New sources of integration at work and dense interpersonal networks

(Pescosolido 1994; Pescosolido and Georgianna 1989) buffer women from loss of family support and from threats to their identity (Girard 1993). Given multiple sources of integration, women suffer less harm from family change than men do or even benefit directly from expanding roles and greater self-fulfillment (Moen, Dempster-McClain, and Williams 1989).

Other arguments make much the same point with respect to homicide victimization. If violence is an expression of unequal and oppressive power relations, traditional gender inequality makes women vulnerable to violence by partners (Browne and Williams 1993; O'Brien 1988). Lacking power within the traditional male-dominated relationship, wives have few options to avoid intimate violence; similarly, teenage girls abused by parents may have few options other than running away from home, thereby risking victimization on the street. Reducing gender stratification by giving women more power, resources, and control within family relationships should reduce their vulnerability to intimate homicide (Brewer and Smith 1995; Simpson 1991; Simpson and Elis 1995; Steffensmeier and Allan 1996). Conversely, since males less often become the victims of intimate partners but remain vulnerable to violence outside the family, they do not benefit from changing marital relationships. To the contrary, single and divorced men, more than married men, involve themselves in activities that increase their risk of homicide victimization. Social change toward gender inequality should, as a result, reduce the levels of homicide deaths of women relative to men.

Along with its benefits for power relationships in families, gender equality improves women's economic opportunities. Patriarchal power relations can make women vulnerable to violence through economic marginality (Steffensmeier and Allan 1996). Since victimization of women usually involves conflict with intimates rather than with strangers or acquaintances (Kruttschnitt 1995; Ogle, Maier-Katkin, and Bernard 1995), when women have access to material resources in the form of work and earnings that create opportunities for them to support themselves outside the traditional family (Messerschmidt 1993), women can afford to set up separate households, move to safer communities, and feel empowered to contact authorities about ex-partners that are threatening. Thus, if discrimination and poverty play a crucial role in homicide offenses by and victimization of men, they should do the same for women (Chesney-Lind and Shelden 1992), and improved economic resources should reduce female homicide offenses and victimization. Greater resources provide greater protection for women from male offenders and thereby increase the sex differential in homicide.

Empirical Evidence. Existing studies have not provided consistent evidence for one or the other of these arguments. Some studies find positive relationships between suicide rates and female labor force participation, divorce, and recent social changes (Davis 1981; Newman, Whittemore, and Newman 1973; Stack 1978; Stack and Danigelis 1985), but other studies find inverse relationships (Hassan and Tan 1989; Kawachi et al. 1999; Yang 1992; Yang and Lester 1988, 1995) or no relationship (Lester 1994; Mäkinen 1997). For homicide, the same ambiguity emerges in the empirical results. A huge literature on variation in aggregate homicide rates across U.S. cities (e.g., Land, McCall, and Cohen 1990; Kposowa, Breault, and Harrison 1995) fails to examine gender and age differences in either victims or offenders. Of the studies examining sex differences, most find no relationship between gender equality and female criminal offending or homicide victimization (Grasmick, Finley, and Glaser 1984; Hartnagel 1982; Kawachi et al. 1999; Miethe and Meier 1994; Smith and Brewer 1992; Smith and Kuchta 1995; Steffensmeier 1980, 1993; Steffensmeier, Allan, and Streifel 1989; Steffensmeier and Streifel 1992), but some find a positive relationship (Yang and Lester 1992) and some find a negative relationship (Bailey and Peterson 1995). The inconsistent results suggest the need to move beyond comparisons of competing and exclusive theories and give more attention to contingency in the consequences of gender equality for suicide and homicide.

Social Change and Institutional Adjustment

A more complex theoretical approach, one that considers how social context may influence the relationship, follows from earlier efforts to understand how the determinants of absolute levels of male and female violent mortality vary across ages, nations, and time periods. The determinants of the gendered dimensions of violent mortality may also vary across the same conditions. If so, an appropriate strategy would avoid searching for a single positive or negative relationship between female status and relative mortality, instead taking the size and direction of the relationship itself as an outcome to be described and explained. Most theories and studies, however, fail to examine the diversity in processes determining gender differences in mortality.

To address such diversity, I present an institutional adjustment hypothesis that combines arguments of protection and inequality by suggesting that both processes occur in sequence. Change initially disrupts traditional values, creating normative uncertainty and role ambiguity among women, provoking backlash among men, and exposing women to male violence. However, institutions eventually adapt to pressures for change, new norms gain wide acceptance, women come to benefit from higher status, and male victimization of women falls. The female advantage in suicide and homicide mortality declines initially but then rises. An institutional adjustment theory thus posits the occurrence of a crisis or disturbance and the adaptation to that crisis, predicts patterns of convergence then divergence, and explains both negative and positive relationships between gender equality and female victimization. The social settings of suicide and homicide gradually change over time in ways that alter the social determinants of mortality outcomes.

Recognizing the contingency of the relationship between gender equality and relative mortality offers a means to integrate ostensibly contrasting arguments. The reduction in protection and inequality arguments emerge as compatible when considering the relative status of women at the time the changes in status occur. The lower the status of women, the weaker their involvement in the world of work, and the stronger their dependence on men and family roles for economic well-being, then the greater the harm of change toward gender equality for relative rates of female suicide and homicide mortality. The higher the status of women, the greater their involvement in the world of work, and the weaker their dependence on men and family roles for economic well-being, then the less the harm (or the greater the benefit) of change toward gender equality for relative rates of female suicide and homicide mortality. In this way, the level of gender equality specifies the relationship between changes in gender equality and violent mortality. The level of gender equality relates to three dimensions of social context—time, age, and nation—that correspond to three dimensions of social context considered in previous chapters on the absolute levels of male and female mortality. I begin with time because of its central place in arguments about social change and institutional adjustment and then consider the dimensions of age and nation in shaping the relationship between gender equality and violent mortality.

Time. Applied to trends over time, the institutional adjustment hypothesis implies the existence of a convex or U-shaped trend in the ratio of male to female violent mortality. Steffensmeier (1984) examines the age-specific suicide rates of males and females in the United States from 1960 to 1978, finding that the gap narrowed in the 1960s but steadied and then widened afterward (see also Burr, McCall, and Powell-Griner 1997). Gartner, Baker, and Pampel (1990) examine differences in homicide, finding for the United States that the gender gap narrowed during the 1950s and again widened afterward. Part of the narrowing in lethal violence before 1970 may have resulted from a lag in the adjustment of norms and values to changing patterns of female employment and sexual independence. Until institutions adjust to new behaviors, violent female deaths may increase.

More specifically, equality brings greater awareness of and increased support for women's problems. The institutional adjustment results in part from the sheer numbers of women facing similar problems and demanding changes, but the women's movement, which reemerged in the 1960s after decades of quiescence, contributed substantially to the ideological support for working women (Chafetz 1995). A more supportive environment for the new roles of women could reverse an upward trend in female suicide. As for homicide, new definitions of spouse abuse as a serious crime, more awareness of the problem, greater prosecution of abusers, and development of shelters for battered women have helped protect women from intimate violence. After a short-run backlash of male violence against females because of the loss of male power (Brewer and Smith 1995), the more supportive environment for the new roles of women emerged and reduced homicide victimization among females relative to males.

Since employment and family roles of women have changed over time, the argument similarly implies the changing impact of these trends on violent mortality. Consider the consequences of rising female employment first. For suicide, Stack (1987) and Trovato and Vos (1992), using data from the United States and Canada, respectively, demonstrate that the effect of female labor force participation on female suicide shifts from positive, in the early post–World War II period, to zero or negative in the late postwar period. Initially, increases in female labor force participation generate role conflict. At later stages, as cultural supports for women occupying combined roles of wife and worker strengthen, the additional roles bring psychological and social benefits that reduce suicide. Thus, as the suicide gap between men and women increases and then decreases, the effects of female labor force participation on suicide change from positive to negative. Burr, McCall, and Powell-Griner (1997) also demonstrate a reversal from 1970 to 1980 in the relationship between female labor force participation and female suicide for cities in the United States. For homicide, Gartner and McCarthy (1991) find something similar. Increases in female labor force participation narrow the gap in homicide victimization in Canada before 1970 but have little effect after 1970. Their results support the claim that the harm for homicide of rising involvement of women in the labor force eventually, but not immediately, disappears.

The consequences for violent mortality of changes in family roles are similar to those for female labor force participation. Status integration theory suggests that, when relatively rare, the experience and status of divorce raise suicide. As divorce becomes more common, its harmful impact on status integration and suicide declines (Stafford and Gibbs 1988). Accordingly, Stack (1987, 1990) finds that the ratio of suicide among divorced to married persons has fallen in recent decades. Divorce apparently has come to have an increasingly less harmful influence on relative female suicide. Gartner, Baker, and Pampel (1990) reach similar conclusions about the consequences of divorce for homicide. Their results show that when women have relatively low education, fewer resources, and little power, divorce increases homicide of women relative to men; when women have gained higher status, divorce has the opposite effect.

To summarize, these interactive or contingent arguments imply that the size and direction of the influences of general social change, rising female labor force participation, and rising divorce on suicide and homicide mortality of men and women vary with the temporal and institutional context. To the extent that it reflects improvements in women's status, the temporal context defines the meaning that indicators of change have for men and women. The hypothesis thus predicts a curvilinear relationship between time and the relative female advantage in suicide and homicide rates, and changes over time in the effects of female work and divorce. Equivalently, it suggests curvilinear relationships of female work and divorce with the relative female advantage in suicide and homicide rates; as these variables rise over time and contribute to the improved status of women, they come to have less negative and eventually even positive influences on the female mortality advantage.

Age. The argument that trends in gender equality, female labor force participation, and divorce initially increase but, after a period of adjustment, then decrease female violent mortality has implications for age differences in the trends. If younger persons adapt quickly to, and indeed actively strive for, changes in the roles of women and men, then period changes should have a relatively small negative effect on rates of violence among this age group (Austin, Bologna, and Dodge 1991; McIntosh and Jewell 1987). In contrast, middle-aged persons, having been socialized to norms during earlier decades, will have more difficulty adjusting to change. Among middle-aged groups, the narrowing in mortality due to initial changes should be stronger than for younger age groups, as should the widening that follows as women and institutions adjust to the changes.

Thus, the divergence arguments would apply more directly to younger women, while both the convergence and divergence arguments would apply more to middle-aged women. In this way, age defines a context that shapes the meaning of social change for the well-being of men and women.

To complete the specification of age differences, this reasoning can apply to the older ages as well. Among older women, social change might produce more difficulties than adjustment and more convergence than divergence. Compared to the impact of lethal violence on younger age groups, stronger initial negative effects and weaker subsequent positive effects of social change on relative levels of lethal violence may emerge for older persons. However, perhaps changes in gender norms, female labor force participation, and divorce have smaller influences on the lives of older persons than younger persons, and rates of lethal violence will respond little if at all to these social changes. Thus, one might plausibly predict little change in either direction among the elderly.

Although these arguments specify that the strength of the curvilinear trend over time in relative violent mortality rates shifts across age groups, the age group differences in period effects can also be presented in equivalent cohort terms. The institutional adjustment argument predicts the largest female advantage among the most recent cohorts. If the trends among younger women show steady improvement in relative rates of lethal violence, it would imply each new cohort will show successively greater female advantages. If trends in lethal violence among middle-aged women first worsen and then improve, it would be a reflection of how social change harms transition cohorts and offers successively greater female advantages to later cohorts (i.e., those same cohorts showing improvement at younger ages). If trends among older women show worsening, it would stem from the movement of transition cohorts into old age; presumably, the eventual movement of younger cohorts into old age will show improvement in decades to come.

Nation. Although they have received little attention, national differences in the context of relative male and female suicide and homicide victimization relate to arguments of institutional adjustment. Policy regime differences exist across nations in the role the state has played in reproducing traditional gender relations, responding to pressures for equality, and ameliorating gender inequalities in work and income (Lewis 1993; Orloff 1996; Sainsbury 1994). Such differences produce variation in the relative power of men and women across otherwise economically similar nations and shape the context in which the sex differential in violent mortality occurs. Insofar as the relative power and resources of men and women differ across national contexts as they do across temporal contexts, the determinants of the relative levels of male and female suicide and homicide mortality may differ.

To review the discussion of previous chapters, a liberal feminist strategy focuses on ensuring individual rights to equal opportunity and nondiscrimination primarily in public spheres of school, work, and politics. The focus on individual rights and neutral treatment of gender tends to ignore reproductive differences, leaving problems of family and home for women to solve individually. The liberal strategy has emerged most strongly in individualist or pluralist nations such as the United States, where the women's movement maintains autonomy from traditional parties and class-based interest groups. A state feminist strategy focuses on efforts to socialize child care and housework in ways that make work and family less incompatible. To do so, the state intervenes in the domestic sphere as well as in the public sphere; policies give preferential treatment to women to redress past inequalities, counter male domination in positions of power, and integrate work and family responsibilities. The reformist strategy of state feminism tends to emerge in collectivist, egalitarian, and interventionist nations.

The institutional adjustment argument posits that the national environment for women's roles shapes how changes toward equality affect their well-being and therefore their propensity toward suicide and involvement in dangerous and risky behaviors that result in homicide. Nations with institutions that ease the conflict between roles inside and outside the family contribute to a more supportive environment for women. The shift from the protection of family roles to multiple roles and independence from the family in women-friendly nations should occur relatively smoothly and quickly and produce fewer problems that result in victimization of women by suicide and homicide. In contrast, nations without supportive institutions should heighten the initial normative conflict experienced by women at early stages of changes toward gender equality and increase the time it takes for norms to adjust to women's multiple roles. The shift from the protection of family roles to multiple roles and independence from the family in the latter nations should do more to increase victimization of women by suicide and homicide than in the nations with institutions more supportive of women.

In terms of predictions, nations with collectivist and women-friendly institutions should do more than nations with individualist and gender-neutral institutions to reduce or reverse the negative influences of social change, women's work, and family disruption on relative levels of mortality. The more supportive the state or national institutions of women's new roles, the more quickly relative violent mortality rates of women adjust to changes in work and family roles. The less supportive the state or national institutions for women's new roles, the more slowly relative violent mortality rates of women adjust to changes in work and family roles. All countries may well experience the curvilinear patterns of change posited by the institutional adjustment arguments, but some nations may experience them less forcefully than others.

Hypotheses. The theoretical arguments, in sum, specify that the consequences of social changes in female work and family independence for the female advantage in violent mortality vary across time. They further specify that these curvilinear trends vary across ages and nations. A set of subhypotheses thus follow from the more general institutional adjustment hypothesis:

1. averaged across all ages and nations, social changes toward the greater involvement of women in the labor force and reduced dependence of women on family roles will initially lower but will subsequently come to increase the female advantage in suicide and homicide mortality;

2. the reversal of the effects of social changes toward the greater involvement of women in the labor force and reduced dependence of women on family roles on the female advantage in suicide and homicide mortality will occur more quickly at the younger ages than at the older ages; and

3. the reversal of the effects of social changes toward the greater involvement of women in the labor force and reduced dependence of women on family roles on the female advantage in suicide and homicide mortality will occur more quickly among nations with collectivist and women-friendly institutions than among nations with individualist and gender-neutral institutions.

In addition to modifying the trend over time in the gap between male and female violent mortality, age and nation may directly influence relative rates of violent mortality. The gap may decline over the life course and emerge smaller in more egalitarian nations. The interactive hypotheses do not require these results, however; age and nation need not independently affect violent mortality for them to condition the effects of time, female work, and family change. Indeed, if interactive relationships exist, the additive relationships between age or nation and violent mortality may misrepresent the diverse processes. The relationships specified in the hypotheses can be better viewed as intertwined rather than separate.

Measurement Problems

Given the similarities across types of violent mortality, the hypotheses make general predictions. Relative rates of suicide and homicide mortality should respond similarly to changes in gender roles. However, they need not respond identically. Suicide and homicide mortality have special characteristics that may strengthen or weaken the support they provide for the hypotheses. If so, each type of lethal violence should be examined separately from the other rather than as a single category.

In comparing types of violent mortality, the previous chapters noted that the ages of homicide offenders and victims, unlike those for suicide, could differ. These age differences might weaken the observed relationship between the social sources of interpersonal violence and the characteristics of homicide victims. The study of sex differences in homicide adds to the potential disparity between the characteristics of offenders and victims. Since men often murder women and women rarely murder men, both female and male victimization respond primarily to the criminal actions of males. Rising female independence may increase female homicide deaths in the private arena through the actions of men threatened by female power or in the public arena through the actions of men finding greater opportunities for crime and violence against women. The study of homicide victimization rather than offending makes it difficult to determine if social changes most affect the violent behavior of men or the exposure of women. Because cross-gender homicide exists and cross-gender suicide does not, suicide may provide a better test of the hypotheses concerning sex differences in violent mortality.[7] Still, since both homicide and suicide, to different degrees, reflect changes in women's roles, they both deserve study.

While cross-gender murders make for some difficulties, the study of sex differences in suicide mortality has a special advantage over the study of absolute levels of suicide mortality. Critics of suicide statistics have made much of the tendency to undercount suicides by including them in the categories for accidents or unknown deaths (Day 1987; van Poppel and Day 1996). Yet the study of sex differences minimizes the undercount bias in suicide. Bias occurs only when the errors of measurement differ for men and women. To attribute age, nation, and time differences in the sex differential in suicide to measurement error, the stigma of suicide for women must not only exceed that for men but it must also do so to varied degrees across the ages, nations, and time periods under study.

To illustrate this advantage, consider a common measure of relative mortality that simply divides one rate by the other. The ratio of the male rate to the female rate shows the proportional excess of the male deaths over female deaths. If suicide rates are undercounted by the same percentage for males and females, the bias in both the numerator and denominator of the ratio cancels out.

Although the problems of undercount bias for relative suicide mortality rates appear less serious than they do for absolute rates of suicide mortality, three potential problems remain. First, if families and physicians view the stigma of suicide as more serious for women than for men, then the downward bias in suicides would be greater for women than for men and would inflate the female suicide advantage.[8] To answer this concern, note that, with social changes equalizing the roles of men and women, the impact of a female suicide stigma on the female suicide advantage should steadily decline. The change in measurement, like the underlying forces of equality, should contribute to convergence in suicide rates as predicted by the reduction in protection arguments. The existence and change in measurement bias can, in short, implicitly help evaluate the theoretical arguments. In addition, previous chapters controlled for measurement bias by including accident and unknown death rates in equations predicting suicide death rates. The same strategy can be used for relative rates of suicide mortality. For example, sex differences in accident and unknown mortality can be used to predict sex differences in suicide. Differences between models without and with these controls can provide information on the extent of bias and its influence on the effects of other determinants.

Second, another measurement problem especially important for sex comparisons stems from differential access of women and men to the most lethal weapons. Even if desires to commit suicide do not differ by sex, greater access by men to firearms may produce higher rates of suicide among them than among women (Canetto and Lester 1995; Kushner 1985, 1995).[9] Since access to weapons by men and women varies across nations and time periods, it may strongly affect cross-national and temporal comparisons of suicide mortality. However, the female access to lethal weapons represents a component of gender equality. As social conditions equalize the roles of men and women, differential access to lethal weapons should become less important for sex differences in suicide mortality. Although the data cannot separate out its influence from other influences, changes in access to firearms may reduce observed male and female differences in suicide mortality and heighten the trend toward convergence.

Third, the study of the sex differential in suicide mortality raises the issue of the "gender paradox in suicide" (Canetto and Sakinofsky 1998). Although females attempt suicide more often than males do, they die less often than males from the attempts (the difference in part relates to access to the most lethal means of killing). The high rates of nonfatal suicide attempts by women may inflate sex differences in suicide mortality because, although social conditions may produce similar problems among men and women, women respond to the problems by attempting suicide while men respond not only by attempting but by actually accomplishing suicide. However, disparities between men and women in the lethality of suicide attempts again relate to forces of social change. Traditional cultural expectations view suicide as masculine behavior and attempting suicide as female behavior. Social differences between men and women affect how they express their anguish, which affects the outcome of suicide. Yet social changes should modify gender-based definitions of suicidal behavior. As roles of men and women converge, women should come to have the same deadly intentions as men and their rates of suicide mortality will increase relative to men. Rather than viewing the gender paradox as a source of bias, one can treat it as part of the social conditions that affect relative male and female suicide.

Conclusion

The separate study of male and female mortality in previous chapters allowed only brief comparisons of sex differences in suicide and homicide. Although similarities exist between absolute levels of violent mortality and sex differences in violent mortality, arguments about the consequences of gender equality warrant the more precise comparisons that come from examining relative rates of mortality. Indeed, much debate exists over the effects of increased female work and related family changes on relative female mortality. A reduction-in-protection argument claims that similar patterns of work between men and women will reduce or eliminate the female mortality advantage; a reduction-in-inequality argument claims, in opposition, that the traditional lower status and restricted work opportunities of women mask the potential for an even larger female mortality advantage. Contributing to the debate, the empirical evidence has not yet identified clear support for either convergence or divergence in violent mortality rates between men and women.

Just as much of the diversity in the effects of cohort size on mortality results from varied relationships across ages, nations, and time, much of the diversity in the effects of female work and related changes on relative mortality also may result from varied relationships across ages, nations, and time. An institutional adjustment hypothesis explains how processes of change differ across these contexts. It predicts that changes toward gender equality in an environment supportive of traditional roles will initially reduce the female advantage in mortality but will subsequently increase the female advantage as the environment becomes more supportive of women's independence. It predicts, further, that changes in the direction of influence of gender equality will occur more quickly at younger ages and in nations with collectivist or women-friendly institutions. Both theories of protection and inequality receive support in the hypothesis but only when limited to time, age, and national contexts unsupportive and supportive, respectively, of women's work outside the family. Finally, the nature of homicide mixes the separate behaviors of offenders and victims and, therefore, may provide weaker support for the hypothesis than suicide.

As applied to female suicide and homicide victimization, the institutional adjustment hypothesis provides a special perspective on the more general sex differential in life expectancy. Whereas the overall female advantage has grown for decades and only recently leveled off, the violent mortality advantage of women has, according to the hypothesis, followed a different pattern of change—it has declined and then risen. Given their more immediate response to changing gender roles, suicide and homicide mortality may provide a clearer demonstration of the causal effects of gender equality than heart disease or cancer mortality. Perhaps suicide and homicide mortality may even foretell of changes to come in other types of mortality but, if not, can still bring useful insights to debates over the consequences of gender equality.

The next two chapters test the arguments presented in this chapter about relative mortality rates for men and women. The tests use the same data, measures, and methods as the previous two chapters, except that the dependent variables measure relative rather than absolute suicide and homicide rates. Thus, the sample consists of 18 nations over the 40 years from 1955 to 1994 and includes seven adult age groups (15–24, 25–34, 35–44, 45–54, 55–64, 65–74, 75 and over).[10] Pooling data for these nations, years, and ages creates a sample size of 5,040. As discussed in previous chapters, the suicide and homicide data come from the World Health Organization and measure deaths per 100,000 in the specified sex and age group for each nation and year. The substantive variables—the female labor force participation rate, the marriage, divorce, and total fertility rates, the unemployment rate, and national product—vary only by nation and year. The lack of age-specific figures for these measures weakens the results, but using the crude measures is better than ignoring the substantive determinants altogether.

With pooled data, the models of relative suicide and homicide rates require controls for the nation, time, and age dimensions that structure the data. National differences are represented by a set of dummy variables, but time and age differences are treated as quadratics to capture the predicted U-shaped relationships. The substantive variables are also treated as quadratics to capture nonlinearity. As described in appendix B, the model estimates come from a version of generalized least squares (GLS) recommended by Beck and Katz (1995) that adjusts for serial correlation and heteroscedasticity. The model coefficients and t-ratios reported in the tables that follow in chapters 10 and 11 have the same interpretation as in ordinary regression but have been adjusted for problems stemming from the nonrandom structure of the data.

CHAPTER 10

Sex Differences in Suicide Rates

The study of sex differences in suicide mortality raises issues and tests arguments that the separate study of male and female suicide rates neglect. Measures of female suicide rates relative to male rates tap different processes than measures of absolute rates of male and female suicide and need not relate to social conditions in the same way as measures of absolute rates. In examining the gap between female and male suicide, then, this chapter addresses a new set of theoretical issues relating to changes in the status of women and the national institutions that promote or obstruct those changes rather than to changes in cohort size. It tests a hypothesis of institutional adjustment that posits an increase and then a decrease in relative female suicide mortality, similar curvilinear relationships for dimensions of women's status related to work involvement and family ties, and variation across ages and nations in the curvilinear relationships of time, female work, and family ties to relative female suicide rates.

Testing these predictions for relative rates of female and male mortality requires a measure that combines the two sex-specific rates. First, a common measure of the sex differential simply divides one rate by the other. The ratio of male suicide rates to female suicide rates describes the proportional excess of the former over the latter for each nation, year, and age group. As a measure of excess male suicide, the ratio also represents the size of the female advantage (i.e., the greater the male excess, the greater the female advantage). However, ratio measures remain sensitive to the size of the denominator: they are undefined if the women's suicide rate equals zero and tend toward infinity as the rate approaches zero. Moreover, taking male suicide rates as the denominator changes the implicit standard of comparison, can alter the ranking of the ratio values, and makes results dependent on an arbitrary choice. The lack of symmetry shows in the ratios for the same sample of 18 nations, 40 years, and seven age groups used in previous chapters. After adding one to both the male and female suicide rates to avoid dividing by zero, calculating the male rate divided by the female rate and the female rate divided by the male rate demonstrates the importance of the choice of the numerator and denominator. The correlation between the two ratios equals only $-.76$ when ideally it should equal -1.00.

Second, taking the natural log of the ratio of male and female suicide rates (plus one) solves the problem of symmetry. Equivalent to the log of the male rate minus the log of the female rate, the log of the ratio of male to female suicide rates gives the inverse of the log of the ratio of female to male suicide rates. For the United States in 1994 at ages 15–24, the male to female ratio equals 6.32 and the log of the ratio equals 1.84; the log of 0.158, the reciprocal of 6.32, equals -1.84. The correlation between the two logs across all cases therefore equals -1.00. In terms of interpretation, the logged ratio measures the percentage difference between male and female suicide rates. By discounting absolute differences at high levels of suicide relative to differences at low levels of suicide, the logged ratio assumes that the same difference in the suicide ratio counts less at higher levels.[1] Such a transformation helps normalize skewed variables and corresponds to the logged measures of suicide rates used in previous chapters.

Third, another measure of the sex differential avoids the denominator problem by comparing one rate to the other rate on the basis of a normative standard (Preston 1976). A residual-based measure first computes the linear, symmetric relationship between male and female suicide rates and, then, uses the empirical relationship to predict the expected male suicide rate given a particular female suicide rate. The difference between the actual male rate and the male rate predicted from the female rate and the average relationship thus measures excess male suicide. As a symmetric measure, the residual for female suicide equals the inverse of the male residual and does not depend on the choice of a denominator. One can interpret the measure as deviations from the expected in terms of suicides per 100,000, with positive values indicating relatively high male suicide rates (or a high female advantage) and negative values indicating relatively low male suicide rates (or a low female advantage).

An orthogonal or symmetric regression of male suicide rates on female suicide rates across all ages, nations, and years gives the following equation (where SR_m^* equals the predicted male suicide rate and SR_f equals the female suicide rate):

$$SR_m^* = 5.17 + 2.196 \times SR_f.$$

The intercept reflects the lower female suicide rates compared to male rates: when the female suicide rate equals zero, the predicted male rate equals 5.17. The slope shows that for each additional female suicide per 100,000 population, male suicides increase, on average, by 2.196 per 100,000 population. As female suicide rates rise, male suicide rates rise more than twice as fast. Based on the equation, the measure of the female advantage in suicide computes the residual from the predicted male suicide rate. The higher the score, the larger the relative male suicide rate and the greater the female advantage. The residual deviation has both positive and negative scores, with negative scores meaning that the female advantage and the male disadvantage in suicide is smaller than average.

For example, the male and female suicide rates for the United States in 1994 for persons ages 15–24 equal 23.4 and 3.7, respectively. Substituting the female rate into the regression equation gives a predicted male rate of 13.3, and the residual deviation measure of the female advantage equals 10.1. Hence, 10 more male suicides per 100,000 population occurred in the United States than would be expected from female suicides. If the female suicide rate had been used as the dependent variable and as the basis for the residual, the score would equal −10.1.

All three measures have advantages. The suicide ratio has an appealingly simple interpretation but depends on the arbitrary choice of the denominator. The residual deviation measure is symmetric and maintains the original units of the suicide rates but requires the unfamiliar interpretation of residuals. The logged ratio is symmetric but shifts the focus to percentage differences. The correlation between the suicide ratio and the logged suicide ratio equals .929, while the correlations of the two ratios with the residual deviation measure equal .738 and .822.[2] The analyses to follow compare the results for all three measures.

Descriptive Statistics

To describe the dependent variables and their patterns across nations, table 32 lists the means for the three measures for each of the 18 nations and for all nations combined. The means for all nations demonstrate the predominance of male suicide. According to the mean suicide ratio of 2.76, male suicide rates on average exceed female suicide rates by 176%. The mean for the logged ratio indicates that logged male suicide rates exceed logged female suicide rates by 0.93. The mean for the residual deviation measure equals zero because the standardization procedure takes scores as deviations from the average excess in male suicide or the average female advantage.

Table 32. Mean Relative Suicide Rates by Nation and Time Period

Nation	Suicide Ratio	Logged Ratio	Residual Deviation
Australia	2.87	.992	.226
Austria	2.79	1.00	5.54
Belgium	2.48	.865	1.02
Canada	3.30	1.15	3.27
Denmark	2.05	.684	−10.9
Finland	4.43	1.42	21.4
France	2.90	1.04	8.14
Germany	2.34	.834	−3.12
Ireland	3.01	.960	−2.18
Italy	2.54	.884	−.670
Japan	1.68	.489	−21.6
Netherlands	1.79	.542	−8.56
New Zealand	2.94	.954	−.864
Norway	3.23	1.09	.845
Sweden	2.75	.961	2.78
Switzerland	2.81	1.00	4.92
United Kingdom	2.05	.667	−7.10
United States	3.61	1.21	6.77
Total	2.76	.930	.00
1955–64	2.83	.940	.593
1965–74	2.56	.857	−1.94
1975–84	2.60	.885	−1.35
1985–94	3.03	1.04	2.70

The nation-specific means show considerable variation around the average. According to the suicide ratio and the logged ratio, Finland has the largest male excess in suicide, followed by the United States, Canada, and Norway. At the other extreme, Japan, the Netherlands, Denmark, and the United Kingdom have low relative rates. The patterns relate slightly to the levels of suicide overall. The correlations of male suicide rates with the ratio and logged ratio equal, respectively, .23 and .28. The patterns likewise do not relate clearly to any regional or cultural grouping of nations. Both Scandinavian and English-speaking nations range from low to high on the suicide differential. As a result, the correlations of the suicide ratio and logged ratio with collectivism equal only −.077 and −.080 and with women-friendly institutions equal only .065 and .116.[3]

The national differentials do not show any relationship to another commonly studied national characteristic—the percentage of Catholics. Among predominately Catholic nations, France and Ireland have low relative female suicide rates, Austria has moderate relative female suicide rates, and Belgium and Italy have high relative female suicide rates. Further, the correlations between the percentage of Catholics and the two measures of the sex differential in suicide rates equal only −.014 and .033. National Catholicism affects neither the absolute levels of suicide rates for men and women nor the relative rates.

The residual deviation measure requires a special interpretation but ranks the nations similarly. Positive scores denote excess male suicide (a female advantage), and negative scores denote low male suicide relative to the average or standard (a smaller female advantage). Finland again has the highest male excess, followed by France, the United States, Austria, and Switzerland. Canada and Norway rank highly on the ratio measures but near the middle on the residual deviation measure. At the other extreme, Japan, Denmark, the Netherlands, and the United Kingdom rank lowest on the residual deviation measure, just as they do on the ratio measures. Again, the national patterns for the residual deviation measure do not match regional, cultural, or political groupings. The measure has correlations of only −.014 and .243 with the measures of collectivist and women-friendly institutions, respectively.

Perhaps more important than national differences for the test of the institutional adjustment hypothesis are the trends over time in relative suicide rates. Table 32 presents a preliminary view of these trends by listing means for four time periods. For each measure, the means decline from the 1950s to the early 1970s but rise afterward. The residual deviation, for example, shows the lowest mean female advantage of −1.94 in the 1965–74 period. The reversal of the direction of change offers initial evidence of curvilinear trends in relative suicide rates.

The general trend in relative suicide rates might, however, vary by age group. Table 33 investigates age differences by presenting means across all nations for the four time periods within each of three broad age groups: 15–34, 35–54, and 65 and over. First, consider age differences in the size of the sex differential. The mean suicide ratio of 2.75 for persons ages 15–34 declines during middle age to 2.37 and then rises during old age to 3.33. The logged suicide ratio and the residual deviation measure reveal the same pattern across ages: suicide rates among men and women emerge as most similar during middle age.

The trends over time within age groups replicate the curvilinear pattern found for all age groups combined. The female advantage in suicide declines and then increases, but the timing of the reversal varies across age groups. Among those under age 35, the reversal occurs early, while among those age 35 and over, the reversal occurs later. For example, the mean suicide ratio for youth bottoms out at 2.32 in the 1965–74 period; the

Table 33. Mean Relative Suicide Rates by Age and Time Period

Year	Young (15–34)			Middle Aged (35–64)			Old (65+)		
	Suicide Ratio	Logged Ratio	Residual Deviation	Suicide Ratio	Logged Ratio	Residual Deviation	Suicide Ratio	Logged Ratio	Residual Deviation
Time period means:									
1955–64	2.39	.807	−3.80	2.55	.876	−.795	3.68	1.17	7.07
1965–74	2.32	.790	−3.38	2.25	.761	−4.30	3.27	1.07	3.05
1975–84	2.85	1.00	.853	2.17	.735	−5.34	3.01	.994	2.44
1985–94	3.44	1.19	4.46	2.53	.891	−1.54	3.37	1.10	7.28
Total	2.75	.947	−.467	2.37	.816	−3.00	3.33	1.08	4.96
OLS trend coefficients:									
Time	−.030	−.007	−.026[a]	−.065	−.026	−.742	−.094	−.024	−.816
Time^2	.0016	.0005	.0076	.0016	.0006	.0173	.0020	.0005	.0198
Year of minimum value	1963	1961	1956	1974	1976	1975	1978	1978	1975

[a] Not statistically significant; all other coefficients are significant at the .01 level.

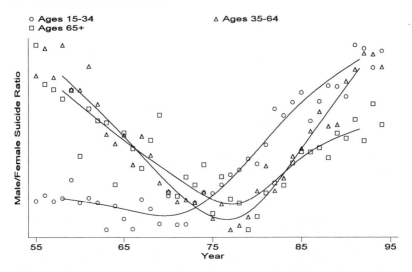

Figure 14. Male/Female Suicide Ratio Trends, 18-Nation Means

same ratio bottoms out at 2.17 in the 1975–84 period among the middle aged, and at 3.01 in the 1975–84 period among the elderly.

To describe these trends more precisely, figure 14 plots the yearly suicide ratios averaged across all nations for the three age groups. Since the ratios fluctuate considerably from year to year, the graph smooths the curves using a moving-average and spline function.[4] In figure 14, all age groups display the curvilinear, U-shaped trend in relative suicide rates, but the trend for youth differs from the trends at older ages. For persons 15–34, a slight decline in the female advantage occurs during the 1950s and 1960s, and a large increase begins in the early 1970s. Rates for the two older age groups decline more dramatically until the mid-1970s and rise almost as dramatically afterward. The figures for the logged suicide ratio and the residual deviation measure identify nearly the same curvilinear patterns in the trends.

Modeling the sex differential in suicide rates as a function of time and time squared efficiently summarizes and compares the nonlinear relationships. Within each age group, regressing the measure of the sex differential on time and time squared yields the coefficients listed in the bottom rows of table 33. All the time coefficients are negative and all the time-squared coefficients are positive, which indicates that the female advantage initially declines, then subsequently increases. For the suicide ratio, for example, the unstandardized coefficient for time equals -0.030 and the unstandardized coefficient for time squared equals 0.0016. Based on these two coefficients, the minimum value of the differential—indicating the greatest similarity in male and female suicide rates—occurs in 1963. Before that year, female suicide rates rose more quickly or declined more slowly than male suicide rates did; after those years, male suicide rates rose more quickly or declined more slowly than female suicide rates did.

Although they illustrate the same general curvilinear pattern, the regression coefficients and year of reversal differ across age groups. The differentials bottom out early among the young, by the early 1960s. For middle-aged persons, they shift direction in the mid-1970s, while for older persons they do not shift direction until the mid- to late 1970s. Consistent with predictions, female suicide rates relative to male suicide rates rise and then decline for all age groups but shift direction earlier for younger persons.

The interaction between time and age in table 33 represents a crude way to capture cohort effects without introducing the identification problems associated with measuring age, time, and birth cohort directly. Since the effects of time vary by age group, they show the impact of cohorts filtering through different ages. The age and time results indicate that newer cohorts entering the younger ages did not experience the same disruption from social change or benefit from the subsequent adjustment as much as did the older cohorts.

Multivariate Results

Additive Effects. Next, I examine the effects of the substantive variables on sex differentials in suicide rates net of the influence of the nation, time, and age variables that structure the data. Table 34 presents multivariate results for time, age, and three time-varying substantive variables—the female labor force participation rate, the divorce rate, and the marriage rate—related to women's status. These variables differ across nations and years but not across age groups. Still, when treated as second-order polynomials, they can capture the nonlinearity specified by the institutional adjustment hypothesis. (The models also include dummy variables for each nation, but because their coefficients reflect the patterns shown earlier, they are not included in table 34).

Most, but not all of the variables in the multivariate equation have the curvilinear coefficients predicted by the institutional adjustment hypothesis. As indicated by the negative and positive coefficients for time and time squared, the female advantage in suicide rates first declines then rises.

Table 34. Unstandardized Coefficients and *t*-Ratios for Regression of Measures of Relative Suicide Rates on Female Work and Family Variables—Additive Models

Independent Variables	Suicide Ratio		Logged Ratio		Residual Deviation	
	Coefficient	*t*-Ratio	Coefficient	*t*-Ratio	Coefficient	*t*-Ratio
Time	−.065	6.44	−.019	7.13	−.522	6.44
Time^2	.0018	7.54	.0006	9.05	.016	8.23
Age	−.117	13.7	−.033	14.7	−.910	12.7
Age^2	.0013	15.4	.0004	16.3	.010	14.6
FLFP	.062	1.82	.020	2.20	.456	1.70
FLFP^2	−.0010	2.06	−.0003	2.63	−.009	2.26
Marriage rate	.671	3.50	.233	4.53	6.08	4.05
Marriage rate^2	−.047	3.57	−.017	4.71	−.418	4.07
Divorce rate	−.192	1.25	−.059	1.45	−.375	0.31
Divorce rate^2	.054	2.03	.018	2.47	.185	0.87
Constant	2.16		.630		−9.23	
df	5,012		5,012		5,012	
R^2—OLS	.4375		.4941		.4986	

Note. FLFP = female labor force participation.

Across ages, the female advantage in suicide rates drops from youth to middle age but then rises again in old age.[5] Of the substantive variables, the marriage rate most consistently relates nonlinearly to the sex differentials in suicide rates and most clearly supports the institutional adjustment hypothesis. Because the marriage rate declines over time, it has a positive coefficient for the unsquared term and a negative coefficient for the squared term; declining marriage initially lowers the female advantage but later increases it.

The coefficients for the divorce rate support the predictions for the ratio measures but not for the residual deviation measure. For the ratio measures, negative and positive coefficients suggest that rising divorce rates initially contribute to equality in male and female suicide rates but later contribute to the female advantage. The coefficient for the unsquared term does not reach statistical significance, which suggests a small or near-zero initial decline in the female suicide advantage; the significant coefficient for the squared term, however, demonstrates the rise in the advantage after a period of little change. The coefficients of the divorce rate and the divorce rate squared for the residual deviation measure have the expected signs but do not reach statistical significance.

The coefficients for the female labor force participation rate do not, however, support the predictions. The signs of the coefficients indicate a rising female advantage before a declining female advantage—just the opposite of predictions. Perhaps the crude measure of female work, which does not distinguish between homemakers and retirees, full- and part-time employment, and low- and high-status jobs, cannot fully capture the harm or benefit of labor force involvement. In addition, the national context may hide the harm or benefit of female work in the additive models. Before rejecting the hypothesis with regard to female work, some additional analyses are needed.

Some simple computations can summarize the strength of the curvilinear relationships. Creating a new variable from the sum of the unsquared and squared terms multiplied by their coefficients in table 34 and substituting these new variables into a regression produces a measure of the combined explanatory power of each quadratic.[6] For the logged suicide ratio, the curvilinear terms for age have the largest summary standardized coefficient of 0.328; the time terms follow in size with a standardized coefficient of 0.188. The marriage rate, divorce rate, and female labor force participation rate, again treated as summaries of the quadratic terms, have standardized coefficients of 0.108, 0.074, and 0.054, respectively. The polynomial specification performs better than the linear specification does, but the substantive variables have relatively weak effects.

Other variables show no linear or curvilinear effects on the sex differential in suicide. The equations delete the total fertility rate and real national product because of their lack of influence. Another equation examines the effects of the unemployment rate and the unemployment rate squared on the sex differential for the shorter time span from 1959 to 1994. Neither term for unemployment has a significant effect on the sex differential or changes the effects of the other determinants. The results indicate that unemployment affects male and female suicide rates similarly.

Collectivist and Women-Friendly Institutions. Although the theoretical discussion emphasizes the impact of national context on the processes that cause female and male suicide rates, the results thus far assume that the effects of the determinants do not vary across nations. Averaged over all nations, the effects of time in table 34 show a decrease in the sex differential in suicide rates during the 1950s and 1960s and an increase in the differential during the 1970s and 1980s. If national characteristics ease the adjustment process, the decline and subsequent increase may prove smaller in some nations than in others. The nonlinear effects of the female labor force participation rate, the divorce rate, or the marriage rate could likewise respond to the specifying influence of national environments.

If the effects of time vary by nation, it will show in the coefficients for product terms of time and time squared by the two measures of national context, collectivist and women-friendly institutions. According to the theoretical arguments, the interaction terms should moderate the initial decline in the female advantage. Nations with weak collectivist or women-friendly institutions should experience a strong reversal in the consequences of social change, and nations with strong collectivist or women-friendly institutions should experience a more linear increase in the female advantage in suicide. The first four rows of table 35 display coefficients for time, time squared, time by collectivism, and time squared by collectivism for each of the three measures of relative suicide rates. The next four rows display the same coefficients for the interactions with the measure of women-friendly institutions.

To interpret these results, consider an example. For the suicide ratio, the coefficients for time and time squared represent effects at the mean of zero for collectivism. The significant and negative coefficient for time and the significant and positive coefficient for time squared replicate the general

Table 35. Unstandardized Coefficients and *t*-Ratios for Regression of Measures of Relative Suicide Rates on Time, Collectivism, and Gender Scale—Nation Interaction Models

Independent Variables	Suicide Ratio		Logged Ratio		Residual Deviation	
	Coefficient	*t*-Ratio	Coefficient	*t*-Ratio	Coefficient	*t*-Ratio
Time:						
Collectivism						
Time	−.064	7.13	−.019	7.75	−.495	6.60
Time^2	.0017	7.96	.0005	9.34	.014	7.70
Time × collectivism	.012	1.26	.005	2.19	.058	0.75
Time^2 × collectivism	−.0006	2.73	−.0002	3.88	−.0036	2.01
Gender						
Time	−.063	6.98	−.018	7.55	−.493	6.55
Time^2	.0017	7.76	.0005	9.06	.013	7.59
Time × gender	.015	1.31	.007	2.18	.048	0.49
Time^2 × gender	−.0007	2.55	−.0003	3.76	−.0048	2.12
FLFP:						
Collectivism						
FLFP	−.060	1.73	−.016	1.69	−.365	1.27
FLFP^2	.0012	2.27	.0004	2.54	.0078	1.82
FLFP × collectivism	.079	2.42	.027	3.07	.775	2.87
FLFP^2 × collectivism	−.0015	3.16	−.0005	3.89	−.0139	3.51
Gender						
FLFP	−.060	1.69	−.017	1.80	−.511	1.75
FLFP^2	.0011	2.07	.0003	2.43	.0089	2.12
FLFP × gender	.046	0.92	.013	0.93	.532	1.29
FLFP^2 × gender	−.0013	1.77	−.0004	1.96	−.0134	2.31

Note. FLFP = female labor force participation.

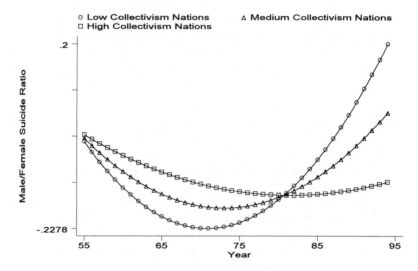

Figure 15. Male/Female Suicide Ratio Trends by Collectivism

curvilinear pattern found previously. More important, the coefficient for time by collectivism is positive (but not significant) and the coefficient for time squared by collectivism is negative and significant. The interaction terms thus balance the additive terms—collectivism moderates the negative effect of time and moderates the positive effect of time squared. Compared to the average, collectivist nations experience a smaller initial decline and a smaller rebound in the female suicide advantage and, thereby, weaken the negative consequences of social change for women's relative suicide. Conversely, individualist nations experience a larger initial decline in the female advantage than the average and, then, experience a larger rebound than the average. The interactions emerge stronger for the logged suicide ratio and weaker for the residual deviation measure but demonstrate much the same patterns.

The results for the interactions of time with the measure of women-friendly institutions confirm the existence of national differences in the consequences of social change for sex differences in suicide. Again, the signs of the coefficients for the time interaction terms contrast with the signs of the coefficients for time and time squared. The opposite signs mean that nations with women-friendly institutions experience a smaller drop and smaller rebound in the female advantage in suicide with social change than do nations without such institutions. In terms of strength, the coefficients involving women-friendly institutions differ little from those for collectivism. Both class-based and gender-based policies ease the harm of social change for female suicide mortality.

Some simple calculations can illustrate the differences across nations. Using the coefficients for the logged suicide ratio and collectivism, the coefficients for time and time squared can be calculated at three levels of collectivism. (The results differ little for levels of women-friendly institutions.) When collectivism equals −1.5 (roughly the value for the United States), the coefficients equal −0.026 and 0.0008; when collectivism equals 0 (roughly the value for Germany), the coefficients equal −0.019 and 0.0005; when collectivism equals 1.5 (roughly the value for Sweden), the coefficients equal −0.011 and 0.0002. Figure 15, which graphs the curves defined by these three sets of coefficients, depicts the differences implied by these three sets of coefficients. Individualist nations show the largest initial drop and the largest reversal, while collectivist nations show a smaller decrease and increase. In visual terms, then, the graph supports the hypothesis about differences across nations in the adjustment of institutions to social change.

Similar if somewhat weaker results emerge when testing for national

Table 36. Unstandardized Coefficients for Regression of the Logged Suicide Ratio on Time and Female Labor Force Participation Polynomials—Nation-Specific Models

Nation	Logged Ratio Coefficients		Logged Ratio Coefficients		Collectivist Institutions Score	Gender Institutions Score
	Time	Time^2	FLFP	FLFP^2		
Australia	−.037	.0011	−.157	.0028	−1.00	−.91
Austria	.011	−.0001	.065	−.0010	.83	.81
Belgium	−.024	.0005	−.278	.0049	.23	.83
Canada	−.026	.0007	−.080	.0013	−1.23	−.68
Denmark	−.019	.0005	−.117	.0014	1.17	.69
Finland	−.004	.0001	.107	−.0013	.53	.69
France	−.014	.0003	−.272	.0040	−.84	1.29
Germany	−.010	.0004	−.119	.0021	.06	.20
Ireland	−.036	.0010	.337	−.0060	−.55	−.52
Italy	−.016	.0005	.059	−.0007	−.65	−.06
Japan	−.013	.0005	−.489	.0067	−.32	−1.22
Netherlands	−.012	.0004	−.039	.0008	1.02	−.20
New Zealand	−.031	.0010	.015	.0000	−.83	−.91
Norway	−.019	.0003	−.015	.0001	1.68	.39
Sweden	−.021	.0003	−.111	.0011	1.51	1.15
Switzerland	−.016	.0003	−.265	.0034	.71	−.85
United Kingdom	−.032	.0011	−.465	.0071	−.76	−.50
United States	−.023	.0007	−.157	.0024	−1.62	−.78

Note. FLFP = female labor force participation.

differences in the influence of female labor force participation. Table 35 presents the effects of the female labor force participation rate, the female labor force participation rate squared, collectivism by the female labor force participation rate, and collectivism by the female labor force participation rate squared. It also presents the coefficients for the interactions of the female labor force participation rate with women-friendly institutions. At the mean of the collectivism scale, the coefficients for female work and female work squared exhibit the expected negative and positive signs. The coefficients for the product terms have the opposite signs of the coefficients for the nonproduct terms, reaffirming that collectivist institutions moderate the harm of female work for relative female suicide rates. Weaker results emerge for the interactions involving the measure of women-friendly institutions. The findings for female labor force participation support the predictions about national differences in the processes determining the sex differential in suicide but not as strongly as the findings for the time variable.

Similar tests do not reveal differences across nations in the curvilinear effects of the marriage and divorce rates, however. The coefficients of the product terms for these variables do not reach statistical significance. Both divorce and marriage have effects on relative suicide rates that reverse direction, but the reversal appears similar across all nations.

National Differences. If the product-term coefficients seems excessively abstract, the differences across nations in the influence of time and female work on the sex differential in suicide can be presented in another form. Using product terms for each nation produces unstandardized coefficients for time and time squared and for female work and female work squared for each nation.[7] Table 36 lists the nation-specific coefficients for the polynomials predicting the logged suicide ratio. A negative coefficient for time and a positive coefficient for time squared indicate in rough terms an initial decline in excess male suicide deaths that eventually becomes an increase. Such a pattern of coefficients appears for Australia, Canada, Ireland, New Zealand, the United Kingdom, and the United States—all nations with low collectivism scores. High-collectivist nations such as Austria, Finland, and the Netherlands, in contrast, have a positive or small negative coefficient for time. Although several nations (particularly Sweden, Norway, and Belgium) deviate from the expected pattern, a tendency exists for different trends in the relative female advantage in suicide rates to emerge in the two types of nations.

A crude but helpful way to summarize the relationship between collectivism and the nonlinear trend in relative suicide rates involves correlating collectivism scores with the quadratic coefficients for the 18 nations. The collectivism scores correlate .464 and −.646 with the time and time-squared coefficients predicting the logged suicide ratio. The women-friendly institutions scores similarly correlate .470 and −.642 with the time and time-squared coefficients. Confirming previous findings, both collectivist and women-friendly institutions moderate the consequences of social change for women's relative well-being. The correlations indicate that nations with collectivist and women-friendly institutions tend to have small negative coefficients for time and small positive coefficients for time squared, thus reflecting a weaker nonlinear relationship with the female advantage in suicide rates. Other nations tend to have relatively large negative coefficients for time and relatively large positive coefficients for time squared, indicating a stronger response and reversal of relative female suicide to social change.

Table 36 also presents nation-specific coefficients for the female labor force participation rate polynomials. According to these results, collectivist and women-friendly institutions affect the influence of female work less clearly than they affect the influence of time. At one extreme, Japan, the United Kingdom, Belgium, France, and Switzerland have the largest negative coefficients for female work and the largest positive coefficient for female work squared. At the other extreme, Ireland, Italy, Finland, and Austria have positive coefficients for female work and negative coefficients for female work squared. The pattern thus corresponds only loosely to the measures of collectivist and women-friendly institutions. The correlations with the unsquared and squared female work coefficients equal only .142 and −.170 for collectivism and .157 and −.137 for women-friendly institutions. The direction of the correlations matches the expected pattern of differences across nations, but the small size of the correlations emphasizes the weakness of the relationships. The female labor force participation rate does not do as well as the time variables in capturing changes in relative female suicide rates.

Measurement Error

Concerns about measurement error in suicide statistics have less validity for relative suicide rates than they have for absolute suicide rates. Measurement bias can affect relative rates only when the efforts to hide suicides differ for men and women and when the efforts vary across the nations and years. Yet little evidence suggests that such bias exists and can explain the curvilinear effects of social change and women's equality on relative suicide rates. To explain these results, changes in gender equality would have to reduce misclassified female suicide initially but then lead to an increase in misclassified female suicide rates that again exaggerates the female advantage. Given this unlikely scenario, the results of the analysis discount the possibility that they could spuriously stem from flaws in official suicide statistics.

Still, tests can help demonstrate the robustness of the empirical results in the presence of measurement error. If the false classification of many suicide deaths as accidental deaths or as deaths from unknown causes spuriously produces relationships between time or women's status and relative suicide rates, then controlling for relative levels of accident and unknown mortality as independent variables should substantially weaken the previous results. Such a weakening seems unlikely, however. The correlation between the logged suicide ratio and the logged accident ratio equals only $-.157$, and the correlation between the logged suicide ratio and the logged unknown mortality ratio equals only $-.164$. Not surprisingly, then, if the other relative mortality measures are included as independent variables predicting the logged suicide ratio, they do not have significant effects.[8]

Another way to control for the misclassification of male and female suicide rates comes from adding the accident and unknown mortality ratios to the dependent suicide ratio. Again, if the false classification of many suicide deaths as accident deaths or as death from unknown causes spuriously produces relationships, controlling for accident and unknown mortality in the dependent variable should eliminate the curvilinear effects of time and other variables. In fact, the model for the dependent variable combining suicide, accident, and unknown mortality ratios changes the results only slightly. Time, age, the marriage rate, and the divorce rate continue to have nonlinear effects, but the t-ratios for the coefficients sometimes decline to below statistical significance. Some changes in the models might be expected given the substantial variation added to the dependent variable by accident and unknown mortality. Still, since the adjustment weakens but does not eliminate the results supportive of the hypotheses, it increases confidence in the robustness of the findings.

Conclusion

By testing arguments about institutional adjustment to social change, this chapter moves beyond simplistic claims that gender equality produces either convergence or divergence in the suicide rates of men and women.

These arguments combine claims about protection and inequality by suggesting that both processes occur in sequence: change initially disrupts traditional values, creating normative uncertainty and role ambiguity among women, but institutions eventually adapt to pressures for change, new norms gain wide acceptance, and anomie declines. Because the social context gradually changes over time in ways that alter the social determinants of mortality, the female advantage in suicide rates should decline initially, but then rise. The institutional adjustment hypothesis thus predicts curvilinear effects of time, female labor force participation, and divorce or nonmarriage on relative suicide rates. Increases at low levels of these variables initially reduce the female advantage in suicide rates, but increases at higher levels of these variables augment the female advantage.

Recognizing the contingency of the relationship between gender equality and relative suicide mortality emphasizes the importance of the social and political context of gender change. The lower the status of women, the weaker their involvement in the world of work and the stronger their attachment to family roles, the greater the harm of change toward gender equality for suicide mortality. The higher the status of women, the greater their involvement in the world of work and the weaker their dependence on men and family roles for economic well-being, the less the harm (or the greater the benefit) of change toward gender equality for suicide mortality. In this way, the level of gender equality specifies the relationship between changes in gender equality and suicide rates.

The level of gender equality relates to three dimensions of social context—time, age, and nation. The institutional adjustment hypothesis predicts that, over time, the initial movement from low status to higher status may produce higher female suicide rates but that the adjustment of institutions to women's new roles and status eventually reduces relative female suicide rates. Across ages, the hypothesis predicts quicker adjustment to changes in inequality among younger women than among older women. And across nations, it predicts that slower adjustment will occur in individualist nations with institutions less supportive of women's ability to combine work and family roles than in collectivist nations with institutions more supportive of women's new roles. Variation in the speed of adjustment to gender change across ages and nations, as reflected in the nonlinear determinants of relative female suicide rates, can help identify the presence of institutional supports for women.

The results confirm the institutional adjustment hypothesis across a variety of nations, time periods, and age groups. Nonlinear effects on the sex differential in suicide rates emerge most consistently for time, age, and the marriage rate and less consistently for the female labor force participation rate and the divorce rate. At low levels of these variables, increases tend to reduce the female advantage and promote convergence in male and female suicide rates; at higher levels of these variables, increases tend to raise the female advantage and promote divergence in male and female suicide rates. The results also reveal that the adjustment process, or the reversal of the effects on the female advantage from negative to positive, occurs relatively more quickly among younger persons than among older persons. Similarly, the process occurs less intensely in collectivist nations than in individualist nations and in nations with women-friendly institutions than in nations without such institutions.

Despite measurement bias, differential access to lethal means of death, and the tendency of men and women to respond to personal problems in different ways, the trends and patterns observed in reported suicide rates for men and women relate as expected to macrolevel social, political, and economic determinants, support plausible arguments of institutional adjustment, and identify the benefits of some institutional strategies promoting gender equality relative to others. These findings suggest moving beyond simple predictions of convergence and divergence in male and female suicide rates. Likewise, they suggest avoiding a search for general relationships between social equality between men and women and their relative suicide rates. Instead, studies should attend to the political context of changing gender roles and their demographic consequences.

CHAPTER 11

Sex Differences in Homicide Rates

Despite results for relative suicide rates that generally support the contextual arguments for institutional adjustment, results for homicide rates may well differ. Because homicide reflects the direction of aggressive behavior toward others rather than toward self, it should not respond to social conditions in the same way as suicide. Indeed, since figures on homicide mortality identify characteristics of victims rather than offenders, a comparison of male and female homicide mortality rates cannot isolate the behavior of offenders as well as suicide mortality rates can. Changes in relative female victimization result from changes in any combination of four types of gender-based homicides: male-male, male-female, female-male, and female-female. The potential for cross-sex murder adds a new dimension to the study of sex differences in mortality but also adds measurement difficulties.

To simplify some of the complexities, it helps to assume that, since men often murder women and women rarely murder men, men make up the vast majority of homicide offenders. If so, female victimization primarily reflects the violent behavior of men, and it changes in two ways. On the one hand, improvements in women's status and diversification of their social roles may threaten men in ways that lead them to act more violently toward women and that make women more available as targets of male violence.[1] On the other hand, improvements in women's status may weaken the sense of dominance and control felt by men that justifies violence and may give women the economic opportunity to escape from potentially violent relationships.[2] The first possibility follows a reduction-in-protection perspective, which predicts convergence in male and female victimization rates. The second possibility follows a reduction-in-inequality perspective, which predicts divergence in male and female victimization rates. The institutional adjustment hypothesis suggests, in-

stead, that the two processes emerge in sequence, with convergence in relative homicide rates preceding divergence. Despite the limitations of homicide mortality data, some inferences about male and female violence might
emerge from information on the victim's sex.

This chapter examines the gap between male and female homicide victimization to gain further insight into the consequences for mortality of
changes in the status of women and the national institutions that promote
or obstruct those changes. It again tests a hypothesis of institutional adjustment that posits (1) an increase and then a decrease in relative female
homicide, (2) curvilinear relationships for variables related to women's
status, such as female work and family ties, and (3) variation across ages
and nations in the curvilinear relationships of time, female work, and family ties to relative female homicide rates.

Tests of these predictions for relative rates of female and male homicide
begin with the same three measures of the sex differential in mortality used
for relative suicide rates. First, the homicide ratio divides the male rate by
the female rate to describe the proportional excess of male victimization
for each nation, year, and age group. This measure changes with the choice
of the denominator, however, and has an excessively skewed distribution.[3]
Second, taking the natural log of the ratio of male and female homicide
rates (plus one) solves the problem of symmetry and measures percentage
differences between male and female homicide rates. By correcting for
skewness created by a nation such as the United States with extremely high
homicide rates, the logged ratio also minimizes the influence of outliers.
Since the two ratios correlate at .938 with each other, but the logged measure has better statistical qualities, I drop the homicide ratio from some of
the later analyses.

Third, the residual deviation measure corrects for symmetry and pre-
serves the original units of the homicide rates. An orthogonal or symmetric
regression of male homicide rates on female homicide rates across all ages,
nations, and years gives the following equation (where HR_m^* equals the
predicted male homicide rate and HR_f equals the female homicide rate):

$$HR_m^* = -1.456 + 3.620 \times HR_f.$$

The slope shows that, for each additional female homicide per 100,000
population, male homicides increase, on average, by 3.620 per 100,000
population—more than three and a half times greater than female homicides increase. Because of the steep slope, the intercept falls below zero.[4]
Based on the equation, then, the measure of the female advantage in homicide computes the residual from the predicted male homicide rate. The

higher the score, the larger the relative male homicide rate and the greater the female advantage. The residual deviation measure has correlations of .719 and .723 with the homicide ratio and logged homicide ratio.

Descriptive Statistics

To describe the dependent variables and their patterns across nations, table 37 lists the means for the three measures for each of the 18 nations and for all nations combined. The means for all nations demonstrate the predominance of male homicide but also show smaller gaps between rates for men and women than exist for suicide rates. According to the mean homicide ratio of 1.56, male homicide rates on average exceed female suicide rates by 56%. The mean for the logged ratio indicates that logged male homicide rates exceed logged female homicide rates by 0.34. Likely because of male killings of females, the means are smaller than the means of 2.76 for the suicide ratio and 0.93 for the logged suicide ratio. Just as it does

Table 37. Mean Relative Homicide Rates by Nation and Time Period

Nation	Homicide Ratio	Logged Ratio	Residual Deviation
Australia	1.47	.332	−1.11
Austria	1.30	.175	−1.02
Belgium	1.21	.120	−1.19
Canada	1.65	.468	−.725
Denmark	1.07	−.037	−.692
Finland	2.39	.764	.360
France	1.55	.366	.375
Germany	1.27	.216	−.505
Ireland	1.53	.289	.964
Italy	2.14	.694	1.53
Japan	1.39	.294	.151
Netherlands	1.38	.275	.765
New Zealand	1.59	.267	−.233
Norway	1.48	.272	.415
Sweden	1.36	.237	−.092
Switzerland	1.17	.074	−.621
United Kingdom	1.25	.194	.177
United States	2.92	1.04	1.45
Total	1.56	.336	0.00
1955–64	1.49	.279	.278
1965–74	1.52	.312	.122
1975–84	1.63	.378	−.141
1985–94	1.61	.373	−.259

for suicide, however, the mean for the residual deviation measure equals zero because it treats scores as deviations from the average excess in male homicide.

The nation-specific means show considerable variation around the average. According to the homicide ratio, those nations with the highest male homicide rates—the United States, Italy, and Finland—also have the highest excess in male homicide victimization and the highest female advantage in homicide victimization. Those nations with the smallest sex differential include nations such as Denmark, Belgium, and Switzerland, which have low male homicide mortality. Ironically, women in the United States have the highest homicide mortality rates in the developed world but also have the lowest relative homicide mortality rates because of the extremely high rate of male homicide mortality. It appears that, where overall homicide rates are low, most murders involve intimate partners and deaths of both men and women. Where overall homicide rates are high, many more murders involve conflict between male acquaintances and strangers rather than between male and female intimates, which increases the prevalence of male victims relative to female victims.

In statistical terms, the smaller variation across nations in homicide mortality among women means that the sex differential relates most closely to variation in male homicide mortality. The correlations between male homicide rates and the homicide ratio and logged ratio equal .655 and .584, while the correlations between female homicide rates and the two ratio measures equal .207 and .134. The dominant influence of male rates on the ratio measures appears in the high positive correlation of male homicide rates with the female relative advantage. More surprising, but consistent with the figures for the United States, high female homicide rates also correlate positively with the female advantage because high female rates are associated with even higher male rates.

The ordering of the nations for the residual deviation measure differs in some ways from the ordering for the ratios. The United States and Italy have the highest scores, but Finland falls closer to the mean of zero. Belgium, Australia, and Austria have the lowest residual scores.

The national patterns in the sex differentials relate only weakly to regional, cultural, or political groupings of nations. Demonstrating variation within regions and cultures, Finland has one of the largest sex differentials, while Denmark has one of the smallest. Among English-speaking nations, the United States has one of the largest sex differentials, while Australia has one of the smallest. In terms of political groupings, the collectivism scale has correlations of −.262 and −.277 with the homicide ratio and the logged ratio. Because the ratio measures relate closely to levels of male homicide and because collectivist nations have lower levels of male homicide, collectivism correlates negatively with the female advantage. More independent of the levels of male homicide, the residual deviation measure has a correlation of only −.079 with collectivism. The measure of women-friendly institutions has weak negative correlations (the largest being −.084) with all three measures.

More important than national differences for the test of the institutional adjustment hypothesis are the trends over time in relative homicide rates. Table 37 presents a preliminary view of these trends by listing means for four time periods. For the ratio measures, the mean sex differential rises from the 1950s to the early 1980s but levels off in the late 1980s and early 1990s. The homicide ratio of 1.61 in 1984–94, for example, increases by 0.12 from the ratio of 1.49 in 1955–64. In contrast, the residual deviation measure of the female advantage declines over time.

To describe trends for each measure more precisely, figure 16 plots the yearly figures for the homicide ratio, the logged homicide ratio, and the residual deviation measure averaged across all nations and all age groups. Since the ratios fluctuate considerably from year to year, the graph smooths the curves using a moving-average and spline function.[5] In the figure, the

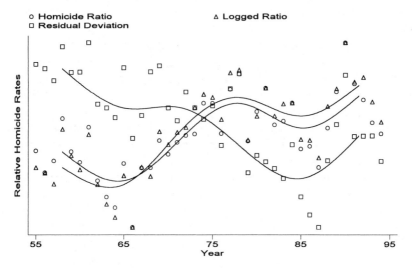

Figure 16. Relative Homicide Trends, 18-Nation Means

ratios generally trend upward, with the fastest rate of increase in the late 1960s and early 1970s. The residual deviation generally trends downward during the same time period. The only similarity appears in the late 1980s and early 1990s, when all measures of the female advantage turn upward. The figure starkly portrays the differences in the measures.

The divergent trends described in table 37 and figure 16 raise measurement concerns. Perhaps either the ratio or residual deviation approach has flaws that distort the patterns of change. Since the residual deviation relates less closely to the level of male homicide, it may do better in isolating changes in female homicide mortality from changes in male homicide mortality. Alternatively, the homicide trends for males and females may differ so little that the relative rates capture little more than random error. In any case, none of the measures of relative homicide rates reveal the U-shaped trend found for the suicide rate or offer support for the institutional adjustment hypothesis.

Consider next the trends in relative homicide rates within age groups. Table 38 investigates age differences by presenting means across all nations for four time periods within each of three broad age groups: 15–34, 35–64, and 65 and over. Averaged across all time periods, the mean homicide ratio of 1.58 for persons ages 15–34 rises during middle age to 1.65 and then falls during old age to 1.41. The residual deviation measure reveals the same pattern across ages, moving from negative to positive and back to negative. Female and male homicide rates emerge as most similar during old age and least similar during middle age.

The trends over time within age groups again demonstrate divergence across the measures. For the youngest age group, the homicide ratio declines slightly and then rises, while the logged ratio rises steadily. The residual deviation measure fluctuates downward and then upward. For the middle-aged group, the trend for the homicide ratio and logged ratio better fits the trend over all age groups: it rises until the late 1980s and early 1990s when it levels off. The residual deviation measure, in contrast, falls steadily. For the oldest age group, the homicide ratio and logged ratio change little until a drop in the last decade. The residual deviation measure declines steadily. The ratio and residual deviation measures again move in opposite directions, and none of the trends follow the expected U-shaped pattern.

To present a more formal test of the trends, the bottom rows of table 38 list the coefficients within each age group from regressing the measures of the sex differential on time and time squared. For the homicide and logged ratios, the coefficients describe either a rise in the female homicide

Table 38. Mean Relative Homicide Rates by Age and Time Period

Year	Young (15–34)			Middle Aged (35–64)			Old (65+)		
	Homicide Ratio	Logged Ratio	Residual Deviation	Homicide Ratio	Logged Ratio	Residual Deviation	Homicide Ratio	Logged Ratio	Residual Deviation
Time period means:									
1955–64	1.50	.272	.196	1.51	.317	.403	1.45	.228	.173
1965–74	1.47	.296	−.090	1.60	.373	.369	1.44	.237	−.035
1975–84	1.62	.394	−.495	1.77	.466	.272	1.43	.230	−.408
1985–94	1.73	.447	−.231	1.73	.451	−.089	1.32	.184	−.543
Total	1.58	.352	−.155	1.65	.402	.239	1.41	.220	−.203
OLS trend coefficients:									
Time	−.007	.002	−.091*	.016*	.010*	.005	.000	.001	−.038
$Time^2$	.0004*	.0001	.0019*	−.0002	−.0001	−.0005	−.0001	−.0001	.0003

*$p < .05$.

advantage or no significant change. The coefficients provide no support for the institutional adjustment hypothesis and most often favor the reduction-in-inequality argument. Again, however, the results for the residual deviation measure offer altogether different conclusions. Among the young, the negative coefficient for time and the positive coefficient for time squared demonstrate the predicted decline and subsequent increase in the female advantage. The middle-aged and older age groups show no significant change. In one sense, the residual deviation measure offers partial support for the institutional adjustment hypothesis. The hypothesis predicts quicker change among the young than the old, and a reversal indeed occurs among the young but not among the old. Yet the weakness of the time relationships and the inability to replicate them for other measures make this conclusion suspect.

These preliminary results are not encouraging for the institutional adjustment hypothesis. Perhaps the extremely high level of male homicide rates in the United States unduly influences the results and distorts relationships among other nations without skewed values. The United States may, in particular, greatly influence the regression model used to compute the residual deviation scores. Therefore, I replicated the measures without the United States and then used the new measures to examine the trends in relative female homicide rates. Without the United States, the regression model used to create the residual deviation measure does change to weaken the slope relating male and female homicide rates. Otherwise, however, the subsample trends do not provide more support for the hypothesis. For the logged ratio, time has positive effects at the young and middle ages and no effects at the older ages. For the revised residual deviation measure, a U-shaped trend emerges for the young but not for the middle aged and old. Again, only one measure for one age group supports the institutional adjustment hypothesis.

Absolute Female Homicide Mortality

A problem with the relative measures of homicide mortality—and a possible source of the weak support for the predictions thus far—comes from the large influence of exogenous variation in male homicide mortality on the relative rates. Measuring female rates relative to male rates ideally isolates unique trends in female rates by controlling for common causes of both male and female homicide mortality. In practice, however, the low variability in female homicide mortality relative to male homicide mor-

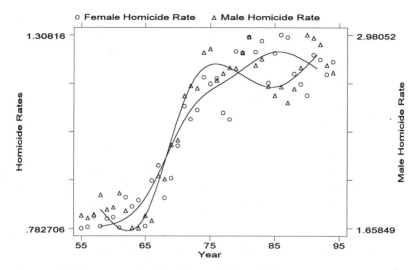

Figure 17. Homicide Rate Trends, 18-Nation Means

tality means that much of the variation in relative rates stems from the killing of men by other men. Even if female mortality remains constant, the female advantage increases with a rise in male homicide and decreases with a decline in male homicide. In the United States, for example, the female advantage during the 1980s expanded with the outbreak of gang- and drug-related male homicides in large cities. Perhaps as a result, relative female rates of mortality do not match the pattern of change found for relative female suicide rates.

To illustrate the problem, consider the smoothed trends in absolute levels of male and female homicide mortality in figure 17. By using separate scales for the gender-specific rates, the graph displays the close match between the male and female trends. Both rates increase dramatically during the late 1960s and early 1970s, then level off. The trend for female homicide rates rises and then falls, as predicted by the institutional adjustment hypothesis, but the similar trends among males in the relative measures mask the changes in female homicide victimization. The close correspondence between the two curves instead emphasizes the small gaps that occur at various times.

By eliminating the possibly excessive influence of male rates on the relative measures, the female homicide mortality rate by itself might reveal the influence of the consequences of changing gender roles for women. The absolute measure of female homicide mortality does not control for trends that affect male and female homicide victimization similarly but, given the predominance of male homicide, may work better than relative measures. If female homicide rates more closely match changes in gender equality than the relative rates, this would argue for consideration of both types of measures. Thus, I replicate the previous results using the female homicide mortality rate and the logged female homicide mortality rate.

First, the collectivist and women-friendly institutions measures correlate in the expected direction with the absolute measures of female homicide mortality. Note that the absolute rates differ in ordering from the relative rates: the higher the value, the worse the position of women. Collectivist and women-friendly institutions have correlations of $-.322$ and $-.116$ with the female homicide rate, and correlations of $-.275$ and $-.073$ with the logged female homicide rate. Consistent with expectations, the higher the collectivism and support for women, the lower the female homicide rate. However weak the relationships, they make more sense than those for relative homicide rates, where collectivist and women-friendly institutions reduce the female advantage.

Second, the trends over time across age groups for female homicide rates fit the predictions of the institutional adjustment hypothesis. Table 39 replicates table 38 with the two measures of female homicide rates. Particularly among the young, the female homicide rate rises steadily but levels off in later time periods. Reflecting the slowed rate of increase, the coefficients for the time term are positive and the coefficients for the time

Table 39. Mean Female Homicide Rates and Logged Rates by Age and Time Period

	Young (15–34)		Middle Aged (35–64)		Old (65+)	
Year	Female Rate	Logged Rate	Female Rate	Logged Rate	Female Rate	Logged Rate
Time period means:						
1955–64	.916	.576	.809	.526	.722	.469
1965–74	1.17	.679	.980	.598	.837	.537
1975–84	1.49	.814	1.16	.687	1.01	.629
1985–94	1.53	.822	1.21	.721	.965	.617
Total	1.27	.723	1.04	.633	.883	.563
OLS trend coefficients:						
Time	.045*	.019*	.026*	.011*	.022*	.012
Time²	−.0006*	−.0003*	−.0003	−.0001	−.0003	−.0002*

*$p < .05$.

squared term are negative. The coefficients for the squared term do not reach statistical significance for middle-aged persons, which means they have not experienced the same reversal as younger persons. Reflecting the different coefficients, the trend for the homicide rate bottoms out in 1993 for the young and in 1999 for the middle aged. The trend stems from a general overall decline in homicide rather than from changes unique to women but does provide some support for the hypothesis.

While recognizing the weakness of the absolute measures—they ignore similar male homicide rates rather than risk overcorrecting for them—the national and temporary patterns in female homicide rates make sense. It seems worthwhile to include a measure of absolute female homicide along with the relative measures in the multivariate analyses to follow.

Multivariate Results

Additive Effects. Perhaps multivariate analyses of the substantive variables will provide more consistent information on the determinants of the sex differential in homicide mortality. To examine the curvilinear effects of time, age, and substantive variables on sex differences in homicide rates, I first examine the regression results for two of the relative homicide rate measures—the logged ratio and the residual deviation—and then for one of the absolute rate measures—the logged female homicide rate. Table 40 presents these results.

The coefficients for the quadratic terms rarely show the expected curvilinear effects on the two measures of relative homicide rates. Age and age squared have significant positive and negative effects, respectively, indicating the rise in the female advantage from youth to middle age, and a decline in the advantage from middle age to old age. Otherwise, the results reveal few significant coefficients. In contrast to the predictions, the female labor force participation rate raises the female advantage initially and later reduces the advantage, and the marriage rate initially reduces the advantage and then increases it. The divorce rate has contrasting coefficients across the two measures of relative homicide, and other measures, such as the total fertility rate and GDP have no effects (and are excluded from the model). Further, results without the outlying cases of the United States do no more to support the institutional adjustment hypothesis. The coefficients generally prove insignificant or highly sensitive to the sample, specification, or dependent variable.

When regressed on the logged female homicide rate, the time and marriage rate variables exhibit the expected effects. The logged female homi-

Table 40. Unstandardized Coefficients and t-Ratios for Regression of Measures of Relative and Absolute Female Homicide Rates on Female Work and Family Variables—Additive Models

Independent Variables	Logged Ratio		Residual Deviation		Logged Female Homicide Rate	
	Coefficient	t-Ratio	Coefficient	t-Ratio	Coefficient	t-Ratio
Time	.003	1.13	−.017	1.14	.009	4.13
Time^2	−.0001	1.22	.0002	0.68	−.0002	3.15
Age	.017	8.22	.070	6.20	−.003	2.21
Age^2	−.0002	9.48	−.0007	6.28	.0000	0.11
FLFP	.023	2.58	.120	2.50	.004	0.62
FLFP^2	−.0002	1.51	−.0014	2.04	−.0000	0.46
Marriage rate	−.017	1.90	−.417	1.39	−.089	2.17
Marriage rate^2	.0087	2.27	.0342	1.68	.006	2.15
Divorce rate	.054	1.26	−.643	2.83	.068	2.16
Divorce rate^2	−.0135	1.82	.075	1.89	.0020	0.35
Constant	−.242		−9.68		1.02	
df	5,012		5,012		5,012	
R^2—OLS	.3463		.1567		.5337	

Note. FLFP = female labor force participation.

cide rate initially increases over time then declines. It also declines initially with increases in the marriage rate but then increases; or, as the marriage rate declines, the logged female homicide rate increases but then declines. The female labor force participation rate has no influence on the logged female homicide rate, while the divorce rate has a positive linear influence. Although superior to those for the relative measures, these results for the absolute measure still offer as much evidence that is inconsistent as as evidence that is consistent with the institutional adjustment hypothesis.

A final test examines the linear and curvilinear effects of the unemployment rate on the sex differential in homicide rates and the logged female homicide rate for the shorter time span of 1959–94 (results not presented). Neither term for unemployment has a significant effect on the sex differential or the absolute rate. Like the previous findings, those for unemployment offer little support for any of the theories of sex differences in homicide.

Collectivist and Women-Friendly Institutions. The weak and inconsistent results thus far for the sex differential measures may stem from the combination of diverse sets of nations in the equations. Since the theoretical discussion emphasizes the impact of national context on the processes that determine female and male homicide rates, the results may vary across nations. If so, the effects of variables in some nations may counter the opposite signed effects in other nations and produce average relationships of near zero. Table 41 tests this possibility by including interaction terms of time by measures of collectivist and women-friendly institutions for the logged ratio and the residual deviation measure. The first four rows of the table display coefficients for time, time squared, time by collectivism, and time squared by collectivism for two measures of relative homicide rates. The next four rows display the same coefficients for the interactions with the measure of women-friendly institutions.

In brief, none of the time interaction coefficients reaches statistical significance. The trends in the homicide sex differential do not vary across nations.[6] The last eight rows of the table present the same tests for differences across nations in the effects of the female labor force participation rate. For the logged ratio, female work initially improves the advantage but

Table 41. Unstandardized Coefficients and t-Ratios for Regression of Measures of Relative and Absolute Female Homicide Rates on Time, Collectivism, and Gender Scale—Nation Interaction Models

Independent Variables	Logged Ratio		Residual Deviation		Logged Female Homicide Rate	
	Coefficient	t-Ratio	Coefficient	t-Ratio	Coefficient	t-Ratio
Time:						
Collectivism:						
Time	.005	2.01	−.034	2.58	.013	7.38
Time^2	−.000	0.68	.0004	1.22	−.0002	3.78
Time × collectivism	.001	0.47	−.003	0.23	−.004	2.17
Time^2 × collectivism	−.0000	0.26	−.0002	0.66	.0001	3.10
Gender:						
Time	.005	1.98	−.035	2.67	.013	7.28
Time^2	−.0000	0.64	.0004	1.28	−.0002	3.71
Time × gender	−.004	1.10	−.033	1.96	.0006	0.24
Time^2 × gender	.0001	1.10	.0004	1.04	.0000	0.64
FLFP:						
Collectivism:						
FLFP	.047	5.27	.006	0.12	.037	5.33
FLFP^2	−.0006	4.45	−.0004	0.61	−.0004	3.73
FLFP × collectivism	−.032	3.82	−.028	0.63	−.021	3.17
FLFP^2 × collectivism	.0005	4.21	.0003	0.39	.0003	3.57
Gender:						
FLFP	.043	4.59	−.003	0.06	.034	4.73
FLFP^2	−.0005	3.77	−.0004	0.50	−.0003	3.12
FLFP × gender	−.025	1.94	−.064	0.92	−.013	1.27
FLFP^2 × gender	.0004	2.44	.0007	0.73	.0002	1.75

Note. FLFP = female labor force participation.

later reduces it; collectivism moderates the initial improvement and the subsequent worsening. As in previous tables, the pattern of coefficients here makes little theoretical sense.

Unlike the relative measures, however, the interactions involving the logged female homicide rate demonstrate the expected national differences. Consider an example. The coefficients for time and time squared in the first rows represent effects at the mean of zero for collectivism. The significant and positive coefficient for time and the significant and negative coefficient for time squared indicate an inverted U-shaped pattern. The collectivism interaction terms moderate the positive time and negative time-squared coefficients. In short, the initial rise and the subsequent drop in female homicide mortality is smaller in collectivist nations than in individualist nations. The measure of women-friendly institutions does not have these same moderating effects.

To illustrate the differences across nations, I use the coefficients for the logged female rate to calculate the effects of time and time squared for three levels of collectivism. When collectivism equals -1.5 (roughly the value for the United States), the coefficients equal 0.019 and -0.00035; when collectivism equals 0 (roughly the value for Germany), the coefficients equal 0.013 and -0.00020; when collectivism equals 1.5 (roughly the value for Sweden), the coefficients equal 0.007 and -0.00005. Individualist nations show the largest initial rise and the largest reversal, while collectivist nations show a smaller rise but, also, a smaller subsequent drop. The interactions of collectivism (but not the women-friendly institutions measure) with female labor force participation also demonstrate the existence of contextual influences. Increases in female labor force participation initially raise the female homicide rate, but eventually the effect wears off. Yet the initial increase and subsequent rebound appear smaller in collectivist nations than in individualist nations.

National Differences. The interactions suggest more puzzles than answers. Few national differences in the effects of time or the female labor force participation rate emerge for the relative measures. Perhaps examining the trends for specific nations will offer more insight into the patterns. Using the product terms for each nation produces unstandardized coefficients for time and time squared and for female work and female work squared for each nation.[7] Table 42 lists the nation-specific coefficients for the time polynomials predicting the logged homicide ratio, the residual deviation measure, and the logged female homicide mortality rate.

Table 42. Unstandardized Coefficients for Regression of Measures of Relative and Absolute Female Homicide Rates on Time Polynomials—Nation-Specific Models

Nation	Logged Ratio		Residual Deviation		Logged Female Homicide Rate	
	Time	Time^2	Time	Time^2	Time	Time^2
Australia	.003	−.0000	−.055	.0009	.011	−.0002
Austria	−.006	−.0000	−.130	.0016	.024	−.0004
Belgium	.018	−.0002	−.003	−.0008	.005	.0001
Canada	.018	−.0004	−.111	.0024	.040	−.0009
Denmark	.005	.0001	−.030	.0000	.010	−.0001
Finland	.006	−.0003	.072	−.0033	.002	.0010
France	−.034	.0006	−.187	.0031	.014	−.0002
Germany	−.015	.0002	−.164	.0031	.030	−.0006
Ireland	.018	−.0002	−.046	.0016	.017	−.0003
Italy	−.009	.0005	−.004	.0016	−.007	.0001
Japan	−.015	.0001	.032	−.0005	−.018	.0002
Netherlands	.013	−.0002	−.019	.0001	.011	−.0001
New Zealand	.014	−.0001	.027	−.0008	.000	.0001
Norway	.017	−.0003	−.004	−.0005	.011	−.0001
Sweden	.018	−.0002	−.029	.0007	.013	−.0002
Switzerland	−.003	.0000	−.029	−.0008	.007	.0001
United Kingdom	.017	−.0002	−.078	.0019	.028	−.0006
United States	.021	−.0005	.156	−.0034	.042	−.0008

The results in the table most obviously highlight the differences between the United States and other nations. For the relative homicide measures, the United States exhibits the strongest positive effects of time and the strongest negative effects of time squared. More than in any other nation, the female advantage rises then declines. The trend does not fit processes of institutional adjustment but, instead, likely relates to the rise of gang- and drug-related homicides among young men during the late 1970s and the 1980s and to the decline of such murders in recent years. The female advantage simply rises with the increases in male homicide victims and falls with their decline.

Some variation in the trends emerge among the other nations. According to the results in table 42, the central European nations of Austria, France, Germany, Italy, and Switzerland exhibit negative effects of time and positive effects of time squared for both measures of relative homicide. These conservative nations, which have scores near the middle of the collectivism scale and scores often near the bottom of the women-friendly institutions scale, experience a worsening in the female homicide advantage that contrasts with the experience not only of the United States but also of social democratic nations such as Sweden and Norway. Again, however, the pattern in central Europe may stem as much from low homicide mortality among men as from high homicide mortality among women.

The last columns of table 42 list the nation-specific coefficients of time and time squared for the logged female homicide rate. The United States again differs from other nations but in the opposite direction from the relative homicide rates. Reflecting the rise and fall in homicide rates, the United States has the largest positive effect of time and the largest negative effect of time squared. At the other extreme, Japan and Italy have negative coefficients for time and positive coefficients for time squared.

Although they are not listed in the table, the nation-specific coefficients for the female labor force participation rate reveal similar differences across nations. The United States shows the strongest initial increase in the logged female homicide mortality rate with a rise in female work but shows the strongest decrease, as well. Australia, Denmark, New Zealand, and Norway, a diverse mix of countries, have the weakest effects of female work and female work squared. However, differences in effects across countries are smaller with this determinant than with time.

Some correlations can help summarize the national patterns implied by these numerous coefficients. Collectivism has no relationship with the nation-specific time trends in relative homicide rates. For the coefficients of the unsquared and squared terms, respectively, collectivism has correlations of .078 and −.056 for the logged homicide ratio and of −.039 and −.114 for the residual deviation measure. Measures of women-friendly institutions have correlations of −.202 and .264 with the coefficients for the logged homicide ratio and correlations of −.331 and .199 with the coefficients for the residual deviation measure. The relationships implausibly indicate that the upward increase in the female advantage is weaker among nations with institutional supports for working women.[8]

The correlations with the logged female homicide rate again differ. The measure of women-friendly institutions has weak correlations of .019 and .101 with the effects of time and time squared, respectively, on the logged female homicide mortality rate. Collectivism has stronger correlations of −.267 and .401 with the logged female homicide mortality rate. Consistent with predictions, high-collectivist nations experience a weaker increase in female homicide victimization over time and a smaller subsequent decrease.[9] As in previous analyses, the results for the logged female homicide rate provide more support than the relative measures for the institutional adjustment hypothesis.

Conclusion

The effort here to move beyond simplistic claims that gender equality produces either convergence or divergence in the homicide rates of men and women by testing arguments about institutional adjustment to social changes has met with little success. The institutional adjustment hypothesis predicts curvilinear effects of time, female labor force participation, divorce, and marriage on relative homicide rates. Yet little evidence of curvilinear relationships emerges in the analyses. The time trend differs substantially for different measures of relative homicide rates, only rarely matches the U-shaped relationship predicted by the institutional adjustment hypothesis, and varies across ages in ambiguous ways. In the multivariate models, the substantive variables seldom have the predicted curvilinear effects and appear highly sensitive to the measure of relative homicide rates, the specification of the model, and the nations included in the sample. Further, national differences in relative homicide rates make little sense: nations like the United States, with the highest rates of female homicide mortality, have the highest female advantage.

The weak results stem in part from two kinds of measurement problems. First, the trends of male and female homicide victimization correspond closely because increasing violence committed by males produces deaths of both males and females. Given similarities in changes in male and female homicide victimization rates, changes over time in sex differences reflect, to a large degree, random error, and alternative measures give contradictory results. Thus, when males kill females as well as other males, homicide rates tend to blur differences between mortality of the two sexes. Second, when differences between male and female homicide mortality do emerge, they often reflect greater swings in male homicide than in female homicide. High male homicide mortality makes relative female homicide rates in the United States the lowest in the developed world. Conversely, low homicide nations such as Sweden or Switzerland have high relative rates of female homicide mortality. The prevalence of acquaintance and stranger homicides in nations such as the United States, which usually involve other forms of criminal activity or conflict among males, raises male homicide victimization and reduces relative female victimization.

To help deal with these measurement problems, the analyses examine absolute female homicide rates. The results for this measure more strongly support the institutional adjustment hypothesis. The rate increases (i.e., worsens women's victimization) over time but then eventually declines; changes in the marriage rate have curvilinear effects; and the curvilinear effects of time and the female labor force participation rate emerge more strongly in individualist nations than in collectivist nations. The contingency of the relationships for this dependent variable emphasizes the importance of the social and political context of gender change. The lower the status of women, the weaker their involvement in the world of work, and the stronger their attachment to family roles, the greater the harm of change toward gender equality for homicide mortality. The higher the status of women, the greater their involvement in the world of work, and the weaker their dependence on men and family roles for economic well-being, the less the harm (or the greater the benefit) of change toward gender equality for homicide mortality.

Despite the support it gives to the hypothesis, the measure of absolute female homicide mortality rates has its own problems. The trends and patterns for females differ little from the trends and patterns for males. The curvilinear trend and differences across nations in female homicide victimization may spuriously result from larger trends that affect both males and females and have little to do with gender inequality. Alternatively and more positively, the similarity in male and female homicide victimization may result from similarities in the consequences of gender change for both sexes. Gender change may initially increase murder of both men and women as men respond with generalized violence to changes in their relationships with women and may later reduce violence as men come to accept new gender roles. It is likely that forces both unrelated and related to gender change affect male and female homicide rates.

Presented alone, the results in this chapter would offer little support for the institutional adjustment hypothesis and the importance of national context. The analyses would appear too selective in the search for evidence that favors the hypothesis. That the results only occasionally match predictions for relative rates and that they more often match predictions for a measure of female homicide that does not control for male homicide indicates limitations in the study of homicide mortality and in the theory of institutional adjustment. Yet the strong evidence for institutional adjustment in relative suicide rates in the last chapter justifies a thorough search for similarities with relative homicide rates and an emphasis on the results that support the hypothesis.

To conclude, then, weak evidence exists for the institutional adjustment hypothesis with regard to homicide, but the evidence is sometimes consistent with the stronger results for relative suicide rates. Even the weak findings for homicide rates suggest moving beyond simple predictions of convergence and divergence in male and female homicide rates. Likewise, they suggest avoiding a search for general and invariant relationships between social equality between men and women and their relative homicide rates. Instead, studies should still attend to the political context of changing gender roles and examine how these changing roles shape the direction and strength of the relationship.

Conclusion

In brief review, the book's quantitative study of 18 high-income democracies during the post–World War II period demonstrates that the effects of cohort change and female work on fertility, suicide and homicide mortality, and sex differences in suicide and homicide mortality vary across contexts or institutional environments. The importance of the institutional or sociopolitical context in shaping the relationship between demographic causes and outcomes shows not in invariant relationships but in relationships that vary in predictable ways. Thus, the effects of both relative cohort size and female labor force participation rates on aspects of both fertility and mortality emerge stronger in individualist than in collectivist nations, in earlier postwar decades than in more recent decades, in gender inegalitarian contexts than in gender egalitarian contexts, at younger ages than at older ages, and among men than among women.

Again, in brief review, these findings can contribute in several ways to the comparative literatures in demography and political sociology. First, they identify links between topics seldom considered together. Demographic characteristics, such as cohort size or female work, and sociopolitical characteristics, such as collectivism or women-friendly institutions, combine to influence diverse demographic outcomes. Although lacking a single dependent variable, the analyses reveal a common theme: that institutions specify the relationships of exogenous population and labor force changes with fertility and mortality. This integrative theme helps make sense of the apparent diversity of topics and variables in this study as well as the diversity of findings of previous studies on these topics and variables.

Second, the findings integrate otherwise competing theories. By attending to institutional contingency, the models move beyond the contrast between exclusive theories and the presentation of one-dimensional empirical results and, thereby, transcend debates over which single set of factors dominates models of fertility and mortality. In studies of mortality, for example, theories positing disadvantages of cohort size and theories positing advantages of cohort size, or theories positing benefits of female work

243

and theories positing harm of female work, each make sense and receive empirical support when limited to the appropriate institutional contexts across nations, time periods, and ages. Variations in institutional context thus provide a means to integrate competing arguments. They make contingent what many consider to be invariant relationships and challenge the validity of unconditional generalizations about the determinants of fertility and mortality.

Third, the findings demonstrate the utility of interactive statistical models. Rather than focusing on average relationships, the models demonstrate how relationships vary from the average and reflect the complexity of the contingent theoretical arguments. They incorporate the influence of national, temporal, and age group contexts as facilitating or inhibiting influences—rather than as direct, additive influences—on the relationships of cohort size and female work with fertility and mortality. By contextualizing the relationships, the nonadditive models capture the disparate directions and sizes of the statistical effects and demonstrate the logical patterns that lie behind the ostensibly inconsistent results of previous studies.

To be sure, the basic thesis of the book receives stronger support in some areas than in others, and the findings reveal considerable complexity. Yet overall the findings offer extensive evidence in favor of the contextual approach I have taken in this book. A summary of the evidence can helpfully demonstrate that point. The paragraphs below review the results in order of the previous chapters. Like the chapters, the review considers how the independent variables (relative cohort size and female labor force participation) relate to the dependent variables (fertility rates, suicide rates, homicide rates, sex differences in suicide rates, and sex differences in homicide rates) but also how the relationships vary across the contextual variables (collectivism, gender equality, time, age, and sex). My review here summarizes the evidence in terms of strong, moderate, or weak support for the hypotheses.

Relative cohort size on fertility: strong support. The evidence on the relationship between these two variables strongly supports the contextual hypotheses. Averaged across all nations and years, relative cohort size only weakly reduces fertility. However, the negative effect of relative cohort size consistently emerges stronger in individualist nations than in collectivist nations, in earlier time periods than in later time periods, and at lower levels of female work than at higher levels. Under certain conditions, relative cohort size has a large influence on fertility, but under other conditions it has little or no effect.

Female labor force participation and fertility: strong support. Again in support of the contextual hypotheses, the negative effect of female work on fertility emerges stronger in individualist nations than in collectivist nations, in nations with weaker institutions for gender equality than in nations with stronger institutions, and in earlier time periods than in later time periods. A stronger negative relationship at lower levels of female work than at higher levels also implies the existence of curvilinearity. The curvilinear relationship between female work and fertility, combined with differences in effects across nations, makes for some complexities in interpretation, but the results nonetheless offer much evidence of how the consequences of female work for fertility can vary.

Relative cohort size and suicide rates: strong support. The relationship between relative cohort size and suicide rates varies consistently across contexts defined by age, sex, nation, and time. Among men, but less so among women, large cohorts have higher suicide rates at younger ages but lower rates at older ages. Further, the age differences in the effect of relative cohort size emerge more strongly in individualist nations than in collectivist nations and in earlier time periods than in later time periods. Again, relative cohort size has more negative consequences in some contexts than in others.

Relative cohort size and homicide rates: weak support. The contextual influences on the relationship between relative cohort size and homicide rates emerge less clearly than for suicide rates. The relationship changes from negative for youth to near zero for middle-aged and elderly persons but does not differ greatly by sex. Further, the age differences in the effect of relative cohort size vary little across nations or time. Although coefficients generally have the expected signs, their small size and inconsistency can only offer partial support for the hypotheses. The weak results likely stem from the nature of homicide: since persons in large cohorts can kill those of other ages and sexes, it tends to diffuse the age and sex differences in the impact of cohort size on homicide victimization.

Female labor force participation and sex differences in suicide rates: moderate support. As indicators of the general movement toward gender equality, female work and several related variables have U-shaped relationships with the female advantage in suicide. This curvilinearity shows the importance of the social and political context of gender change: the lower the status of women, the greater the harm of change toward gender equality for their suicide morality; the higher the status of women, the greater the benefit of change toward gender equality for their suicide mortality. Further, the effects of social change on sex differences in suicide mortality emerge more strongly in individualist nations than in collectivist nations and at younger ages more than at older ages. However, because the relationships hold more strongly for time and the marriage rate than for the female labor force participation and divorce rates, they warrant only moderate support for the hypotheses.

Female labor force participation and sex differences in homicide rates: weak support. Little evidence exists for a curvilinear relationship between female work or related measures of changes in women's status and sex differences in homicide rates. Further, the effect varies in ambiguous ways across age, nation, and time. The results come closer to the predictions for absolute female homicide rates than for female homicide rates relative to males but overall only weakly support the hypotheses. Again, this may result partly from males killing females as well as other males, thus masking the sex-specific consequences of female work and other components of gender equality.

In summary, except for homicide, the results consistently favor the hypotheses and offer substantial if not complete evidence for my arguments. To be fair, I present the weak results for homicide along with the stronger results for fertility and suicide and can also note that even for homicide, the results at least weakly or occasionally support the hypotheses. Despite some qualifications, the findings warrant further efforts to understand the importance of the social and political context in shaping demographic relationships.

Further study of these sorts of relationships may be important for another reason. Although I explain patterns over a relatively long time period in the book and use relatively recent data (at least compared to most comparative studies), the last half of the 1990s and the first decade of the twenty-first century may define new contexts that need study. Indeed, critics might assert that, because the late 1990s reflect the culmination of new forms of globalization, the findings presented here have already become outdated. Recent increases in the mobility of capital across national boundaries, the ability of firms with capital resources to relocate to other parts of the globe, the membership in tariff-free trading blocs such as the European Union, the unemployment rate in collectivist Sweden, and the prosperity in the liberal United States all suggest that national differences have declined and will continue to decline. If this proves to be so, the institutional environments demonstrated to shape demographic relationships for most of the post–World War II time period may lose their importance and the previous findings may no longer apply to the new economic order.

Despite the importance of globalization, the consequences of recent changes for the welfare state, and implicitly for my contextual demographic arguments, tend to be overstated. As Esping-Andersen (1996) states, "Popular perceptions notwithstanding, the degree of welfare state rollback, let alone significant change, has so far been modest" (10). Globalization may block expansion of some programs and development of new initiatives but does not force contraction or fundamentally reshape the welfare state. Rather, Rieger and Leibfried (1998) argue that global competitive pressures make national welfare programs all the more important to the economic well-being of citizens. Historically, smaller, natural resource–poor European nations that required free trade for economic growth have had larger welfare states in order to cushion the harm of swings in the world economy; many governments viewed their welfare state and institutions for consensus decision making as components of, rather than obstacles to, international competitiveness. Further integration into the world economy may therefore make radical changes in the welfare state all the more unlikely.

The persistence of national structures of social policy in the modern global economy further implies the persistence of national institutional differences. Despite facing similar global pressures, nations have in the past and will continue in the future to maintain their uniqueness by responding to the pressures with distinctive policies (Castles and Pierson 1996). In Esping-Andersen's (1996) words, "One of the most powerful conclusions in comparative research is that political and institutional mechanisms of interest representation and political consensus building matter tremendously in terms of managing welfare, employment, and growth objectives. . . . Welfare states seek to adapt, [but] they do so very differently. A major reason has to do with institutional legacies, inherited system characteristics, and the vested interests that these cultivate" (6).

For example, Sweden can no longer maintain full employment, cannot afford the generous benefits of the recent past, and has moved, at the margins, away from universalism in eligibility. It nonetheless contrasts strikingly with the United States and many other nations. Where 1996 total government outlays in Sweden made up 65.3% of GDP—a substantial drop from 69.8% in 1994—the same 1996 figure for the United States equaled only 35.6% (Organization for Economic Cooperation and Development 1998). Where 86.6% of the Swedish labor force belongs to one of the three major unions, unions members comprise only 14.5% of the American labor force (Europa Publications 1998, 3205, 3221, 3644). And where the leftist, labor-based Swedish Social Democratic Party remains a dominant political force, the Democratic Party in the United States still lacks a strong socialist, labor union base and social democratic agenda. If Sweden and the United States are to become alike in their politics, public policies, and institutions, they have a long way to go before reaching that point. Similarly, neither Germany nor France, despite periods of rule by rightist parties (now replaced by leftist coalitions), have imitated the United States by dismantling their programs of social protection.

As global economic trends have not yet eliminated national political and policy differences, common global trends toward gender equality have not eliminated national differences in state approaches to issues of gender equality. Neither the strategic goal of providing opportunities for part-time employment, public child care, and paid maternity leave in Sweden nor the strategic goal of treating men and women identically or neutrally in the United States have changed substantially in the past several years. Although few new initiatives have emerged in either country, it is also true that the efforts of some groups to dismantle existing women-friendly institutions or to encourage adoption of other strategies have met with little success. Women may, as Jackson (1998) argues, be destined for equality, but the paths to equality continue to differ across nations.

These arguments suggest that the institutional forces and national differences that have been found to be important in determining fertility and mortality in high-income nations will not fade in the near future. If, contrary to these suggestions, the institutional context does change, it would not negate the value of these findings for previous decades. Because the theoretical framework offered in this book attends to contextual contingency, it can still take account of sociopolitical convergence across nations. Invariant propositions that imply the continuance into future decades of previously observed relationships are often negated by new data and new circumstances. A contextual approach, however, recognizes that the changing institutional environment can reshape the processes determining fertility and mortality, and models can incorporate the changed environment. Just as the 1951–94 period demonstrated the declining influence of relative cohort size and female work, the next decades may demonstrate new relationships. Far from becoming outdated by recent and future changes, the results for previous decades offer a strategy for understanding demographic changes to come.

Statistical Models and Estimation I

This appendix reviews the statistical problems and solutions involved in analyzing pooled cross-section and time-series data. First, use of time-series data with an inherent ordering creates problems of serial correlation. Rather than producing random errors, the dependence of variable values on values of previous years creates ordering over time in the size and direction of the errors. Serial correlation leaves ordinary least squares (OLS) estimates unbiased but makes them inefficient without a lagged dependent variable (and biased in the presence of a lagged dependent variable). Second, the use of multiple nations of diverse size and social characteristics makes for heteroscedasticity or differences in the size of errors across nations. With numerous time points within each nation, the nation-specific variance in the errors can be calculated and compared. If the variances differ, they again produce unbiased but inefficient estimates. Third, nations with shared regional location, cultural background, or historical experiences may generate similar patterns of errors that violate the assumption of randomness. This cross-sectional correlation of the errors also makes for inefficient estimates. Fourth, stable national influences on outcomes may produce spurious relationships. If cultural influences across nations, for example, both lower fertility and raise female work, they might bias the estimates without controls or adjustments for this between-unit heterogeneity.

Generalized least squares (GLS) procedures deal with the first three problems by using estimates of the error parameters from the first-stage OLS residuals to produce consistent second-stage estimates of the coefficients (Judge et al. 1988; Kmenta 1986). Strictly speaking, the procedure may be referred to as modified, pseudo, or feasible GLS estimation because the error parameters are themselves estimated rather than known a priori. Since feasible GLS requires estimation of the error parameters, it can introduce substantial randomness, especially with a small number of cases within panel units. Based on Monte-Carlo simulations, Beck and Katz (1995) demonstrate that the most effective strategies of adjustment for problems of serial correlation, heteroscedasticity, and contemporaneous correlation in practical research situations limit the number of error parameters. Following Beck and Katz (1995), I rely on a feasible GLS variant that estimates minimal error parameters.

To deal with serial correlation, Beck and Katz find that use of a single autoregression parameter common to all nations gives more efficient estimates than specifying parameters unique to each nation. The GLS models of fertility thus assume a common first-order autoregressive process. To correct for serially correlated errors, the two-stage procedure uses OLS residuals to estimate one serial correlation parameter and then uses the generalized least squares matrix to subtract out the overtime redundancy in the variables produced by the autocorrelation.

To deal with heteroscedasticity, Beck and Katz (1995) recommend the use of a panel-based variant of a heteroscedastic-consistent covariance matrix to estimate standard errors. Alternative procedures adjust the estimates in proportion to the unit-specific error variances (Judge et al. 1988; Kmenta 1986) but again require estimating 18 separate error variances, which reduces the efficiency of the estimates. The models therefore estimate the panel-corrected standard errors of Beck and Katz.

To deal with cross-sectional correlation of the errors, the model may be treated as a system of 18 equations in which the residuals for each nation correlate with those of other nations. A form of seemingly unrelated regressions appropriate for pooled cross-section time-series data uses the cross-national correlations of the residuals (after removing the serial correlation within nations) to adjust for the lack of independence across nations. The 18 nations, however, require an 18×18 matrix of coefficients. Beck and Katz (1995) demonstrate the problems of estimating the numerous error parameters used in this procedure and recommend, except in the presence of correlations .75 and over, avoiding this adjustment. Since the cross-sectional correlations in the fertility models do not reach these levels, I do not adjust for them.

Finally, estimation of unbiased pooled models often requires controls for between-nation heterogeneity in the form of fixed effects or varying intercepts (Hsaio 1986; Stimson 1985). Fixed effects estimators restrict the analysis to within-nation change by taking the independent and dependent variables as deviations from nation-specific means. Where possible, the fertility models partially capture these time-invariant, nation-specific effects with the theoretically defined concepts of collectivism and women-friendly institutions. Yet, since the contextual variables seldom capture all the heterogeneity, fixed effects models can give superior estimates of autocorrelations, variances, and coefficients. In contrast to random effects models, which summarize nation-specific influences in the form of a random variable, the fixed effects models are easily estimated by including dummy variables for all nations (less one) in the model and proceeding with GLS adjustments for autocorrelation and heteroscedasticity. Similar sorts of fixed effects models can control for between-period heterogeneity with time dummy variables.

At the same time, however, fixed effects models have limitations. Tam (1997) argues that models with unit-specific dummy variables magnify the distorting influence of measurement error. Ignoring between-unit variance not only reduces the efficiency of the estimates but, in the presence of correlated measurement error, also biases the estimates. Tam's critique applies most to panel data where the number of cross-sectional units greatly exceeds the number of time points. With 700 plus cases and more time points than nations in this pooled cross-national time-series data, the use of 17 dummy variables does not create as serious a problem as panel data for thousands of persons over two or three time points. Still, I examine GLS estimates with and without adjustment for between-nation heterogeneity throughout the analyses.

The tables in chapters 4 and 5, either for GLS or fixed effects GLS models, present unstandardized coefficients and t-ratios obtained from the xtgls procedure in Stata (1999), with the options corr[ar1] to specify a first-order autoregressive process common to all nations and pcse p[c] to specify panel-corrected standard errors. The resulting coefficients and t-ratios are interpreted as usual. Goodness-of-fit measures present more problems with the models because the GLS estimates in essence transform the original variables before minimizing the sum of the squared errors. Stata therefore does not present a variance-explained measure in its output (Beck and Katz also do not report the variance explained in their GLS analyses). As a rough guide, I list the OLS variance explained for each model to identify the explanatory power of the determinants. However, given the limitations of this or any other measure of the pseudo-variance explained, the interpretations and tests of the hypotheses focus on the coefficients, their strength, and their significance.

Buse (1973) presents a "measure of the proportion of the generalized sum of squares of the dependent variable which is attributable to the influence of the explanatory variables. It also has the properties usually associated with R^2: its range is zero to one; it is zero when all the estimated coefficients except the constant are zero; and it is monotonically related to the F-statistic used in testing the null hypothesis that all coefficients except the constant are zero" (107). Although computed in some GLS programs, Stata output does not list the Buse measure.

APPENDIX B

Statistical Models
and Estimation II

The study of suicide and homicide mortality involves data measured separately for seven age groups as well as for nations and years. The age-specific figures allow for two types of analyses. First, the analyses can treat age-specific mortality rates as separate dependent variables, with nations and years as the units of analysis. The 18 nations and 40 years provide 720 cases, but the age-specific figures allow for separate analyses of each of the seven age groups. For example, the analyses can examine models for persons ages 15–24, then for persons ages 25–34, and so on. While useful for detailed description, the separate age group analyses become cumbersome and redundant: numerous sets of coefficients make for difficulties in interpretation and generalization and may incorrectly imply that all coefficients differ significantly across age groups. Although tests for differences across models could simplify the results, the numerous and unwieldly statistical comparisons limit the usefulness of such tests.

Second, the analyses I use extend the pooled approach to include age as well as nations and years. Rather than separate variables, the age-specific figures can represent separate units of observation nested within each nation and year. Instead of 720 cases combining nations and years, the analyses have 5,020 (720 × 7) cases combining nations, years, and ages. The suicide or homicide mortality rate continues to serve as the dependent variable, but the rate differs for each nation, each year, and each age group. One can visualize the data matrix as stacking 40 years of time series for each of the 18 nations for the first age group, then adding the 40 years of time series for each of the 18 nations for the next age group, and so on until reaching the 40 years of time series for each of the 18 nations for the oldest age group. Within the stacked matrix, the mortality rate comprises a single variable that has different values for each observation (i.e., for each nation-year-age). For some variables, the size of the sample pooled by nation, year, and age exaggerates the available information. Although each case has its own mortality rate and its own measure of relative cohort size, the other independent variables differ only by nation and year (i.e., the independent variables have the same values for each age group). However, even crude variables averaged across all age groups help capture more general characteristics of nations and time periods that relate to the age-specific rates of mortality.

In the models, the additive coefficients represent effects averaged across ages as well as across nations and years. Although the additive coefficients assume unvarying effects, interaction coefficients can represent age, nation, and time differences in the relationships between the determinants and outcomes. The modeling strategy can begin simply but can systematically and sequentially relax the initial additive constraints to help capture the complexity inherent in the age-specific rates and the pooled data.

A few equations can help explain this second approach to the analyses. Referring to cases for each age group j, nation i, and year t, the additive model takes the following form:

$$Y_{itj} = \alpha + \Sigma\beta_j A_j + \Sigma\beta_i N_i + \Sigma\beta_t T_t + \Sigma\beta_k X_k + e_{itj}.$$

In this additive model, the mortality rate (Y) is a function of age, nation, and year in the form of additive terms for A_j (j dummy variables for age), N_i (i dummy variables for nation), T_t (t polynomial terms for time), and e_{itj} (the error term). These variables represent controls for sources of between-age, -nation, and -time heterogeneity that help identify the non-spurious influence of the other independent variables, X_k.

However, the model averages the effects of the independent variables across nations, time, and age groups. Tests of the hypotheses concerning differences in effects across nations, time, and ages require a more complex model. To allow for variation in the effects of independent variables across ages, for example, the equation adds multiplicative interaction terms:

$$Y_{itj} = \alpha + \Sigma\beta_j A_j + \Sigma\beta_i N_i + \Sigma\beta_t T_t + \Sigma\beta_k X_k + \Sigma\beta_{kj} X_k A_j + e_{itj}.$$

The set of coefficients β_{kj} represents the changes in effect of the X_k variables across the j age groups. Similar interaction terms can capture variation in the effects of the X variables across nation, time, or nation-specific measures of collectivism and women-friendly institutions.

The same estimation problems described in appendix A apply to these equations because the error term e_{itj} likely does not satisfy the assumptions of ordinary least squares. Pooling by age groups as well as by nations and years introduces an additional source of dependence in the observations.

Applied to the pooled nation-time-age data, the Beck and Katz (1995) feasible-GLS procedure differs from that described in appendix A only in the addition of the age groups. With age as another component of the panel, the data have $n \times j$ cross-sectional units and t time units. Thus, the estimates (1) adjust for a common autoregressive parameter computed from the t cases within each combination of nation and age group; (2) compute panel adjusted standard errors with the combined nation and age group defining the panel units; and (3) use variables for nation and age to control for cross-sectional heterogeneity.

The controls for between-unit heterogeneity become especially important given the added age dimension in the pool data. The large age differences in victimization by suicide and homicide require age-based control variables in the models. Nation differences also likely will prove important in the models. However, the models do not include controls for combined age-nation variables that would represent each cross-sectional unit in the analysis. As a result, the limitations of the fixed effects estimates described by Tam (1997) do not apply to these models.

As before, the tables in chapter 7–11 present GLS unstandardized coefficients and t-ratios obtained from the xtgls procedure in Stata (with the options corr[ar1] to specify a first-order autoregressive process common to all nation-ages and pcse and p[c] to specify panel-corrected standard errors). The resulting coefficients and t-ratios are interpreted as usual. The tables also present the OLS variance explained as a rough guide to the explanatory power of the determinants. However, the limitations of this or any other measure of the pseudo-variance explained suggest the value of focusing on the coefficients, their strength, and their significance.

Notes

1. The Demographic Consequences of Changing Cohort Size and Female Work

1. Easterlin's argument about cohort size emphasizes changes in the processes determining fertility and mortality outcomes. It considers how changes in the composition of a population affect the process by which a population characteristic produces demographic outcomes; cohort size thereby affects the age-specific behavior and age-standardized outcomes rather than the crude or aggregated outcomes. Testing for the existence of changes in process independent of changes in composition therefore requires age-specific or age-standardized indicators. Although more complex than compositional arguments, processual arguments may more accurately represent social life. For example, a pure compositional argument would predict a rise in the crude birth rate with an increase in the number of women of childbearing age. However, an increase in the size of the young adult population may also create an oversupply of workers in the labor market. The resulting decline in economic status among young people may reduce fertility. The change in the relationship between age and fertility due to a shifting age distribution may lead to a decline in age-specific fertility, if not the crude birth rate. Moreover, positing the importance of the processes by which population characteristics determine demographic outcomes implies the importance of the contextual environment in which the process occurs. If age and sex have automatic relationships with fertility and mortality because of biological characteristics, they also have more socially determined, processual relationships that likely vary across societies, nations, and contexts.

2. For example, age relates so predictably to demographic behavior in the compositional sense that standard measures control for it automatically. Researchers standardize rates by age composition with measures of the total fertility rate, with estimates of life expectancy, or with age-specific fertility and mortality rates but give less attention to how the influence of population characteristics on demographic outcomes may vary across different contexts.

2. Sociopolitical Sources of Demographic Divergence

1. The influences of cohort size and female work also vary by age, but age defines a separate dimension of study examined in more detail in other chapters.

2. Critics of Esping-Andersen's (1990) three worlds of welfare capitalism argue that New Zealand and Australia differ from other liberal nations and that Italy and Japan differ from other conservative nations (e.g., Castles and Mitchell 1993). However, in responding to these criticisms, Esping-Andersen (1999) highlights the underlying similarities within categories of liberal and conservative nations and asserts the continuing importance of his distinctions. Any grouping necessarily ignores some differences across individual nations, but Esping-Andersen's categories have proven highly influential in organizing or simplifying the diversity of policies that exist across the high-income nations.

3. The distinction made here between collectivism and individualism differs from the meaning of the same terms used in a more psychological context by Triandis (1995). He uses collectivism to refer to identification with families and tribes as well as with classes and nations. Collectivism could refer to the strong kin ties in southern Europe or Japan rather than to the strong ties to national institutions of social protection in northern Europe. In fact, Triandis ranks Italy and Japan as more collectivist than Sweden, where the scheme used here posits the reverse. My use of collectivism and individualism follows the comparative literature on public policy, class conflict, and political sociology.

4. Some of the individual items used in the scales lack data for one or more nations, and one measure reports data only on the European nations. However, the scale construction procedure assigns scores to each nation based on the number of individual items with valid data. For example, the Bradshaw measure of family support reports values for the United Kingdom but not the United States, while the other three measures of family support report values for both nations. Therefore, the combined family support index averages three values for the United States but four values for the United Kingdom. Note also that the scaling procedure standardizes each of the component items before creating the index.

3. Contextual Variation in the Determinants of Fertility

1. Although not central to Easterlin's argument, large cohorts can also experience economic deprivation through price mechanisms. For example, the high demand that large cohorts create for college, housing, and consumer goods can raise prices and thereby make their relatively low income seem even more inadequate.

2. Similar conclusions emerge from cross-national studies of cohort-specific unemployment and income (variables more difficult to measure because of the limitations of comparative data). Bloom, Freeman, and Korenman (1987) find that age structure affects wages in the United States but not in the European nations they study.

3. The rise in immigration in recent decades may contribute to the weakening influence of relative cohort size in the United States. Despite the entrance of smaller birth cohorts into the labor market during the 1980s and 1990s, the entrance of immigrants into the labor force during the same time period reduces the advantages of small birth cohorts. However, immigration does little to explain

national differences in cohort size. Nations with high immigration, like the United States, in fact show stronger effects of relative cohort size than lower-immigration European nations do. As the arguments to follow explain, the individualist and dualist labor market of the United States contributes to the economic deprivation of large cohorts and the demand for low-wage immigrant workers.

4. Lesthaeghe (1983) and colleagues (Lesthaeghe and Meekers 1986; Lesthaeghe and Surkyn 1988) have argued for the importance of cultural contexts in the study of demographic behavior (e.g., an individualist value system reduces the ability of relatives and the community to regulate fertility). This cultural dimension varies across regions and periods and exogenously influences fertility and family behavior. I consider collectivist institutions to be part of the cultural context of decisions regarding childbearing.

5. As illustrated in France, where the generosity of pronatalist state policies and concern with depopulation exceed those in nearly all other countries, feminists view pronatalism as a threat to women's achievement and reproductive freedom (King 1998).

6. Blossfeld et al. (1995) make the same point about the relationship between education and divorce. They find that women with high education have a greater risk of marital disruption only where divorce is uncommon and constitutes a severe violation of norms. As divorce increases and customs become more permissive, the liberating impact of women's high education will decline. Thus, improved education initially destabilizes traditional family relationships, but as families become more differentiated, educational differentials in divorce diminish.

7. Statistics from the International Labour Office ([ILO] 1986, 1991) supplement the OECD figures. For discrepancies in the rates for a given country between the two sources, I adjust the OECD figures to correspond to ILO figures. I also interpolate figures for years lacking data.

8. The correlation between the labor force participation rate for all women and the rate for women ages 25–44 in the ILO data is .95. Although including older women understates the level of participation, the patterns across nations and years are not greatly affected.

4. Relative Cohort Size and the Total Fertility Rate

1. The coefficient for relative cohort size of -0.883 in column 4 of table 5 reflects the effect for the reference period of 1951–61. The effect for the period 1962–72 equals -0.883 plus the coefficient of -1.60 for the interaction term of relative cohort size with the 1962–72 dummy variable. The effects for the other periods also add the coefficients for the interaction terms to the coefficient for relative cohort size in the reference period.

2. Note that the FE-GLS model controls for between-nation heterogeneity with nation-specific dummy variables (coefficients not presented) rather than with the collectivism scale. The dummy variables that control for between-nation heterogeneity subsume stable national differences represented by the collectivism

scale and also capture other stable differences relevant to fertility. Indeed, because the collectivism scale is perfectly collinear with the set of country-specific dummy variables, the fixed effects models cannot include all these variables simultaneously. In other words, the nation dummy variables can control for both the additive effects of collectivism and other stable country-specific unmeasured variables. It is necessary, then, to replicate the first equation, only with the dummy variables (fixed effects) replacing the additive effect of collectivism. The estimates can show the interaction between relative cohort size and the other variables net of the more complete additive controls for stable national differences. These estimates, like those that include collectivism directly, can also demonstrate the predicted contingent effect of relative cohort size.

3. The coefficient for relative cohort size of -1.12 shows its effect when collectivism equals zero (i.e., at medium levels of collectivism). Using a collectivism score of -1.5 to represent low collectivism nations, the effect of relative cohort size equals -1.12 plus -1.5 times the interaction coefficient of 0.891 for relative cohort size by collectivism. Using a collectivism score of 1.5 to represent high collectivist nations, the effect of relative cohort size equals -1.12 plus 1.5 times the interaction coefficient of 0.891. Other values can be used to represent high and low collectivism, but -1.5 and 1.5 reflect values close to the minimum and maximum, respectively.

4. To obtain standardized coefficients here and elsewhere in the chapter, I simply multiply the unstandardized coefficient by the standard deviation of the independent variable as a ratio to the standard deviation of the dependent variable. More complex calculations might use standard deviations for individual countries to calculate nation-specific standardized coefficients but use of the standard deviations for the full set of cases provides a straightforward means of comparing the relative size of coefficients.

5. The calculations in table 7 come from using interaction terms involving both collectivism and time in column 6 of table 6. The coefficient of $-.771$ for relative cohort size shows its effect for the reference time period of 1951–62 when collectivism equals zero. This coefficient plus the coefficient for the interaction of relative cohort size with the dummy variable for 1962–72 (i.e., -1.52) shows the effect for medium-collectivist nations in 1962–72. This coefficient plus the coefficient for the interaction of relative cohort size with the dummy variable for 1984–94 (i.e., $-.222$) shows the effect for medium-collectivist nations in 1984–94. To get the effect for high-collectivist nations, I add the collectivism value of 1.5 times the collectivism interaction coefficient of 1.01 to the effect for medium-collectivism nations. I do the same for the low-collectivist nations, only using the collectivism value of -1.5.

6. The measure of collectivist institutions performs better than the measure of women-friendly institutions in these models. When substituted for the collectivism scale, the gender-based scale does not significantly interact with relative cohort

size. The class-based measure of sociopolitical context proves most relevant to the influence of relative cohort size.

7. Alternative lag structures had little effect on these results. Lagging relative cohort size by 2 years produced slightly stronger effects than a 1-year or 3-year lag. Changing the lags for the other variables made little difference. Because the data for these other variables go back to 1950 rather than to 1949, a 2-year lag would have eliminated the 1951 time point and 18 cases. Thus, I use a 1-year lag for variables other than relative cohort size.

8. With the time-varying independent variables, the GLS and FE-GLS models eliminate the time-period dummy variables.

9. The relationship between female labor force participation and fertility is also biased by endogeneity. Lagging the participation rate helps deal with the problem. Yet, without entering into the debate over the causal priority of these two variables and developing a model for female labor force participation rates in which instrumental variables and two-stage least squares can be used to obtain unbiased estimates, the coefficients must be interpreted with caution.

10. The additive variables in the model are centered or taken as deviations from their means. This only affects the constant in columns 1 and 2 of table 8, which equals the mean total fertility rate across nations and years. In the interaction equation (cols. 3 and 4), the additive coefficients show the effect of each variable at mean relative cohort size (i.e., when relative cohort size is zero) and, therefore, have an interpretation similar to the coefficients in the additive model (cols. 1 and 2).

11. The calculations in table 9 use the interaction of relative cohort size with collectivism and female labor force participation. Since female labor force participation is centered or taken as deviations from the mean, I use -15, 0, and $+15$ to represent low, medium, and high values for female labor force participation and to correspond to rates of 20, 35, and 50. Values for low, medium, and high collectivism equal, as in other calculations, -1.5, 0, and 1.5. The computation includes both types of interactions. For example, the effect for high-collectivist nations with high female labor force participation equals: $-1.26 + (1.5 \times .786) + (15 \times .071)$.

12. Other reasons may explain the delay in the benefits of small cohort size for young persons in the United States. Perhaps early members of the baby-bust cohort may still suffer from the effect of the crowded labor market brought on by preceding baby-boom cohorts, or illegal immigration in recent decades may have kept wages low among the baby-bust cohorts entering the labor force during the 1980s. However, these arguments probably do not explain the large effect of relative cohort size on fertility in the United States, a nation with relatively high legal and illegal immigration.

13. Excluding Japan has little effect on the results. The interaction between relative cohort size and collectivism depends more on the inclusion of Australia, the United States, Canada, and New Zealand. However, excluding Japan along

with the other non-European nations focuses the analysis on the theoretically meaningful subset of European nations.

5. Female Labor Force Participation and the Total Fertility Rate

1. The combined scale of women-friendly institutions can also be treated as a set of five other subscales. Correlating these subscales with the effect of female labor force participation shows the strongest relationship with the measure of maternity leave and the weakest relationship with the measure of legal equality. Despite these differences, the combined scale performs just as well as the individual items.

2. These figures come from the GLS estimates listed in the third column of table 13. The coefficient of female labor force participation shows its effect for the reference period of 1951–61. The effect for the second period equals the coefficient for female labor force participation ($-.043$) plus the coefficient for female labor force participation times the dummy variable for the 1962–72 period (0.003). The effects for the next two time periods are computed in the same way.

3. The quadratic for the female labor force participation rate is analogous to the interaction between the female labor force participation rate and relative cohort size in the previous chapter. As demonstrated by the coefficients for the product terms in table 8 (chap. 4), high levels of female labor force participation can reduce the negative effect of relative cohort size. A similar interpretation applies to the squared term for female labor force participation in table 13. The positive coefficient for the squared term shows that high levels of female labor force participation reduce the negative effect of female labor force participation. Thus, high female labor force participation reduces the harm for fertility of further increases in both relative cohort size and female work.

4. The first derivative of the terms in the GLS curvilinear model in the fifth column of table 13 equals $-0.145 + (2 \times 0.0018 \times X)$, where X refers to the female labor force participation rate. Thus, the effect when the participation rate equals 20 equals $-0.145 + (2 \times 0.0018 \times 20)$ or -0.073.

5. The inflection point equals $-b_1/2b_2$, where b_1 equals the coefficient for the unsquared term and b_2 equals the coefficient for the squared term. For the GLS estimates, the inflection point equals 40.3.

6. The coefficient of collectivism in the model shows its effect when female labor force participation equals zero and, therefore, has little meaning. When female labor force participation takes its mean value of 32.3, the effect of collectivism equals -0.109. At the mean, collectivist nations have slightly lower fertility, but this has less importance than the interactive effect in moderating the influence of female work on fertility.

7. The coefficients for the female labor force participation rate in table 14 of -0.029 and -0.033 represent the average national effect in the first time period rather than the average national effect for the full time period. To obtain the effect for low collectivism nations with a score of -1.5 on the scale, multiply the inter-

action term in the GLS equation in the first column of table 14 of 0.014 by −1.5 and add the coefficient of −0.029. For high collectivist nations, do the same using the collectivism value of 1.5.

8. The coefficients implied by the model in table 14 do not exactly reflect the nation-specific coefficients in table 12 because the model attempts to simplify national differences by using collectivism as a linear term to capture the 18 separate effects in table 12.

9. The calculations use the interaction terms for female work by both time and collectivism in the GLS estimates of column 3. For example, the effect for high collectivist nations in the latest time period would equal −0.040 + 0.020 + 0.014 × 1.5, or 0.001.

10. To get standardized coefficients, I simply multiply the unstandardized coefficients by the ratio of the standard deviation of female work to the standard deviation of fertility.

11. Another way to demonstrate differences across nations in the effect of the female participation rate relies on the nation-specific coefficients analogous to those in table 12. Whereas table 12 calculates the linear effect of the female participation rate for each nation, another analysis calculated the effects of the female participation rate and the female participation–rate squared for each nation. For 18 nations, collectivism has a correlation of 0.283 with the effect of the female participation rate and −0.243 with the effect of the female participation–rate squared; similar correlations hold for women-friendly institutions. The correlations reveal that collectivist and women-friendly institutions weaken the initial decline in fertility that comes with the rising female participation rate and also weaken the later rebound represented by the positive effect of the squared term.

12. To obtain the effect for women-friendly nations, I multiply the coefficient of 0.022 for the interaction term in the GLS equation in the first column of table 16 by 1.29 and add it to the coefficient of −0.025. For women-unfriendly nations, I do the same using the value of −1.22.

13. To get standardized coefficients, I again multiple the unstandardized coefficient by the ratio of the standard deviation of female work to the standard deviation of fertility.

14. The calculations use the interaction terms for female work by both time and gender equality in the GLS estimates of column 3 of table 16. For example, the effect for egalitarian nations in the latest time period would equal −0.035 + 0.019 + 0.023 × 1.29, or 0.014.

6. Cohort Size and Suicide and Homicide Mortality

1. Since then, suicide rates among the elderly have risen. McCall (1991) suggests that the reversal of previous downward trends stems from health problems among the elderly at the oldest ages. Improvements in health prolong the life but not the quality of experience of more and more elderly persons.

2. A somewhat more complex version of this argument takes into account the

generally lower influence of cohort size among the young in recent decades but predicts something different for the elderly. In the United States, the political power of aged interest groups and their sense of group identity may have emerged most strongly in recent years (Preston 1984). This suggests a weaker positive effect of cohort size for the young but a stronger negative effect for the elderly in recent years.

3. One could argue as well that collectivism increases homicide. Although collective social protection may unify groups politically, it may also inhibit communal personal ties that protect individuals from violence. By shifting public protection from family and community to the government and by empowering bureaucratic representatives of the members of encompassing groups, collectivist institutions may reduce local community ties. In some ways collectivism inhibits the atomism and anonymity of modern life, but in other ways it may contribute to it. Ultimately, the competing arguments about the additive effect of collectivism need empirical evaluation.

4. Some argue that paid employment and multiple role identities reduce stress and mortality for working women (Moen, Dempster-McClain, and Williams 1989). I explore this contrasting argument in more detail in later chapters on the sex differential in suicide, but in the meantime I use female labor force participation as an indicator of declining family integration.

5. The results of van Poppel and Day (1996) may stem, in part, from the use of crude rather than age-specific rates. Simpson (1998) argues that many unknown deaths occur among children, which would raise the death rates for groups that tend to exhibit high fertility, such as Catholics, without biasing estimates of suicides. He also argues that it is mistaken to equate unknown deaths and suicides. Sex- and age-specific data on unknown deaths and suicides therefore would improve on the crude comparisons across all ages that van Poppel and Day make.

6. Suicide rates for persons under age 15, which equal zero in all nations and years, can be safely ignored. Homicide rates for persons under age 15 reflect national and temporal differences in child abuse but raise special issues that go beyond this study of relative cohort size.

7. Age-Specific Suicide Rates

1. To highlight visually differences in trends rather than differences in levels of suicide rates, each age-specific curve uses a different scale. Despite what appears to be the case in the graphs, suicide rates for older age groups exceed those for younger age groups.

2. The negative correlations also stem from the failure to control for general tendencies across ages in suicide rates. Older persons have higher suicide rates than do younger persons, regardless of cohort size, but also make up a smaller percentage of the population because of mortality. This apparent negative relationship will disappear with controls for age.

3. At all ages except 35–44 and 45–54, the correlations between the popula-

tion percentage and relative cohort size exceed .800. Yet the correlations equal only .515 for persons ages 35–44 and .173 for persons ages 45–54. The discrepancy at the middle ages suggests that the denominator including persons aged 65 and over has some idiosyncratic characteristics.

4. Although not precisely bivariate correlations, the coefficients are analogous to the correlations that would be obtained if the variables were measured as deviations from nation means. The standardized coefficients with controls for the nation dummy variables provide an easy means to get equivalent results.

5. To obtain these summary results, each correlation in table 19 defines a separate case. Each case also has scores on the age and sex of the group, the measure of cohort size, and the type of model. Correlations relating the correlation coefficients in the table to each of the characteristics provide the summary measures reported in the text.

6. Although the time terms' average changes across all ages, their coefficients match the trend for the older age groups more than the youngest age groups. For males, the older age groups and the time polynomials show a decline in suicide rates in the most recent years, but, as depicted in fig. 10, the youngest age groups fail to experience this decline.

7. The effects come from adding the relative cohort size coefficient of 0.006 for the omitted age group to the coefficients for the product terms of each age group times relative cohort size. For example, the effect for the youngest age group equals 0.006 plus 0.075.

8. As discussed elsewhere, obtaining a simple measure from the GLS estimates of explained variance and an accurate indicator of the enhanced explanatory power of the interactive model presents problems. Lacking a clear test of the increase in explained variance due to the interaction terms, I concentrate on the size and significance of the individual terms and simply report the variance explained from the OLS estimates.

9. In a similar analysis using data up to 1986 and another estimation technique (Pampel 1996), I found much stronger effects of relative cohort size than I do here. The extension of the results here to a longer time period, one for which the influence of cohort size seems to decline, helps account for the weaker results.

10. Given the lack of interaction between age and cohort size for women in table 20, the nation and time interactions in table 21 focus only on male suicide. The comparison of the determinants of male and female suicide rates addresses equally important issues that deserve attention elsewhere (see chap. 10). However, since I desire to examine how the interaction of age and cohort size varies across nations and time periods, and since these variables do not interact in determining female suicide, I concentrate here on the male results.

11. The analysis could also compare four separate models divided by both national context and time. However, these models provide little information beyond that in table 21. Since context and time are orthogonal, the average of the

separate equations would show that the strongest effect of cohort size occurs in individualist nations in the early period, and the weakest effect of cohort size occurs in the collectivist nations in the later period.

12. Recall that the control variables are not measured separately by age but do vary across nations and years. Even so, they may explain some of the age-specific effects of cohort size. Perhaps age differences in suicide and age differences in the effect of cohort size result from differences across countries and time in the measures of family ties.

13. The negative effect appears to result from the high correlation of the divorce rate with the other independent variables. The *t*-ratio falls to marginal levels when included in an equation without female labor force participation, the total fertility rate, and GDP. The total fertility rate, in contrast, has consistent effects in the expected direction on both male and female suicide with other control variables.

8. Age-Specific Homicide Rates

1. It would be ideal to have figures on homicide offenders, but this would shift the focus of the study from mortality and raise difficult problems of measurement. The study of offenders must focus on the ages of persons arrested for homicide. Reliability of arrest data across nations, years, and ages is suspect. Many homicides do not lead to quick arrests, and the number varies across nations, years, and ages. The higher the proportion of homicides involving strangers and acquaintances rather than family members and intimates, the less likely the arrest. These problems have not prevented useful studies of cohort size for the United States (e.g., O'Brien, Stockard, and Isaacson 1999) but do present serious problems in cross-national studies.

2. Again, if reliable and comparable data existed, it would be ideal to know the sex of the murderer. I must, however, concentrate on mortality victims rather than offenders.

3. To highlight visually differences in trends rather than differences in levels of homicide, each age-specific curve uses its own scale. Despite what the format of the graphs seems to indicate, homicide mortality rates for younger age groups exceed those for older age groups.

4. To obtain these summary measures, each correlation in table 24 defines a separate case. Each case also has scores on the age and sex of the group, the measure of cohort size, and the type of model. Correlations relating the correlation coefficients in the table to each of the characteristics provide the summary measures reported in the text.

5. Income inequality measures the share of income going to the richest 20% of households (Bornschier and Heintz 1979), ethnic-linguistic heterogeneity measures on a scale from 0 to 1 the diversity of a nation's population (Bornschier and Heintz 1979), economic discrimination measures work and status disadvantages

of minority groups (Messner 1989), war deaths measure the number of persons killed in foreign wars since the 1950s (Gartner 1990), and the death penalty is coded as 0 for those nations without the penalty and as 1 for those with the penalty (Gartner 1990).

9. Sex Differences in Suicide and Homicide Mortality

1. The study of violent mortality removes the influence of biological differences between men and women in terms of their resistence to degenerative diseases such as heart disease and cancer. Although much debate exists over the genetic advantages of women in longevity, the longer survival of women even under conditions of extreme social disadvantage suggests that biology plays some role—albeit one that is hard to measure—in sex differences in many causes of mortality. Whatever its importance for mortality from degenerative diseases, however, women's biological advantage likely has little relationship to violent mortality. Perhaps women's physiologies make them better able to survive external injuries from gun wounds, stabbings, falls, or poisons, but the advantage is likely small. Relative rates of violent mortality almost exclusively respond to differences in social rather than biological conditions.

2. The study of violent mortality avoids the complex issue of the effects of smoking on sex differences in heart disease, cancer, and related diseases. Because rates of smoking correlate positively with female labor force participation they may contribute to declining sex ratios in mortality and hide other benefits for longevity that come from gender equality (Nathanson 1995; Trovato and Lalu 1998). Limiting mortality to suicide and homicide eliminates the confounding influence of smoking.

3. Although less than perfect, the relationship between suicide or homicide and well-being no doubt exceeds zero. On the one hand, lower rates of suicide and homicide victimization among women do not signify their better well-being in an absolute sense; other indicators of physical and mental health highlight problems of women relative to men. Factors besides well-being also influence relative suicide and homicide levels of men and women. On the other hand, trends in suicide and homicide of women relative to men indicate something about the respective social positions of each gender. Even if levels of suicide and homicide of men and women exaggerate the well-being of women, changes in those relative levels may relate closely to changes in relative social positions.

4. The competing viewpoints sometimes represent ideological positions favoring or opposing changes in the roles of women and men. Perhaps the difficulty in separating demographic and ideological positions helps make the sex differential in mortality a contentious issue of debate. Yet at least at the conceptual level, a relationship between gender equality in status and mortality need not imply that efforts for equality should cease; some may favor equality while recognizing that potential costs in terms of the female mortality advantage occur

along with other substantial benefits. Conversely, opposition to gender equality would remain among some regardless of its consequences for the health risks of women.

5. Some might deny altogether that progress toward gender equality has been made. Such a viewpoint correctly recognizes that women have far to go before obtaining full equality but ignores the enormous changes in the position of women over the past century. For example, in support of his thesis that gender inequality is destined for extinction by the modern economy and polity, Jackson (1998) describes the extraordinarily consistent growth of female employment. Even if not complete, sufficient improvements in women's status have occurred to gauge their influence on suicide and homicide mortality.

6. Lehmann (1995) discusses the tension inherent in Durkheim's theory of suicide differences between men and women.

7. In reporting their finding of no relationship between gender equality and female homicide victimization, Smith and Kuchta (1995) identify a problem that makes it difficult to isolate the consequences of changes in women's behavior for homicide. They note that changes in relative female victimization result primarily from rising male homicide victimization, which in turn stems from drug and gang conflict--activities that rarely involve women. As will become apparent in later chapters, wide fluctuations in male homicide victimization can distort measures of relative female homicide rates.

8. To the contrary, the high rate of female attempted but failed suicides suggests that men feel the stigma associated with suicide more than women do since men take measures to make sure their attempts do not miscarry.

9. Similarly, greater access of men to firearms may result in more homicides among men than women.

10. Unlike Western nations, Japan shows suicide rates that fall with modernization because of the resulting decline in altruistic and fatalist suicide exceeds the increase in anomic and egoistic suicide (Chandler and Tsai 1993). Western nations show clear increases in suicide with modernization because group-oriented suicides have always been rare. This suggests excluding Japan from the analysis of other high-income nations. Yet the analyses to follow in subsequent chapters do not change with the exclusion of Japan.

10. Sex Differences in Suicide Rates

1. For example, the absolute difference of one-half between the suicide ratios of 1.5 and 2.0 translates into logged ratios of 0.405 and 0.693 and a difference of 0.288, while the absolute difference of one-half between the suicide ratios of 4.5 and 5.0 translates into logged ratios of 1.504 and 1.609 and a difference of 0.105. The same absolute difference in the suicide ratio results in smaller logged differences at higher levels of the suicide ratio. In percentage terms, however, a unit difference in the logged ratio has the same meaning. A 50% increase in the suicide

ratio from 1 to 1.5 translates into an increase of 0.405 in the logged suicide rate, and a 50% increase in the suicide ratio from 2 to 3 also translates into an increase of 0.405 in the logged rate.

2. The residual deviation measure can also use the logged male and female suicide rates in the calculations, but the logged residual deviation measure correlates nearly perfectly with the logged ratio measure and provides no information not available from analysis of the logged ratio.

3. The weak correspondence between levels of the sex differential in suicide and national characteristics does not by itself negate the hypothesis about differences in the trends over time across nations. The test of the hypothesis requires comparisons of the determinants of the sex differential across nations rather than comparisons of the levels of the sex differential across nations. A variety of historical, cultural, social, geographical, and economic circumstances besides whether a nation has collectivist and women-friendly institutions affects absolute and relative suicide levels across nations and contributes to the weak correlations. However, when controlling for these differences in the levels of the sex differential, national characteristics may, as specified by the hypothesis, interact with other variables to influence the sex differential.

4. To highlight visually differences in trends rather than differences in levels of the suicide ratios, each age-specific curve uses a different scale. Despite what the format of the graph seems to indicate, suicide ratios are highest for older age groups and lowest for middle-aged groups.

5. The age coefficients relate to different cohort experiences. Because they adapt more quickly to innovative roles and behaviors, young women from new cohorts experience less harm from social change than middle-aged women do. At the oldest ages, women from cohorts born near the turn of the previous century likely experience little harm from changes in gender roles because they adhere to traditional norms. As a result, the suicide rates of middle-aged women are affected most by social changes toward gender equality and, across all nations and years, are most like those of men.

6. Whitt (1986) refers to these as sheath coefficients. To illustrate, a summary variable for time would equal the time variable multiplied by its coefficient of -0.019 plus the time-squared variable multiplied by its coefficient of 0.0006. When entered as a linear term in the regression, the new variable has a single coefficient that summarizes the strength of the two quadratic terms.

7. Previous models contain 17 dummy variables representing each nation minus the reference nation. The product terms multiply time by each of the 17 dummy variables and time squared by each of the dummy variables. The effects of time and time squared represent the trend for the reference nation, and the coefficients for the products of time and time squared by a nation dummy variable show the difference in the time trend between that nation and the reference nation. Adding the coefficients for the interaction terms to the coefficients for time

and time squared gives time and time-squared coefficients for each nation. The same procedure produces coefficients for female work and female work squared for each nation.

8. Controls for accidents without adjustment no doubt overcorrect for measurement bias. Since common forces affect both relative suicide and accident mortality, the overlap between the two types of mortality involves more than measurement error. An instrumental variable solution uses relative female and male deaths from unknown causes—a measure of the quality of death registration systems—to predict the accidental mortality ratio and then uses the predicted accident mortality ratio as a determinant to the suicide ratio. Supporting other results, the coefficients net of the predicted accident mortality variable differ little from the coefficients withouth the control.

11. Sex Differences in Homicide Rates

1. The less likely possibility involves an increase in the rates of women killing other women that exceeds the increase in the rates of women killing men.

2. The less likely possibility here involves a decrease in the rates of women killing other women that exceeds the decrease in the rates of women killing men.

3. The lack of symmetry shows in a correlation between the male/female ratio and the female/male ratio of $-.76$ when ideally it should equal -1.00.

4. Because of the negative intercept, when the female rate equals zero, the observed male rate must exceed the predicted rate.

5. To highlight differences in trends visually rather than differences in levels of measures, each measure uses a different scale.

6. Again, considering the possible undue influence of the United States, I replicated the interaction models with the United States deleted. Only one instance shows the expected results: the interaction of time with collectivism for the residual deviation measure.

7. Previous models contain 17 dummy variables representing each nation minus the reference nation. The product terms multiply time by each of the 17 dummy variables and time squared by each of the dummy variables. The coefficients of time and time squared represent the trend for the reference nation, and the coefficients for the products of time and time squared by a nation dummy variable show the difference in the time trend between that nation and the reference nation. Adding the coefficients for the interaction terms to the coefficients for time and time squared gives time and time-squared coefficients for each nation. The same procedure produces coefficients for female work and female work squared for each nation.

8. Other national determinants of homicide rates examined in chap. 9—income inequality, ethnic-linguistic heterogeneity, economic discrimination, war deaths, and the death penalty—have diverse effects on the measures of relative homicide rates. The correlations for most measures differ greatly in size and direction for two relative measures presented in table 42 and fail to identify mean-

ingful patterns across nations in homicide rates. Like the results for collectivism and women-friendly institutions, the measures of other national characteristics do little to support arguments for contextual influences.

9. The other national characteristics relate meaningfully to the logged absolute female homicide mortality rate. Like collectivism, high income inequality, ethnic-linguistic heterogeneity, economic discrimination, war deaths, and the death penalty lead to large initial increases in the female homicide mortality rate.

References

Adler, Freda. 1975. *Sisters in Crime: The Rise of the New Female Criminal.* New York: McGraw-Hill.

Ahlburg, D. A. 1983. "Good Times, Bad Times: A Study of the Future Path of U.S. Fertility." *Social Biology* 30:17–31.

———. 1986. "A Relative Cohort Size Forecasting Model of Canadian Total Live Births." *Social Biology* 33:51–56.

———. 1987. "Investigating Fertility Fluctuations." Paper read at the European Fertility Conference, Jyvaskyla, Finland.

Ahlburg, D. A., and M. O. Schapiro. 1984. "Socioeconomic Ramifications of Changing Cohort Size: An Analysis of U.S. Post-War Suicide Rates by Age and Sex." *Demography* 21:97–108.

Almgren, G., A. Guest, G. Immerwahr, and M. Spittel. 1998. "Joblessness, Family Disruption, and Violent Deaths in Chicago, 1970–90." *Social Forces* 76: 1465–93.

Archer, Dane, and Rosemary Gartner. 1984. *Violence and Crime in Cross-National Perspective.* New Haven, Conn.: Yale University Press.

Austin, R. L., M. Bologna, and H. H. Dodge. 1991. "Sex Role Change, Anomie and Female Suicide: A Test of Alternative Durkheimian Explanations." *Suicide and Life-Threatening Behavior* 22:197–225.

Bailey, W. C., and R. D. Peterson. 1995. "Gender Inequality and Violence against Women: The Case of Murder." Pp. 174–205 in *Crime and Inequality,* ed. John Hagan and Ruth D. Peterson. Stanford, Calif.: Stanford University Press.

Barrett, David B., ed. 1982. *World Christian Encyclopedia.* Oxford: Oxford University Press.

Beck, N., and J. N. Katz. 1995. "What to Do (and What Not to Do) with Time-Series-Cross-Sectional Data." *American Political Science Review* 89:634–47.

Becker, Gary S. 1991. *A Treatise on the Family.* Cambridge, Mass.: Harvard University Press.

Beer, J. de. 1991. "Births and Cohort Size." *Social Biology* 38:146–53.

Beets, G. C., A. C. Liefbroer, and J. de Jong Gierveld. 1997. "Combining Employment and Parenthood: A Longitudinal Study of Intentions of Dutch Young Adults." *Population and Development Review* 16:457–74.

Bennett, R. R., and J. P. Lynch. 1990. "Does a Difference Make a Difference? Comparing Cross-National Crime Indicators." *Criminology* 28:153–81.

Bernhardt, E. M. 1993. "Changing Family Ties, Women's Position, and Low Fertility." Pp. 80–103 in *Women's Position and Demographic Change,* ed. Nora Federici, Karen Oppenheim Mason, and Sølvi Sogner. Oxford: Clarendon.

Bhrolcháin, M. N. 1992. "Period Paramount? A Critique of the Cohort Approach to Fertility." *Population and Development Review* 18:599–629.

Blanchet, D., and O. Ekert-Jaffé. 1994. "The Demographic Impact of Family Benefits: Evidence from a Micro-Model and from Macro-Data." Pp. 79–104 in *The Family, the Market and the State in Ageing Societies,* ed. John Ermisch and Naohiro Ogawa. Oxford: Clarendon.

Bloom, D. E., R. B. Freeman, and S. D. Korenman. 1987. "The Labour-Market Consequences of Generational Crowding." *European Journal of Population* 3: 131–76.

Blossfeld, Hans-Peter, ed. 1995. *The New Role of Women: Family Formation in Modern Societies.* Boulder, Colo.: Westview.

Blossfeld, Hans-Peter, and Catherine Hakim, eds. 1997. *Between Equalization and Marginalization: Women Working Part-Time in Europe and the United States of America.* Oxford: Oxford University Press.

Blossfeld, H., A. de Rose, J. M. Hoem, and G. Rohwer. 1995. "Education, Modernization, and the Risk of Marriage Disruption in Sweden, West Germany, and Italy." Pp. 200–222 in *Gender and Family Change in Industrialized Countries,* ed. Karen Oppenheim Mason and An-Magritt Jensen. Oxford: Clarendon.

Boling, P. 1998. "Family Policy in Japan." *Journal of Social Policy* 27:173–90.

Bornschier, Volker, and Peter Heintz, eds. 1979. *Compendium of Data for World-System Analysis.* Zurich: University of Zurich Press.

Borschorst, A. 1994. "The Scandinavian Welfare States—Patriarchal, Gender Neutral or Women-Friendly?" *International Journal of Contemporary Sociology* 31:45–67.

Bouvier, L. F., and C. J. DeVita. 1991. "The Baby Boom—Entering Midlife." *Population Bulletin* 46(3):1–35.

Bradshaw, J. 1994. "Simulating Policies: An Example in Comparative Method." Pp. 439–60 in *Comparing Social Welfare Systems in Europe,* ed. Bruno Palier. Oxford: Oxford University Press.

Breault, K. D. 1986. "Suicide in America: A Test of Durkheim's Theory of Religious and Family Integration, 1933–1980." *American Journal of Sociology* 92: 628–56.

Brewer, V. E., and M. D. Smith. 1995. "Gender Inequality and Rates of Female Homicide Victimization across U.S. Cities." *Journal of Research in Crime and Delinquency* 32:175–90.

Brouard, N. 1990. "Classification of Developed Countries according to Cause-of-Death Patterns: A Test of Robustness during the Period 1968–1974." Pp. 250–

68 in *Measurement and Analysis of Mortality: New Approaches,* ed. Jacques Vallin, Stan D'Souza, and Alberto Palloni. Oxford: Clarendon.

Browne, A., and K. R. Williams. 1993. "Gender, Intimacy, and Lethal Violence: Trends from 1976 through 1987." *Gender and Society* 7:78–98.

Burr, J. A., P. L. McCall, and E. Powell-Griner. 1997. "Female Labor Force Participation and Suicide." *Social Science and Medicine* 44:1847–59.

Buse, A. 1973. "Goodness of Fit in Generalized Least Squares Estimation." *American Statistician* 27:106–8.

Butz, W. P., and M. P. Ward. 1979. "The Emergence of Counter-Cyclical U.S. Fertility." *American Economic Review* 69:318–28.

Canetto, S. S., and D. Lester. 1995. "The Epidemiology of Women's Suicidal Behavior." Pp. 35–57 in *Women and Suicidal Behavior,* ed. Silvia Sara Canetto and David Lester. New York: Springer.

Canetto, S. S., and I. Sakinofsky. 1998. "The Gender Paradox in Suicide." *Suicide and Life-Threatening Behavior* 28:1–23.

Castles, Francis G., ed. 1993. *Families of Nations: Patterns of Public Policy in Western Democracies.* Aldershot: Dartmouth.

Castles, F. G., and M. Flood. 1993. "Why Divorce Rates Differ: Law, Religious Belief and Modernity." Pp. 293–326 in *Families of Nations: Patterns of Public Policy in Western Democracies,* ed. Francis G. Castles. Aldershot: Dartmouth.

Castles, F. G., and D. Mitchell. 1993. "Worlds of Welfare and Families of Nations." Pp. 93–128 in *Families of Nations: Patterns of Public Policy in Western Democracies,* ed. Francis G. Castles. Aldershot: Dartmouth.

Castles, F. G., and C. Pierson. 1996. "A New Convergence? Recent Policy Developments in the United Kingdom, Australia, and New Zealand." *Policy and Politics* 24:233–45.

Center for International Comparisons. 1998. Penn World Tables. http://pwt .econ.upenn.edu.

Chafetz, J. S. 1995. "Chicken or Egg? A Theory of the Relationship between Feminist Movements and Family Change." Pp. 63–81 in *Gender and Family in Industrialized Countries,* ed. Karen Oppenheim Mason and An-Magritt Jensen. Oxford: Clarendon.

Chamberlayne, P. 1993. "Women and the State: Changes in Roles and Rights in France, West Germany, Italy, and Great Britain, 1970–1990." Pp. 170–93 in *Women and Social Policies in Europe: Work, Family, and the State,* ed. Jane Lewis. Aldershot: Edward Elgar.

Chandler, C. R., and Y. Tsai. 1993. "Suicide in Japan and in the West: Evidence for Durkheim's Theory." *International Journal of Comparative Sociology* 34: 244–59.

Charles, M. 1992. "Cross-National Variation in Occupational Sex Segregation." *American Sociological Review* 57:483–502.

Chesnais, J. C. 1983. "La notion de cycle en démographie: La fécondité post transitionelle, est-elle cyclique?" *Population* 38:361–90.

———. 1992. *The Demographic Transition: Stages, Patterns and Economic Implications.* Oxford: Clarendon.

———. 1996. "Fertility, Family, and Social Policy in Contemporary Western Europe." *Population and Development Review* 22:729–39.

Chesney-Lind, Meda, and Randall G. Shelden. 1992. *Girls, Delinquency, and Juvenile Justice.* Pacific Grove, Calif.: Brooks/Cole.

Christenson, B. A., and N. E. Johnson. 1995. "Educational Inequality in Adult Mortality: An Assessment with Death Certificate Data in Michigan." *Demography* 32:215–30.

Clark, R. D. 1992. "Family Structure, Liberty, Equality and Divorce: A Cross-National Examination." Pp. 175–196 in *Fertility Transitions, Family Structure, and Population Policy,* ed. Calvin Goldscheider. Boulder, Colo.: Westview.

Cliquet, R. L. 1991. "The Second Demographic Transition: Fact or Fiction?" *Population Studies No. 23.* Strasbourg: Council of Europe.

Coale, Ansley J., and Susan Cotts Watkins, eds. 1986. *The Decline of Fertility in Europe.* Princeton, N.J.: Princeton University Press.

Cohen, L. E., and M. Felson. 1979. "Social Change and Crime Rate Trends: A Routine Activities Approach." *American Sociological Review* 44:588–608.

Cohen, L. E., and K. C. Land. 1987. "Age Structure and Crime: Symmetry versus Asymmetry and the Projection of Crime Rates through the 1990s." *American Sociological Review* 52:170–83.

Coleman, D. 1996. "New Patterns and Trends in European Fertility: International and Sub-National Comparisons." Pp. 1–61 in *Europe's Population in the 1990s,* ed. David Coleman. Oxford: Oxford University Press.

Curtis, Lynn A. 1974. *Criminal Violence: National Patterns and Behavior.* Lexington, Mass.: D.C. Heath.

Cutright, P., and C. M. Briggs. 1995. "Structural and Cultural Determinants of Adult Homicide in Developed Countries: Age and Gender-Specific Rates, 1955–1989." *Sociological Focus* 28:221–43.

Cutright, P., and R. M. Fernquist. 2000. "Effects of Societal Integration, Period, Region, and Culture of Suicide on Male Age-Specific Suicide Rates: Twenty Developed Countries, 1955–1989." *Social Science Research* 29:148–72.

Davis, K., and P. van den Oever. 1982. "Demographic Foundations of New Sex Roles." *Population and Development Review* 8:495–512.

Davis, R. A. 1981. "Female Labor Force Participation, Status Integration and Suicide, 1950–1969." *Suicide and Life-Threatening Behavior* 11:111–23.

Day, L. H. 1987. "Durkheim on Religion and Suicide—A Demographic Critique." *Sociology* 21:449–61.

———. 1995. "Recent Fertility Trends in Industrialized Countries: Toward a Fluctuating or a Stable Pattern." *European Journal of Population* 11:275–88.

Deflem, M., and F. C. Pampel. 1996. "The Myth of Post-National Identity: Popular Support for European Unification." *Social Forces* 75:119–44.

Demeny, P. 1997. "Replacement-Level Fertility: The Implausible Endpoint of the

Demographic Transition." Pp. 94–110 in *The Continuing Demographic Transition,* ed. C. W. Jones, R. M. Douglas, J. C. Caldwell, and R. M. D'Souza. Oxford: Clarendon.

Durkheim, Émile. (1897) 1966. *Suicide.* New York: Free Press.

Easterlin, Richard A. 1973. "Relative Economic Status and the American Fertility Swing." Pp. 170–233 in *Family Economic Behavior: Problems and Prospects,* ed. Eleanor H. B. Sheldon. Philadelphia: Lippincott.

———. 1976. "The Conflict between Aspirations and Resources." *Population and Development Review* 2:417–25.

———. 1978. "What Will 1984 Be Like? Socioeconomic Implications of Recent Twists in Age Structure." *Demography* 15:397–432.

———. 1987a. *Birth and Fortune: The Impact of Numbers on Personal Welfare.* Chicago: University of Chicago Press.

———. 1987b. "The New Age Structure of Poverty in America: Permanent or Transient?" *Population and Development Review* 13:195–208.

Easterlin, R. A., and G. A. Condran. 1976. "A Note on the Recent Fertility Swing in Australia, Canada, England and Wales, and the United States." Pp. 140–51 in *Population, Factor Movements, and Economic Development: Studies Presented to Brinley Thomas,* ed. Hamish Richards. Cardiff: University of Wales Press.

Ekert, O. 1986. "Effets et limites des aides financières aux familles: Une expérience et un modèle." *Population* 41:327–48.

Elder, G. H. 1981. "Scarcity and Prosperity in Postwar Childbearing: Explanations from a Life Course Perspective." *Journal of Family History* 6:410–33.

Ellison, C. G., J. A. Burr, and P. L. McCall. 1997. "Religious Homogeneity and Metropolitan Suicide Rates." *Social Forces* 76:273–99.

Ermisch, J. F. 1979. "The Relevance of the 'Easterlin Hypothesis' and the 'New Home Economics' to Fertility Movements in the Great Britain." *Population Studies* 33:39–58.

———. 1980. "Time Costs, Aspirations, and the Effect of Economic Growth on German Fertility." *Oxford Bulletin of Economics and Statistics* 42:125–43.

———. 1996. "The Economic Environment for Family Formation." Pp. 144–62 in *Europe's Population in the 1990s,* ed. David Coleman. Oxford: Oxford University.

Esping-Andersen, Gøsta. 1985. "Power and Distributional Regimes." *Politics and Society* 14:222–55.

———. 1990. *The Three Worlds of Welfare Capitalism.* Princeton, N.J.: Princeton University Press.

———, ed. 1996. *Welfare States in Transition: National Adaptations in Global Economies.* London: Sage

———. 1999. *Social Foundations of Postindustrial Economies.* Oxford: Oxford University Press.

Europa Publications. 1998. *Europa World Yearbook.* Vol. 2. London: Europa Publications.

Feldman, J. J., D. M. Makuc, J. C. Kleinman, and J. Cornoni-Huntley. 1989. "National Trends in Educational Differentials in Mortality." *American Journal of Epidemiology* 129:919–33.

Fernquist, R. M., and P. Cutright. 1998. "Societal Integration and Age-Standardized Suicide Rates in Twenty-One Developed Countries, 1955–1989." *Social Science Research* 27:109–27.

Fox, John, ed. 1989. *Health Inequalities in European Countries.* Aldershot: Gower.

Fries, J. 1980. "Aging, Natural Death, and the Compression of Mortality." *New England Journal of Medicine* 303:130–36.

———. 1989. "Compression of Morbidity: Near or Far?" *Milbank Quarterly* 67:208–32.

Fukuyama, Francis. 1995. *Trust: Social Virtues and the Creation of Prosperity.* New York: Free Press.

Gartner, R. 1990. "The Victims of Homicide: A Temporal and Cross-National Comparison." *American Sociological Review* 55:92–106.

Gartner, R., K. Baker, and F. C. Pampel. 1990. "Gender Stratification and the Gender Gap in Homicide Victimization." *Social Problems* 37:593–612.

Gartner, R., and B. McCarthy. 1991. "The Social Distribution of Femicide in Urban Canada, 1921–1988." *Law and Society Review* 25:287–311.

Gartner, R., and R. N. Parker. 1990. "Cross-National Evidence on Homicide and the Age Structure of the Population." *Social Forces* 69:351–71.

Gauthier, Anne Hélène. 1996a. "The Measured and Unmeasured Effects of Welfare Benefits on Families: Implications for Europe's Demographic Trends." Pp. 297–331 in *Europe's Population in the 1990s,* ed. David Coleman. Oxford: Oxford University Press.

———. 1996b. *The State and the Family: A Comparative Analysis of Family Policies in Industrialized Countries.* Oxford: Clarendon.

Gauthier, A. H., and J. Hatzius. 1997. "Family Benefits and Fertility: An Econometric Analysis." *Population Studies* 51:295–306.

Gelb, Joyce. 1989. *Feminism and Politics: A Comparative Perspective.* Berkeley: University of California Press.

Gibbs, J. P., and W. T. Martin. 1964. *Status Integration and Suicide: A Sociological Study.* Eugene: University of Oregon Press.

Gillis, John R., Louise Tilly, and David Levine, eds. 1992. *The European Experience of Declining Fertility, 1850–1970: The Quiet Revolution.* Cambridge, Mass.: Blackwell.

Girard, C. 1993. "Age, Gender, and Suicide: A Cross-National Analysis." *American Sociological Review* 58:553–74.

Goldscheider, Frances K., and Linda J. Waite. 1991. *New Families, No Families? The Transformation of the American Home.* Berkeley: University of California Press.

Golini, Antonio. 1998. "How Low Can Fertility Be? An Empirical Exploration." *Population and Development Review* 24:59–73.

Goode, W. J. 1960. "A Theory of Role Strain." *American Sociological Review* 25: 483–96.

Gornick, J. C., and J. Jacobs. 1998. "Gender, the Welfare State, and Public Employment: A Comparative Study of Seven Industrialized Countries." *American Sociological Review* 63: 688–710.

Gornick, J. C., M. K. Meyers, and K. E. Ross. 1998. "Public Policies and the Employment of Mothers: A Cross-National Study." *Social Science Quarterly* 79: 35–54.

Grasmick, H. G., N. J. Finley, and D. L. Glaser. 1984. "Labor Force Participation, Sex-Role Attitudes, and Female Crime." *Social Science Quarterly* 65: 703–17.

Guibert-Lantoine, C., and A. Monnier. 1997. "The Demographic Situation of Europe and the Developed Countries Overseas: An Annual Report." *Population: An English Selection* 9: 243–68.

Hagan, J., J. Simpson, and A. R. Gillis. 1987. "Class and Household: A Power Control Theory of Gender and Delinquency." *American Journal of Sociology* 92: 788–816.

Hakim, C. 1997. "A Sociological Perspective on Part-Time Work." Pp. 22–70 in *Between Equalization and Marginalization: Women Working Part-Time in Europe and the United States of America,* ed. Hans-Peter Blossfeld and Catherine Hakim. Oxford: Oxford University Press.

Hammarström, A. 1994. "Health Consequences of Youth Unemployment—Review from a Gender Perspective." *Social Science and Medicine* 38: 699–709.

Hantrais, L. 1994. "Comparing Family Policy in Britian, France, and Germany." *Journal of Social Policy* 23: 135–60.

———. 1997. "Exploring the Relationships between Social Policy and Changing Family Forms within the European Union." *European Journal of Population* 13: 339–79.

Hartnagel, T. F. 1982. "Modernization, Female Social Roles, and Female Crime: A Cross-National Investigation." *Sociological Quarterly* 23: 477–90.

Hassan, R., and G. Tan. 1989. "Suicide Trends in Australia, 1901–1985: An Analysis of Sex Differentials." *Suicide and Life-Threatening Behavior* 19: 362–80.

Heitlinger, Alena. 1993. *Women's Equality, Demography and Public Policies: A Comparative Perspective.* New York: St. Martin's.

Henry, Andrew F., and James F. Short, Jr. 1954. *Suicide and Homicide: Some Economic, Sociological, and Psychological Aspects of Aggression.* Glencoe, Ill.: Free Press.

Hernes, Helga. 1987. *Welfare State and Women Power.* Oslo: Norwegian University Press.

Hewlett, Sylvia Anne. 1986. *A Lesser Life: The Myth of Women's Liberation in America.* New York: William Morrow.

Hicks, A., and D. Swank. 1992. "Politics, Institutions, and Welfare Spending in Industrialized Democracies, 1960–82." *American Political Science Review* 86: 658–74.

Himes, C. L., S. H. Preston, and G. A. Condran. 1994. "A Relational Model of Mortality at Older Ages in Low Mortality Countries." *Population Studies* 48: 269–91.

Hindelang, M. J., M. R. Gottfredson, and J. Garofalo. 1978. *Victims of Personal Crime: An Empirical Foundation for a Theory of Personal Victimization.* Cambridge, Mass.: Ballinger.

Hirschi, T., and M. Gottfredson. 1983. "Age and Explanation of Crime." *American Journal of Sociology* 89: 552–84.

Hoem, B. 1995. "The Way to the Gender-Segregated Swedish Labour Market." Pp. 279–96 in *Gender and Family Change in Industrialized Countries,* ed. Karen Oppenheim Mason and An-Magritt Jensen. Oxford: Clarendon.

Hoem, J. M. 1990. "Social Policy and Recent Fertility Change in Sweden." *Population and Development Review* 16:735–48.

———. 1993. "Public Policy as the Fuel of Fertility: Effects of Public Policy Reform on the Pace of Childbearing in Sweden in the 1980s." *Acta Sociologica* 36:19–31.

Höhn, C. 1991. "Policies Relevant to Fertility." Pp. 247–56 in *Future Demographic Trends in Europe and North America: What Can We Assume Today?* ed. Wolfgang Lutz. London: Academic Press.

Holden, C. 1986. "Youth Suicide: New Research Focuses on a Growing Social Problem." *Science* 233:839–41.

Holinger, P. C., D. Offer, and M. A. Zola. 1988. "A Prediction Model of Suicide among Youth." *Journal of Nervous and Mental Disease* 176:275–79.

Horiuchi, S., and J. R. Wilmoth. 1998. "Deceleration in the Age Pattern of Mortality at Older Ages." *Demography* 35:391–412.

House, J. S., R. C. Kessler, and A. R. Herzog. 1990. "Age, Socioeconomic Status, and Health." *Milbank Quarterly* 68:383–411.

Hsaio, C. 1986. *Analysis of Panel Data.* New York: Cambridge University Press.

Huinink, J., and K. U. Mayer. 1995. "Gender, Social Inequality, and Family Formation in West Germany." Pp. 168–199 in *Gender and Family Change in Industrialized Countries,* ed. Karen Oppenheim Mason and An-Magritt Jensen. Oxford: Clarendon.

Inglehart, Ronald. 1990. *Culture Shift in Advanced Industrial Society.* Princeton, N.J.: Princeton University.

Inkeles, A. 1981. "Convergence and Divergence in Industrial Societies." Pp. 3–38 in *Directions of Change: Modernization Theory, Research and Realities,* ed. Mustafa O. Attir, Burkhart Holzner, and Zdenek Suda. New York: Westview.

International Labour Office. 1986. *Economically Active Population: Estimates and Projections.* Geneva: International Labour Office.

———. 1991 and various years. *Yearbook of Labour Statistics.* Geneva: International Labour Office.

———. 1992 and various years. *The Cost of Social Security.* Geneva: International Labour Office.

Jackson, Robert Max. 1998. *Destined for Equality: The Inevitable Rise of Women's Status.* Cambridge, Mass.: Harvard University Press.

Jones, E. F., J. D. Forrest, N. Goldman, S. K. Henshaw, R. Lincoln, J. I. Rosoff, C. Westoff, and D. Wulf. 1985. "Teenage Pregnancy, Contraception, and Family Planning Services in Industrialized Countries." *Family Planning Perspectives* 17:53–63.

Jones, Elise F., Jacqueline Darroch Forrest, Stanley K. Henshaw, Jane Silverman, and Aida Torres. 1989. *Pregnancy, Contraception, and Family Planning Services in Industrialized Countries.* New Haven, Conn.: Yale University Press.

Judge, George G., William E. Griffiths, R. Carter Hill, and Tsoung-Chao Lee. 1988. *Introduction to the Theory and Practice of Econometrics.* 2d ed. New York: Wiley.

Kamerman, Sheila B., and Alfred J. Kahn, eds. 1991. *Child Care, Parental Leave, and the Under 3s: Policy Innovation in Europe.* New York: Auburn House.

Kannisto, Väinö. 1994. *Development of Oldest-Old Mortality, 1950–1990: Evidence from Twenty-Eight Developed Countries.* Odense, Denmark: Odense University Press.

Kannisto, V., J. Lauritsen, A. R. Thatcher, and J. W. Vaupel. 1994. "Reductions in Mortality at Advanced Ages: Several Decades of Evidence from Twenty-Seven Countries." *Population and Development Review* 20:793–810.

Karvonen, L., and P. Selle. 1995. "Introduction: Scandinavia: A Case Apart." Pp. 3–24 in *Women in Nordic Politics: Closing the Gap,* ed. Lauri Karvonen and Per Selle. Aldershot: Dartmouth.

Kawachi, I., B. P. Kennedy, V. Gupta, and D. Prothrow-Stith. 1999. "Women's Status and the Health of Women and Men: A View from the States." *Social Science and Medicine* 48:21–32.

Kerr, Clark, J. T. Dunlop, Frederick Harbison, and Charles Myers. 1964. *Industrialism and Industrial Man.* New York: Oxford University Press.

Kertzer, D. I. 1997. "The Proper Role of Culture in Demographic Explanation." Pp. 137–57 in *The Continuing Demographic Transition,* ed. C. W. Jones, R. M. Douglas, J. C. Caldwell, and R. M. D'Souza. Oxford: Clarendon.

Keyfitz, N. 1991. "Subreplacement Fertility: The Third Level of Explanation." Pp. 235–46 in *Future Demographic Trends in Europe and North America: What Can We Assume Today?* ed. Wolfgang Lutz. London: Academic Press.

King, L. 1998. "France Needs Children: Pronatalism, Nationalism, and Women's Equity." *Sociological Quarterly* 39:33–52.

Klinger, A. 1991. "Survey of Recent Fertility Trends and Assumptions Used for Projections." Pp. 147–68 in *Future Demographic Trends in Europe and North America: What Can We Assume Today?* ed. Wolfgang Lutz. London: Academic.

Kmenta, Jan. 1986. *Elements of Econometrics.* 2d ed. New York: Macmillan.

Kolberg, J. E. 1991. "The Gender Dimension of the Welfare State." *International Journal of Sociology* 21:119–48.

Korpi, Walter. 1989. "Power, Politics, and State Autonomy in the Development of Social Citizenship: Social Rights during Sickness in Eighteen OECD Countries since 1930." *American Sociological Review* 54:309–28.

Korpi, W., and J. Palme. 1998. "The Paradox of Redistribution and Strategies of Equality: Welfare State Institutions, Inequality, and Poverty in the Western Countries." *American Sociological Review* 63:661–87.

Kposowa, A. J., K. D. Breault, and B. M. Harison. 1995. "Reassessing the Structural Covariates of Violent and Property Crimes in the USA: A Country-Level Analysis." *British Journal of Sociology* 46:79–105.

Krull, C., and F. Trovato. 1994. "The Quiet Revolution and the Sex Differential in Quebec's Suicide Rates: 1931–1986." *Social Forces* 72:1121–47.

Kruttschnitt, C. 1995. "Violence by and against Women: A Comparative and Cross-National Analysis." Pp. 89–107 in R. Barry Ruback and Neil Alan Weiner. *Interpersonal Violent Behaviors: Social and Cultural Aspects.* New York: Springer.

———. 1996. "Contributions of Quantitative Methods for the Study of Gender and Crime, or Bootstrapping Our Way into the Theoretical Thicket." *Journal of Quantitative Criminology* 12:135–61.

Kunst, A. E., and J. P. Mackenbach. 1994. "The Size of Mortality Differences Associated with Educational Levels in Nine Industrialized Countries." *American Journal of Public Health* 84:932–37.

Kushner, H. I. 1985. "Women and Suicide in Historical Perspective." *Signs* 10: 537–52.

———. 1995. "Women and Suicidal Behavior." Pp. 35–57 in *Women and Suicidal Behavior,* ed. Silvia Sara Canetto and David Lester. New York: Springer.

Land, K. C., P. L. McCall, and L. E. Cohen. 1990. "Structural Covariates of Homicide Rates: Are There Any Invariances across Time and Social Space?" *American Journal of Sociology* 95:922–63.

Lauritsen, J. L., R. J. Sampson, and J. H. Laub. 1991. "The Link between Offending and Victimization among Adolescents." *Criminology* 29:265–92.

Lee, R. D., and J. B. Casterline. 1996. "Introduction." Pp. 1–18 in *Fertility in the United States: New Patterns, New Theories,* ed. John B. Casterline, Ronald D. Lee, and Karen A. Foote. New York: Population Council.

Lehmann, J. M. 1995. "Durkheim's Theories of Deviance and Suicide: A Feminist Reconsideration." *American Journal of Sociology* 100:904–30.

Lester, D. 1991. "Size of Youth Cohort and Suicide Rate in Japan." *Perceptual and Motor Skills* 73:508.

———. 1994. "Gender Equality and the Sex Differential in Suicide Rates." *Psychological Reports* 75:1162.

Lesthaeghe, R. 1983. "A Century of Demographic and Cultural Change in Western Europe: An Exploration of Underlying Dimensions." *Population and Development Review* 9:411–35.

———. 1992. "Beyond Economic Reductionism: The Transformation of the Reproductive Regimes in France and Belgium in the Eighteenth and Nineteenth Centuries." Pp. 1–44 in *Fertility Transitions, Family Structure and Population Policy,* ed. Calvin Goldscheider. Boulder, Colo.: Westview.

———. 1995. "The Second Demographic Transition in Western Countries: An Interpretation." Pp. 17–62 in *Gender and Family Change in Industrialized Countries,* ed. Karen Oppenheim Mason and An-Magritt Jensen. Oxford: Clarendon.

Lesthaeghe, R., and D. Meekers. 1986. "Value Changes and the Dimensions of Familism in the European Community." *European Journal of Population* 2: 225–68.

Lesthaeghe, R., and J. Surkyn. 1988. "Cultural Dynamics and Economic Theories of Fertility Change." *Population and Development Review* 14: 1–45.

Lewis, J. 1992. "Gender and the Development of Welfare Regimes." *Journal of European Social Policy* 3: 159–73.

———, ed. 1993. *Women and Social Policies in Europe: Work, Family and the State.* Aldershot: Edward Elgar.

———. 1997. "Gender and Welfare Regimes: Further Thoughts." *Social Politics* 4: 160–77.

Lijphart, Arend. 1984. *Democracies: Patterns of Majoritarian and Consensus Government in Twenty-One Countries.* New Haven, Conn.: Yale University Press.

Lijphart, A., and M. M. L. Crepaz. 1991. "Corporatism and Consensus Democracy in Eighteen Countries: Conceptual and Empirical Linkages." *British Journal of Political Science* 21: 235–56.

Lopez, Alan D., Graziella Caselli, and Tapani Valkonen, eds. 1995. *Adult Mortality in Developed Countries: From Description to Explanation.* Oxford: Clarendon.

Lutz, Wolfgang, ed. 1991. *Future Demographic Trends in Europe and North America: What Can We Assume Today?* London: Academic.

MacDonald, M. M., and R. R. Rindfuss. 1978. "Relative Economic Status and Fertility: Evidence from a Cross-Section." *Research in Population Economics* 1: 291–307.

Macunovich, D. J. 1995. "The Butz-Ward Model in Light of More Recent Data." *Journal of Human Resources* 30: 229–55.

———. 1996. "Relative Income and Price of Time: Exploring Their Effects on U.S. Fertility and Female Labor Force Participation." *Population and Development Review* 22: 223–57.

———. 1998. "Fertility and the Easterlin Hypothesis: An Assessment of the Literature." *Journal of Population Economics* 11: 53–111.

Mäkinen, I. 1997. "Are There Social Correlates of Suicide?" *Social Science and Medicine* 44: 1919–29.

Manton, K. G., E. Stallard, and H. D. Tolley. 1991. "Limits to Human Life Expectancy: Evidence, Prospects, and Implications." *Population and Development Review* 17: 603–37.

Manton, K. G., and J. W. Vaupel. 1995. "Survival after the Age of Eighty in the

United States, France, England, and Japan." *New England Journal of Medicine* 333:1232–35.

Mare, R. D. 1990. "Socio-Economic Careers and Differential Mortality among Older Men in the United States." Pp. 367–87 in *Measurement and Analysis of Mortality: New Approaches,* ed. Jacques Vallin, Stan D'Souza, and Alberto Palloni. Oxford: Clarendon.

Mason, K. O. 1997. "Gender and Demographic Change: What Do We Know?" Pp. 158–82 in *The Continuing Demographic Transition,* ed. C. W. Jones, R. M. Douglas, J. C. Caldwell, and R. M. D'Souza. Oxford: Clarendon.

Matland, R. E. 1995. "How the Election System Structure Has Helped Women Close the Representation Gap." Pp. 281–309 in *Women in Nordic Politics: Closing the Gap,* ed. Lauri Karvonen and Per Selle. Aldershot: Dartmouth.

Maxim, P. S. 1985. "Cohort Size and Juvenile Delinquency: A Test of the Easterlin Hypothesis." *Social Forces* 63:661–81.

McCall, P. L. 1991. "Adolescent and Elderly White Male Suicide Trends: Evidence of Changing Well-Being?" *Journal of Gerontology* 46:543–51.

McCall, P. L., and K. C. Land. 1994. "Trends in White Male Adolescent, Young-Adult and Elderly Suicide: Are There Common Underlying Structural Factors." *Social Science Research* 23:57–81.

McDonald, P. 1997. "Gender Equity, Social Institutions, and the Future of Fertility." Working papers in demography, Research School of Social Sciences, Australian National University, Canberra.

McIntosh, J. L., and B. L. Jewell. 1987. "Sex Difference Trends in Completed Suicide." *Suicide and Life-Threatening Behavior* 16:16–27.

Menard, S. 1992. "Demographic and Theoretical Variables in the Age-Period-Cohort Analysis of Illegal Behavior." *Journal of Research in Criminology* 29: 178–99.

Menard, S., and D. S. Elliot. 1990. "Self-Reported Offending, Maturational Reform, and the Easterlin Hypothesis." *Journal of Quantitative Criminology* 6: 237–67.

Messerschmidt, James W. 1993. *Masculinities and Crime: Critique and Reconceptualization of Theory.* Lanham, Md.: Rowman & Littlefield.

Messner, S. 1989. "Economic Discrimination and Societal Homicide Rates: Further Evidence on the Cost of Inequality." *American Sociological Review* 54: 597–611.

Miethe, Terance D., and Robert F. Meier. 1994. *Crime and Its Social Context: Toward an Integrated Theory of Offenders, Victims, and Situations.* Albany: State University of New York Press.

Misra, J., and F. Akins. 1998. "The Welfare State and Women: Structure, Agency, and Diversity." *Social Politics* 5:259–85.

Moen, P., D. Dempster-McClain, and R. M. Williams. 1989. "Social Integration and Longevity: An Event-History Analysis of Women's Roles and Resilience." *American Sociological Review* 54:635–47.

Morgan, S. P. 1996. "Characteristic Features of Modern American Fertility." Pp. 19–66 in *Fertility in the United States: New Patterns, New Theories,* ed. John B. Casterline, Ronald D. Lee, and Karen A. Foote. New York: Population Council.

Mósesdóttir, L. 1995. "The State and Egalitarian, Ecclesiastical and Liberal Regimes of Gender Relations." *British Journal of Sociology* 46:623–42.

Nathanson, C. A. 1995. "Mortality and the Position of Women in Developed Countries." Pp. 135–57 in *Adult Mortality in Developed Countries: From Description to Explanation,* ed. Alan D. Lopez, Graziella Caselli, and Tapani Valkonen. Oxford: Clarendon.

Newman, J. F., K. R. Whittemore, and H. G. Newman. 1973. "Women in the Labor Force and Suicide." *Social Problems* 21:220–30.

Nimwegan, Nico van, Jean-Claude Chesnais, and Pearl Dykstra, eds. 1993. *Coping with Sustained Low Fertility in France and the Netherlands.* Amsterdam: Swets & Zeitlinger.

Norris, Pippa. 1987. *Politics and Sexual Equality: The Comparative Position of Women in Western Democracies.* Boulder, Colo.: Rienner.

O'Brien, R. M. 1988. "Exploring the Intersexual Nature of Violent Crimes." *Criminology* 28:601–26.

———. 1989. "Relative Cohort Size and Age-Specific Crime Rates: An Age-Period–Relative Cohort Size Model." *Criminology* 27:57–78.

O'Brien, R. M., J. Stockard, and L. Isaacson. 1999. "The Enduring Effects of Cohort Characteristics on Age-Specific Homicide Rates, 1960–1995." *American Journal of Sociology* 104:1061–95.

O'Connell, M. 1978. "The Effect of Changing Age Distributions on Fertility: An International Comparison." *Research on Population Economics* 1:233–45.

O'Connor, J. S. 1993. "Gender, Class and Citizenship in the Comparative Analysis of Welfare State Regimes: Theoretical and Methodological Issues." *British Journal of Sociology* 44:501–18.

O'Connor, Julia S, Ann Shola Orloff, and Sheila Shaver. 1999. *States, Markets, Families: Gender, Liberalism, and Social Policy in Australia, Canada, Great Britain and the United States.* Cambridge: Cambridge University Press.

Ogle, R. S., D. Maier-Katkin, and T. J. Bernard. 1995. "A Theory of Homicidal Behavior among Women." *Criminology* 33:173–93.

Olsen, R. J. 1994. "Fertility and the Size of the U.S. Labor Force." *Journal of Economic Literature* 32:60–100.

Oppenheimer, V. K. 1976. "The Easterlin Hypothesis: Another Aspect of the Echo Effect to Consider." *Population and Development Review* 2:433–57.

———. 1982. *Work and the Family: A Study of Social Demography.* New York: Academic Press.

———. 1994. "Women's Rising Employment and the Future of the Family in Industrial Societies." *Population and Development Review* 20:293–342.

Oppenheimer, V. K., M. Kalmijn, and N. Lim. 1997. "Men's Career Development and Marriage Timing during a Period of Rising Inequality." *Demography* 34:311–30.

Organization for Economic Cooperation and Development. 1996 and various years. *Labor Force Statistics.* Paris: Organization for Economic Cooperation and Development.

———. 1998. *National Accounts, 1984–1996.* Paris: Organization for Economic Cooperation and Development.

Orloff, A. S. 1993. "Gender and the Social Rights of Citizenship: The Comparative Analysis of Gender Relations and Welfare States." *American Sociological Review* 58:303–28.

———. 1996. "Gender in the Welfare State." *Annual Review of Sociology* 22: 51–78.

Palme, Joakim. 1990. *Pension Rights in Welfare Capitalism.* Stockholm: Swedish Institute for Social Research, Univeristy of Stockholm.

Pampel, F. C. 1994. "Population Aging, Class Context, and Age Inequality in Public Spending." *American Journal of Sociology* 100:153–95.

———. 1996. "Cohort Size and Age Specific Suicide Rates: A Contingent Relationship." *Demography* 33:341–56.

Pampel, F. C., and P. Adams. 1992. "The Effect of Demographic Change and Political Structure on Family Allowance Expenditures." *Social Service Review* 66:524–46.

Pampel, F. C., and H. E. Peters. 1995. "The Easterlin Effect." *Annual Review of Sociology* 21:163–94.

Pampel, F. C., J. B. Williamson, and R. Stryker. 1990. "Class Context and Pension Response to Demographic Structure in Advanced Industrial Democracies." *Social Problems* 37:535–50.

Pappas, G., S. Queen, W. Hadden, and G. Fisher. 1993. "The Increasing Disparities in Mortality between Socioeconomic Groups in the United States, 1960 and 1986." *New England Journal of Medicine* 329:103–9.

Pescosolido, B. A. 1994. "Bringing Durkheim into the Twenty-First Century: A Network Approach to Unresolved Issues in the Sociology of Suicide." Pp. 264–95 in *Emile Durkheim: Le Suicide 100 Years Later,* ed. David Lester. Philadelphia: Charles Press.

Pescosolido, B. A., and S. Georgianna. 1989. "Durkheim, Suicide, and Religion: Toward a Network Theory of Suicide." *American Sociological Review* 54: 33–48.

Pescosolido, B. A., and R. Mendelsohn. 1986. "Social Causation or Social Construction of Suicide? An Investigation into the Social Organization of Official Rates." *American Journal of Sociology* 51:80–101.

Pinelli, A. 1995. "Women's Condition, Lower Fertility, and Emerging Union Patterns in Europe." Pp. 82–101 in *Gender and Family Change in Industrialized Countries,* ed. Karen Oppenheim Mason and An-Magritt Jensen. Oxford: Clarendon.

Pollak, R. A., and S. C. Watkins. 1993. "Cultural and Economic Approaches to Fertility: Proper Marriage or Mésalliance?" *Population and Development Review* 19:467–96.

Preston, Samuel H. 1976. *Mortality Patterns in National Populations.* New York: Academic Press.

———. 1984. "Children and the Elderly: Divergent Paths for America's Dependents." *Demography* 21:435–57.

Preston, S., and P. Taubman. 1993. "Socio-Economic Differences in Adult Mortality and Health Status." Pp. 279–318 in *Demography of Aging,* ed. Linda G. Martin and Samuel H. Preston. Washington D.C.: National Academy Press.

Ragin, Charles C. 1987. *The Comparative Method: Moving beyond Qualitative and Quantitative Strategies.* Berkeley: University of California Press.

Retherford, R. D., N. Ogawa, and S. Sakamoto. 1996. "Values and Fertility Change in Japan." *Population Studies* 50:5–25.

Rieger, E., and S. Leibfried. 1998. "Welfare State Limits to Globalization." *Politics and Society* 26:363–90.

Rindfuss, R. R., and K. L. Brewster. 1996. "Childrearing and Fertility." Pp. 258–89 in *Fertility in the United States: New Patterns, New Theories,* ed. John B. Casterline, Ronald D. Lee, and Karen A. Foote. New York: Population Council.

Rindfuss, R. R., K. L. Brewster, A. L. Kavee. 1996. "Women, Work, and Children." *Population and Development Review* 22:457–82.

Rindfuss, Ronald R., and James A. Sweet. 1977. *Post-War Fertility Trends and Differentials in the United States.* New York: Academic Press.

Robinson, W. C. 1997. "The Economic Theory of Fertility over Three Decades." *Population Studies* 51:63–74.

Rockett, I. R. H. 1998. "Injury and Violence: A Public Health Perspective." *Population Bulletin* 53:1–40.

Rockett, I. R. H., and G. S. Smith. 1989. "Homicide, Suicide, and Motor Vehicle Crash, and Fall Mortality: United States' Experience in Comparative Perspective." *American Journal of Public Health* 79:1396–1400.

Rogers, R. G. 1995. "Sociodemographic Characteristics of Long-Lived and Healthy Individuals." *Population and Development Review* 21:33–58.

Rogers, R. G., and R. Hackenberg. 1987. "Extending Epidemiologic Transition Theory: A New Stage." *Social Biology* 34:234–43.

Rosenfeld, R. A., and G. E. Birkelund. 1995. "Women's Part-Time Work: A Cross-National Comparison." *European Sociological Review* 11:111–34.

Rothenberg, R., H. R. Lentzer, and R. A. Parker. 1991. "Population Aging Patterns: The Expansion of Mortality." *Journals of Gerontology* 40:S66–S76.

Sainsbury, Diane, ed. 1994. *Gendering Welfare States.* London: Sage.

———. 1996. *Gender, Equality, and Welfare States.* Cambridge: Cambridge University Press.

Schmidt, M. G. 1993. "Gendered Labour Force Participation." Pp. 179–237 in

Families of Nations: Patterns of Public Policy in Western Democracies, ed. Francis G. Castles. Aldershot: Dartmouth.

Schmitter, P. C. 1979. "Still the Century of Corporatism?" Pp. 7–52 in *Trends Toward Corporatist Intermediation,* ed. Phillipe C. Schmitter and Gerhardt Lehmbruch. London: Sage.

———. 1981. "Interest Intermediation and Regime Governability in Contemporary Western Europe and North America." Pp. 287–330 in *Organizing Interests in Western Europe: Pluralism, Corporatism, and the Transformation of Politics,* ed. Suzanne Berger. Cambridge: Cambridge University Press.

Schoen, R., Y. J. Kim, C. A. Nathanson, J. Fields, and N. M. Astone. 1997. "Why Do Americans Want Children?" *Population and Development Review* 23: 333–58.

Schultz, Theodore P. 1981. *Economics of Population.* Reading, Mass.: Addison-Wesley.

Siaroff, A. 1994. "Work, Welfare and Gender Equality: A New Typology." Pp. 82–100 in *Gendering Welfare States,* ed. Diane Sainsbury. London: Sage.

Simon, Rita J. 1975. *Women and Crime.* Lexington, Mass.: D. C. Heath.

Simpson, M. 1998. "Suicide and Religion: Did Durkheim Commit the Ecological Fallacy, and Did Van Poppel and Day Combine Apples and Oranges?" *American Sociological Review* 63: 895–96.

Simpson, S. S. 1991. "Caste, Class, and Violent Crime: Explaining Differences in Female Offending." *Criminology* 29: 115–35.

Simpson, S. S., and L. Elis. 1995. "Doing Gender: Sorting Out the Caste and Crime Conundrum." *Criminology* 33: 47–77.

Singh, G., and S. M. Yu. 1996. "Trends and Differentials in Adolescent and Young Adult Mortality in the United States, 1950 through 1993." *American Journal of Public Health* 86: 560–64.

Singh, Rina. 1998. *Gender Autonomy in Western Europe: An Imprecise Revolution.* New York: St. Martin's.

Smith, D. P. 1981. "A Reconsideration of Easterlin Cycles." *Population Studies* 35: 347–64.

Smith, M. D. 1986. "The Era of Increased Violence in the United States: Age, Period, or Cohort Effect?" *Sociological Quarterly* 27: 239–51.

Smith, M. D., and V. E. Brewer. 1992. "A Sex-Specific Analysis of Correlates of Homicide Victimization in United States Cities." *Violence and Victims* 7: 279–86.

Smith, M. D., and E. S. Kuchta. 1995. "Female Homicide Victimization in the United States: Trends in Relative Risks, 1946–1990." *Social Science Quarterly* 76: 665–72.

Stack S. 1978. "Suicide: A Comparative Analysis." *Social Forces* 57: 644–53.

———. 1987. "The Effect of Female Participation in the Labor Force on Suicide: A Time Series Analysis, 1948–1980." *Sociological Forum* 22: 257–77.

———. 1990. "New Micro-Level Data on the Impact of Divorce on Suicide,

1959–1980: A Test of Two Theories." *Journal of Marriage and the Family* 52: 119–27.

Stack, S., and N. Danigelis. 1985. "Modernization and the Sex Differential in Suicide, 1919–1972." *Comparative Social Research* 8: 203–16.

Stafford, M. C., and J. P. Gibbs. 1988. "Change in the Relation between Marital Integration and Suicide Rates." *Social Forces* 66: 1060–79.

Stata. 1999. Stata Statistical Software, release 6.0. College Station, Tex.: Stata Corporation.

Steffensmeier, D. 1980. "Sex Differences in Patterns of Adult Crime, 1965–77: A Review and Assessment." *Social Forces* 58: 1080–1108.

———. 1993. "National Trends in Female Arrests, 1960–1990: Assessment and Recommendations for Research." *Journal of Quantitative Criminology* 9: 411–44.

Steffensmeier, D., and E. Allan. 1996. "Gender and Crime: Toward a Gendered Theory of Female Offending." *Annual Review of Sociology* 22: 459–87.

Steffensmeier, D., E. Allan, and C. Streifel. 1989. "Development and Family Crime: A Cross-National Test of Alternative Explanations." *Social Forces* 68: 262–83.

Steffensmeier, D., and C. Streifel. 1992. "Time-Series Analysis of the Female Percentage of Arrests for Property Crimes, 1960–1985: A Test of Alternative Explanations." *Justice Quarterly* 9: 77–103.

Steffensmeier, D., C. Streifel, and M. D. Harer. 1987. "Relative Cohort Size and Youth Crime in the United States." *American Sociological Review* 52: 702–10.

Steffensmeier, D., C. Streifel, and E. S. Shihadeh. 1992. "Cohort Size and Arrest Rates over the Life Course: The Easterlin Hypothesis Reconsidered." *American Sociological Review* 57: 306–14.

Steffensmeier, R. H. 1984. "Suicide and the Contemporary Woman: Are Male and Female Suicide Rates Converging?" *Sex Roles* 10: 613–31.

Steinmo, Sven, Kathleen Thelan, and Frank Longstreth, eds. 1992. *Structuring Politics: Historical Instiutionalism in Comparative Analysis.* Cambridge: Cambridge Univeristy Press.

Stephens, John D. 1979. *The Transition from Capitalism to Socialism.* London: MacMillan.

Stimson, J. 1985. "Regression in Time and Space: A Statistical Essay." *American Journal of Political Science* 29: 914–47.

Streek, W., and P. C. Schmitter. 1991. "From National Corporatism to Transnational Pluralism: Organized Interests in the Single European Market." *Politics and Society* 19: 133–64.

Summers, R., and A. Heston. 1991. "The PENN World Table (Mark 5): An Expanded Set of International Comparisons, 1950–1988." *Quarterly Journal of Economics* 106: 327–68.

Sweet, J. A., and R. R. Rindfuss. 1983. "Those Ubiquitous Fertility Trends: United States, 1945–1979." *Social Biology* 30: 127–39.

Tam, T. 1997. "Sex Segregation and Occupational Gender Inequality in the United States: Devaluation or Specialized Training?" *American Journal of Sociology* 102:1652–92.

Teitelbaum, Michael S., and Jay M. Winter. 1985. *The Fear of Population Decline.* Orlando, Fla.: Academic Press.

Therborn, G. 1993. "The Politics of Childhood: The Rights of Children in Modern Times." Pp. 241–91 in *Families of Nations: Patterns of Public Policy in Western Democracies,* ed. Francis G. Castles. Aldershot: Dartmouth.

Thornton, A. 1978. "The Relationship between Fertility and Income, Relative Income, and Subjective Well-Being." *Research in Population Economics* 1: 261–90.

Tilly, C. 1995. "To Explain Political Processes." *American Journal of Sociology* 100: 1594–1610.

Travis, R. 1990. "Suicide in Cross-Cultural Perspective." *International Journal of Comparative Sociology* 31:237–48.

Triandis, Harry C. 1995. *Individualism and Collectivism.* Boulder, Colo.: Westview.

Trovato, F. 1987. "A Longitudinal Analysis of Divorce and Suicide in Canada." *Journal of Marriage and the Family* 49:193–203.

Trovato, F., and R. Vos. 1992. "Married Female Labor Force Participation and Suicide in Canada, 1971 and 1981." *Sociological Forum* 7:661–77.

Trovato, F., and N. M. Lalu. 1996. "Narrowing Sex Differentials in Life Expectancy in the Industrialized World: Early 1970's to Early 1990's." *Social Biology* 43:20–37.

———. 1998. "Contributions of Cause-Specific Mortality to Changing Sex Differentials in Life Expectancy: Seven Nations Case Study." *Social Biology* 45:1–20.

Tsuya, N., and K. O. Mason. 1995. "Changing Gender Roles and Below-Replacement Fertility in Japan." Pp.139–67 in *Gender and Family Change in Industrialized Countries,* ed. Karen Oppenheim Mason and An-Magritt Jensen. Oxford: Clarendon.

Uhlenberg, P. 1992. "Population Aging and Social Policy." *Annual Review of Sociology* 18:449–74.

United Nations. 1996 and various years. *Demographic Yearbook.* New York: United Nations.

———. 1999. *World Population Prospects: The 1998 Revision.* New York: United Nations.

Unnithan, N. Prabha, Lin Huff-Corzine, Jay Corzine, and Hugh P. Whitt. 1994. *The Currents of Lethal Violence: An Integrated Model of Suicide and Homicide.* Albany: State University of New York Press.

U.S. Bureau of Census. 1994. *Statistical Abstract of the United States.* Washington D.C.: U.S. Government Printing Office.

Valkonen, T. 1991. "Assumptions about Mortality Trends in Industrialized

Countries: A Survey." Pp. 3–26 in *Future Demographic Trends in Europe and North America: What Can We Assume Today?* ed. Wolfgang Lutz. London: Academic.

Vallin, J. 1993. "Social Change and Mortality Decline: Women's Advantage Achieved or Regained?" Pp. 190–212 in *Women's Position and Demographic Change,* ed. Nora Federici, Karen Oppenheim Mason, and Sølvi Sogner. Oxford: Clarendon.

———. 1995. "Can Sex Differentials in Mortality Be Explained by Socioeconomic Mortality Differentials." Pp. 178–200 in *Adult Mortality in Developed Countries: From Description to Explanation,* ed. Alan D. Lopez, Graziella Caselli, and Tapani Valkonen. Oxford: Clarendon.

van de Kaa, Dirk J. 1987. "Europe's Second Demographic Transition." *Population Bulletin* 42:1–57.

———. 1988. "The Second Demographic Transition." Working paper, Planologisch Demografisch Instituut, Amsterdam

van Poppel, F., and L. H. Day. 1996. "A Test of Durkheim's Theory of Suicide—without Committing the Ecological Fallacy." *American Sociological Review* 61: 500–507.

Waldron, I. 1993. "Recent Trends in Sex Mortality Ratios for Adults in Developed Countries." *Social Science and Medicine* 36:451–62.

Walker, J. R. 1995. "The Effect of Public Policies on Recent Swedish Fertility Behavior." *Journal of Population Economics* 8:233–51.

Watkins, Susan Cotts. 1991. *From Provinces into Nations: Demographic Integration in Western Europe, 1870–1960.* Princeton, N.J.: Princeton Univeristy.

Wennemo, I. 1992. "The Development of Family Policy: A Comparison of Family Benefits and Tax Reductions for Families in Eighteen OECD Countries." *Acta Sociologica* 35:201–17.

Western, B. 1991. "A Comparative Study of Corporatist Development." *American Sociological Review* 56:283–94.

Westoff, C. F. 1991. "The Return to Replacement Fertility: A Magnetic Force?" Pp.227–33 in *Future Demographic Trends in Europe and North America: What Can We Assume Today?* ed. Wolfgang Lutz. London: Academic Press.

Whitt, H. P. 1986. "The Sheaf Coefficient: A Simplified and Expanded Approach." *Social Science Research* 15:174–89.

Whittington, L. A., J. Alm, and H. E. Peters. 1990. "Fertility and the Personal Exemption: Implicit Pronatalist Policy in the United States." *American Economic Review* 80:545–56.

Wilensky, Harold L. 1976. *The "New Corporatism," Centralization, and the Welfare State.* Beverly Hills, Calif.: Sage.

Williams, F. 1995. "Race/Ethnicity, Gender, and Class in Welfare States: A Framework for Comparative Analysis." *Social Politics* 2:127–59.

Williamson, Peter. 1989. *Corporatism in Perspective: An Introductory Guide to Corporatist Theory.* London: Sage.

World Health Organization. 1996 and various years. *World Health Statistics.* Geneva: World Health Organization.

Wright, R. E. 1989. "The Easterlin Hypothesis and European Fertility Rates." *Population and Development Review* 15 : 107–22.

Yang, B. 1992. "The Economy and Suicide: A Time-Series Study of the U.S.A." *American Journal of Economics and Sociology* 51 : 87–99.

Yang, B., and D. Lester. 1988. "The Participation of Females in the Labor Force and Rates of Personal Violence (Suicide and Homicide)." *Suicide and Life-Threatening Behavior* 18 : 270–78.

———. 1992. "The Association between Working and Personal Violence (Suicide and Homicide) in Married Men and Women." *International Journal of Contemporary Sociology* 29 : 67–76.

———. 1995. "Suicidal Behavior and Employment." Pp. 97–108 in *Women and Suicidal Behavior,* ed. Slivia Sara Canetto and David Lester. New York: Springer.

Index

accident deaths, 135–36, 157–58, 189, 220, 270 n. 8 (chap. 10)
age structure, 5, 55, 122–23, 145, 166
Ahlburg, D., 141
Australia, 78, 84, 93, 97, 111, 145, 169, 218, 226, 238, 258 n. 2
Austria, 78–79, 98, 102, 142, 145, 152, 156, 179, 208–9, 218, 226
autocorrelation. *See* serial correlation

baby boom, 57–58, 79–80, 85, 105, 123, 126, 145, 166, 261 n. 12
baby bust, 57–58, 80, 85, 261 n. 12
Baker, K., 196
Beck, N., 204, 250–51, 255
Becker, G., 57
Belgium, 78–79, 84, 97–98, 142, 156, 208, 218–19, 226
Birkelund, G., 73
Bloom, D., 258 n. 2
Blossfeld, H., 66–67, 73, 259 n. 6
Boling, P., 67
Bradshaw, J., 258 n. 4
Brewster, K., 66, 68
Briggs, C., 127
Burr, J., 195
Buse, A., 251–52
Butz, W., 67

Canada, 78–79, 84, 94, 97–98, 145, 163, 169, 208–9, 261 n. 13
Catholic nations, 134–35, 138, 155–57, 179, 208–9, 264 n. 5
childhood economic socialization, 55
children
care of, 69, 248
costs of, 64
preferences for, 66
support of, 47–48

work and, 65
Cohen, L., 13, 126
cohort size, 77, 179, 258nn. 1, 3
age differences and, 17, 142, 257 n. 1
benefits of, 8, 124
competition and, 123
consequences of, 5–6, 123
contingent influence of, 18
diversity in, 90–92
economic status and, 61
effects of, 85–89
evidence concerning, 9
fertility and, 55, 57, 61–69, 80, 94–96, 243–44, 259 n. 1, 260n. 5
collectivism and, 60–61
contextual influences on, 59–60
contingency, 88–89
gender equality and, 61–63
national differences, 82–85
time differences, 80–82, 86–88
harm of, 8
homicide and, 160, 174, 181, 243, 245, 266nn.1–5
age differences and, 128–29, 169–74
contingency, 127
correlations, 166
divergence across ages and nations, 126
evidence concerning, 126–27
hypotheses about, 131–34, 139, 161
national differences in, 129–30, 167, 181, 173–74
sex differences in, 129, 168, 172
time differences in, 124, 131, 167, 181, 173
indirect effects on, 135
low value of, 80
mean, 79
measures, 72, 141, 162
models of, 83, 88–89

cohort size (*continued*)
  mortality and, 135
    controversy on, 9
    varied effects of, 15–16
  national differences, 79, 82
  range, 83
  sex differences, 6, 17–18
  stress as a result of, 124
  suicide and, 243, 245, 264nn. 2–13
    additive results, 152
    age differences in, 128–29, 146, 152–
      53, 158
    contingency, 127
    correlation, 146
    divergence across ages and nations, 126,
      159
    diversity in, 159
    evidence concerning, 125
    hypotheses about, 131–34, 139, 153, 158
    multivariate results for, 148–49
    national differences in, 129–30, 147,
      153–55
    sex differences in, 129, 153, 158
    time differences in, 124, 131, 147–48
  time differences and, 17
  United States and Europe and, 16
  weaknesses within, 14
collectivism, 30–33, 55, 60–62, 74, 243,
    245, 251
  definition of, 31
  female work and, 107
  fertility and, 77, 84–85, 88, 90–96, 103–
    4, 258 n. 3, 259nn. 2, 4, 260nn. 2, 5,
    260 n. 6, 261 n. 11, 263nn. 9–11,
    262nn. 6–8
  generality of, 46–47
  homicide and, 161, 174, 177–78, 181,
    264 n. 3
  homicide sex differences and, 226–27,
    232–39, 269 n. 3, 271nn. 8–9
  mortality and, 129–32, 138
  mortality sex differences and, 198
  national differences in, 46–47
  scales of, 43–47, 107, 117
  suicide and, 154–55, 157–58
  suicide sex differences and, 214–19, 222
collectivist institutions. *See* collectivism
completed cohort fertility, 72
composition, of population, 56, 122, 126,
    257nn. 1–2 (chap. 1)

consensus government, 29, 43
context, 59, 71, 77, 140, 155, 181, 239, 244,
    248
contingency, 71, 158–59, 194–96, 239,
    243
convergence, 27, 197, 220–23, 239
  across nations, 12
  invariant relationships and, 13
  pressures toward, 28
  rejection of, 28
  and social protection, 13
  and support for women, 14
corporatism, 29, 43
cross-sectional correlation, 249–50, 255
crude birth rates, 56, 72
curvilinearity, 196, 204, 209–10, 213, 218,
    220–21, 230, 233, 236, 239, 245
Cutright, P., 127

data, pooled, 75, 137–38, 203–4, 249, 253–
    55
Day, L., 135, 264 n. 5
death penalty, 135, 177, 267 n. 5, 270 n. 8,
    271 n. 9
decommodification, 30, 35, 43
defamilialization, 35
demographic transition, second, 12
Demographic Yearbook, 72, 138
demography, 21–22, 243
Denmark, 78, 163, 179, 208–9, 226, 238
divergence, 27–29, 37, 55, 126, 197, 220–
    23, 239
divorce, 259 n. 6, 266 n. 13
  homicide and, 162, 174, 179
  homicide sex differences and, 233, 239
  mortality sex differences and, 187, 196–
    97, 204
  suicide and, 134–38, 155
  suicide sex differences and, 212–13, 220–
    22
Durkheim, É., 134, 188–89, 191, 268 n. 6

Easterlin, R., 55–58, 60–63, 72, 94–95,
    123–24, 127, 135, 138, 160, 187,
    257 n. 1, 258 n. 1
Easterlin effect
  contextual differences, 60
  hypotheses about, 60
  time differences, 60
  variation in, 59–60

economic discrimination, 135, 160–61, 177, 266 n. 5, 270 n. 8, 271 n. 9
economic theories, 56–57, 61, 116
education, 67–69
employment support, 48
England, 127
Esping-Andersen, G., 247, 258 n. 2
ethnic-linguistic heterogeneity, 135, 177, 266 n. 5, 270 n. 8, 271 n. 9

family allowance spending, 64, 68, 74, 93–94, 96,115, 117
Felson, M., 134
female autonomy, 34, 65
female employment. *See* female work
female labor force participation. *See* female work
female wages, 57, 66–67
female work, 117, 244–45, 259nn. 7–8, 261 n. 7, 266 n. 13
   age differences, 257 n. 1 (chap. 2)
   benefits of, 10
   cohort size and, 90–94, 96
   collectivism and, 107–9
   consequences of, 7
   controversy over, 12
   convergence and, 98
   costs of, 10
   curvilinear relationship, 106, 113
   evidence concerning, 11
   fertility and, 19, 55, 61–66, 70, 99, 243–45, 261nn. 9–11, 262nn. 2–14
      changes in, 104–7
      collectivism and, 103–4
      diversity and, 99–100
      national differences in, 101–4
      in Sweden, 99–100
      in the United States, 100
      women-friendly institutions and, 103–4
   growth of, 6
   homicide and, 162, 174, 179, 233–34, 239
   homicide sex differences and, 11, 243, 246
   institutional adjustment to, 20
   institutional support of, 20–21
   measurement of, 72–73, 118
   mortality and, 20, 131–34, 138, 186–87, 195–97, 204, 264 n. 4
   national differences in, 19–20, 97
   suicide and 155, 212–14, 218, 222,

   suicide sex differences and, 11, 243, 245–46
   time differences and, 19, 98
   varied effects, 18, 21
   women-friendly institutions and, 111–13
feminism
   liberal 32, 198
   socialist 32–33, 198
fertility, 55–56, 77–78, 135, 138, 162, 174, 179, 187, 233, 248, 259 n. 4, 266 n. 13
   age differences and, 3, 39
   cohort size and, 55, 57, 61–69, 80, 94–96, 243–44, 259 n. 1, 260 n. 5
   collectivism and, 37, 60–61
   contextual influences of, 59–60
   contingency, 88–89
   evidence concerning, 57–58
   gender equality and, 61–63
   national differences in, 82–85
   problems with studies about, 58
   time differences in, 80–82, 86–88
   collectivism and, 77, 84–85, 88, 90–96, 103–4, 258 n. 3, 259nn. 4, 2, 260nn. 5, 6, 261 n. 11, 262nn. 6–7, 263nn. 8–11
   convergence in levels of, 36
   data sources for, 72
   divergence in levels of, 37
   economic opportunity and, 60
   economic theories of, 63–64
   factors affecting, 36–37
   female wages and, 63
   female work and, 57, 155, 243–45, 261nn. 9–11, 262–63nn. 2–14
      changes in 104–7
      collectivism and, 103–4
      diversity, 99–100
      national differences in, 101–4
      in Sweden, 99–100
      in the United States, 100
      women-friendly institutions, 103–4
   gender equality and, 39
   hypotheses about, 71
   income effect on, 64
   institutional coherence and, 69
   marriage and, 56
   national differences in, 68, 71, 78
   opportunity costs and, 63
   postponement of, 56

fertility (*continued*)
price effect on, 64
range of, 36
religious differences in, 79
sociological theories about, 63–66
standard deviations of, 79
time differences in, 68–71, 78
Finland, 97–98, 102, 152, 163, 169, 209, 218, 226
France, 79, 142, 156, 208–9, 219, 248, 259 n. 5
Freeman, R., 258 n. 2
full employment, 60–61, 129–30

Gartner, R., 127, 135, 195–96
Gauthier, A., 67
gender equality, 10–11, 62–65, 68, 220–21, 238, 263 n. 14, 267–68 nn. 4–5
class equality and, 33–34
determinants of, 33–34
divergence in, 35
expert judgments regarding, 47
fertility and, 35, 39
homicide and, 35, 186–87, 267 n. 3, 268 n. 7
evidence concerning, 193
hypotheses about, 199–200
institutional adjustment to, 193–94
reduction in inequality and, 191–92, 203
reduction in protection and, 188–91, 203
institutions and, 70
legal aspects of, 48
measurement of, 47, 186
mortality and, 185
movement toward, 31–32
national scores on, 49
reliability measures of, 49
scale measuring, 47–48
suicide and, 35, 267 n. 3
evidence concerning, 193
hypotheses about, 199–200
institutional adjustment to, 193–94
reduction in inequality and, 191–92, 203
reduction in protection and, 188–91, 203
stability in, 49–50
in the United States, 49
validity of measures of, 50
weaknesses of measures of, 50

generalized least squares, 75, 249–55, 261 n. 8
Germany, 59, 67, 78, 84, 98, 122, 127, 142, 237, 248
Girard, C., 126
globalization, 246–48
governability, 30, 43
Granger causality, 59
Great Britain, 59
gross domestic product (GDP), 74, 90–93, 115, 117, 138, 162, 175, 179, 204, 233

Hakim, C., 73
Hatzius, J., 67
Henry, A., 189
Heston, A., 74
heterogeneity, between-unit, 75, 137, 249–51, 255, 259 n. 2
heteroscedasticity, 101, 138, 249–50, 255
Hoem, J., 70
homicide
age differences in, 24, 41, 127, 164–65, 168, 232
changes in, 42
children and, 264 n. 6
cohort size and, 124, 160, 169, 243–45, 266 n. 1–5
age differences in, 128–29, 169, 174
contingency, 127
correlations, 166
divergence across ages and nations, 126
evidence concerning, 126–27
hypotheses about, 131–34, 139, 161
national differences in, 129–30, 167, 173–74
sex differences in, 129, 168, 172
time differences in, 131, 167, 173
collectivism and, 41, 264 n. 3
cross-sex instances of, 223
determinants of, 134–35
divergence in, 40–41
female rates of, 230–36, 239
fertility and, 25
gender equality and, 186–87, 267 n. 3, 268 n. 7
evidence concerning, 193
hypotheses about, 199–200
institutional adjustment to, 193–94

reduction in inequality and, 191–92, 203
reduction in protection and, 188–91
immediacy of response to social circumstance, 25
mean rates of, 162
measurement of, 160–61, 230–31, 233, 266nn. 1–2
models of, 253–54
national differences in, 162–63, 168, 234–38
sex differences in, 41–42, 161–63, 186–87, 270nn. 1–8 (chap. 11)
    additive effect for, 233–34
    age differences in, 227–28
    female work and, 243, 246
    hypotheses about, 224
    mean rates of, 225
    measurement of, 224–25, 228, 239
    national differences in, 225–26, 234–38
    reduction in inequality and, 223, 230
    reduction in protection and, 188–91, 223
    trends in, 227, 270n. 5
social protection and, 41
suicide and, 132–33, 165, 174, 178–80, 182
time differences in, 164–65, 168, 231
victims and offenders, 223
youth and, 126, 160

immigration, 258n. 3, 261n. 12
income, 174
    age differences in, 128
    growth of, 155
    inequality of, 135, 160–61, 266n. 5, 270n. 8, 271n. 9
    potential, 55–56, 67
individual autonomy, 65
individualism, 30–31, 96, 130, 158, 174, 216–17, 222, 239, 245, 251, 258n. 3, 266n. 11
individualist institutions. See individualism
institutional adjustment, 181, 193–94, 203, 205, 212, 220–24, 227, 230, 237, 239
    age and, 196–97
    cohort and, 197
    national differences in, 197–99
    time and, 194–95

International Labour Office, 74, 259n. 7
Ireland, 78–79, 85, 97–98, 100, 102, 142, 152, 163, 156, 169, 208
Isaacson, L., 266n. 1
Italy, 67, 78, 97–98, 142, 152, 156, 161–64, 169, 208, 226, 237–38, 258n. 3

Jackson, M., 248, 267n. 5
Japan, 67–68, 78, 84, 93, 98, 102, 111–12, 122, 127, 142–45, 152, 164, 169, 208–9, 219, 238, 258nn. 2–3, 261n. 13, 268n. 10
jobs, role of flexible schedules, 69

Katz, J., 204, 250–51, 255
Korenman, S., 258n. 2
Kutcha, E., 268n. 7

labor
    demand for, 60
    supply of, 94
Land, K., 126
leftist rule, 30, 43
Lehmann, J., 267n. 6
Leibfried, S., 247
Lesthaeghe, R., 63, 259n. 4

Macunovich, D., 57, 67
marriage, 134, 138, 155, 162, 174, 179, 187, 204, 212–13, 220–22, 233–34, 239
Mason, K., 68
maternity leave, 48, 64, 248
McCall, P., 126, 195, 263n. 1
McCarthy, B., 195
McDonald, P., 68–69
Mendelsohn, R., 137
mortality, 185, 248
    age differences in, 4
    behavioral sources relating to, 40
    convergence, 29
    decline in rates of, 4
    evidence concerning, 39–40
    national differences in, 40
    sex differences in, 4–5, 267n. 1
    smoking and, 267n. 2
    variation in, 4

Netherlands, the, 59, 97, 116, 135, 152, 163, 208–9, 218

New Zealand, 78–79, 84–85, 93, 97–98, 116, 145, 218, 238, 258 n. 2, 261 n. 13
Norway, 84, 98, 208–9, 218, 238

O'Brien, R., 266 n. 1
Oppenheimer, V., 61–62
outliers, 111, 116

Pampel, F., 196
parental leave, 69
Parker, R., 174
part-time work, 248
Penn World Table, 74
Pescosolido, B., 137
Pinelli, A., 68
policies, pronatalist, 64
political sociology, 243
politics, 21–22
population aging, 123, 145, 159, 166
population projections, 7–8, 13
postmaterialism, 65
Powell-Griner, E., 195
power control theory, 189
preschool access, 48
Preston, S., 124, 127, 138, 141, 160
price effect, 67
processual change, 56, 123, 126, 257nn. 1–2

relative cohort size. *See* cohort size
relative economic status, 61, 123
relative income, 56, 61, 135
    ex ante, 62
    ex post, 62
reproductive freedom, 65
Rieger, E., 247
Rindfuss, R., 66, 68
role incompatibility, 68, 70–71
Rosenfeld, R., 73
routine activities theory, 134, 189–91

sample, 23–24, 71, 75, 137, 203, 253
Schapiro, M., 141
Scotland, 127
self-realization, 65
serial correlation, 75–76, 137, 204, 249–50, 255
sex roles, 62
Short, J., 189

Simpson, M., 264 n. 5
Smith, M., 268 n. 7
social contagion, 58
social integration, 134, 155, 189
social security spending, 46, 74, 90–94, 96, 115, 117, 129–30, 135, 138
social welfare spending, 61
sociological theories, 56, 68, 116
sociopolitical context, 55, 62, 96, 116–18, 125, 131, 135, 138
Stack, S., 195–96
standardized coefficients, 253nn. 10, 13, 260 n. 3, 265 n. 4
standard of living, expected, 55–56
Stata, 251–52
Steffensmeier, D., 194
Stockard, J., 266 n. 1
suicide
    age differences in, 24, 41, 121, 124–26, 142–43, 149
    attempted, 202, 268 n. 8
    children and, 264 n. 6
    cohort size and, 145, 243, 245, 264nn. 2–13
        additive relationship, 152
        age patterns of, 128–29, 146, 152–53, 158
        contingency, 127
        correlations between, 146
        divergence, 126, 159
        hypotheses about, 131–34, 139, 153, 158
        multivariate results regarding, 148–49
        national differences in, 129–30, 147, 153–55
        sex differences in, 129, 153, 158
        time differences in, 124, 131, 147–48
    collectivism and, 41
    curvilinearity, 144
    determinants of, 134–35
    divergence in, 40–41
    fertility, in relations to, 25
    gender equality and, 186–87, 267 n. 3
        evidence concerning, 193
        hypotheses about, 199–200
        institutional adjustment to, 193–94
        reduction in inequality and, 191–92, 203
        reduction in protection and, 188–91, 203

homicide and, 122, 132–33,178–80, 182
immediacy of response to social circum-
    stances, 25, 121
lifestyle and, 121
measurement of, 135, 140–41, 157–58,
    189, 200–201, 264 n. 5
models for, 253–54
national differences in, 122, 127, 135,
    142, 149
old age and, 123–24
religion and, 135
role strain in relation to, 189
sex differences in, 186, 205, 269 n. 3
    additive effects, 212–14
    age differences in relation to, 209–10,
        221–22
    changes in, 41–42
    cohort and, 212, 269 n. 5
    collectivism and, 214–17
    female work and, 243, 245–46
    gender equality and, 197
    mean rates of, 207
    measurement of, 205–7, 219–22,
        269 nn. 1–2, 270 n. 8
    national differences in relation to, 208,
        212, 218–19, 221
    reduction in inequality and, 191–92,
        212
    reduction in protection and, 188–91,
        212
    time differences in relation to, 209–10,
        221, 269 n. 4
    women-friendly institutions and, 214–
        17
social integration and, 188–89, 191
social protection and, 41
status integration and, 189
time differences in, 122, 127, 144–
    45,149, 264 n. 1
years of life lost and, 121
youth and, 121–24
Summers, R., 74
Sweden, 67–69, 78–80, 86, 102, 169, 218,
    238–39, 246–48, 258 n. 3
Switzerland, 78, 84, 98, 142, 152, 179, 209,
    219, 226, 237, 239

Tam, T., 251, 255
Triandis, H., 258 n. 3
Trovato, F., 195

unemployment, 60–62, 64, 74, 93, 96, 130,
    135, 155–56, 174–75, 234, 258 n. 2
United Kingdom, 163, 208–9, 218–19,
    258 n. 4
United States, the, 246–48, 258 nn. 3–4,
    261 nn. 12–13, 264 n. 2, 270 n. 6
    female work in, 98, 108, 111, 116
    fertility in, 58–59, 67, 69–70, 72, 78–81,
        84–86, 92–94
    homicide in, 161–63, 169, 175–76, 179
    homicide sex differences in, 226, 230,
        237–39
    mortality in, 122, 124–27, 133, 137–38
    mortality sex differences in, 187, 194–95,
        198
    suicide in, 140, 145, 159
    suicide sex differences in, 208–9, 218
universal benefits, 30, 43, 61
universalism, 30, 43, 61
unknown deaths, 157–58, 220, 279 n. 8

values, 57, 63–65, 68
van Poppel, F., 135, 264 n. 5

Wales, 127
Ward, M., 67
war deaths, 135, 177, 267 n. 5, 270 n. 8,
    271 n. 9
Whitt, H., 269 n. 6
women-friendly institutions, 251, 260 n. 6,
    263 n. 12, 269 n. 3, 271 nn. 8–9
    female work and, 111–13
    fertility and, 55, 73, 103–4
    homicide sex differences and, 232–35,
        237–238
    mortality and, 138, 198,
    scales measuring 117, 258 n. 4
    suicide sex differences and, 214–19
work-parenting conflict. *See* role
    incompatibility
World Health Organization, 137, 161, 203
Wright, R., 59